EZRA POUND AND CONFUCIANISM
REMAKING HUMANISM IN THE FACE OF MODERNITY

Ezra Pound and Confucianism

Remaking Humanism in the Face of Modernity

Feng Lan

UNIVERSITY OF TORONTO PRESS
Toronto Buffalo London

© University of Toronto Press Incorporated 2005
Toronto Buffalo London
Printed in Canada

ISBN 0-8020-8941-0 (cloth)
ISBN 978-1-4426-1311-9 (paper)

Printed on acid-free paper

Library and Archives Canada Cataloguing in Publication

Lan, Feng
Ezra Pound and Confucianism : remaking humanism in the face
of modernity / Feng Lan.

Includes bibliographical references and index.
ISBN 0-8020-8941-0

1. Pound, Ezra, 1885–1972 – Knowledge – Confucianism.   2. Pound,
Ezra, 1885–1972 – Criticism and interpretation.   I. Title.

PS3531.O82Z733 2004   811'.52   C2004-904314-5

University of Toronto Press acknowledges the financial assistance to its
publishing program of the Canada Council for the Arts and the Ontario
Arts Council.

University of Toronto Press acknowledges the financial support for its
publishing activities of the Government of Canada through the Book
Publishing Industry Development Program (BPIDP).

Contents

Acknowledgments vii

A Note on Romanization ix

Introduction: Keeping Confucian 'Blossoms' from Falling   3

1 Five Types of 'Misreading' in Pound's Confucian Translations
   1. The Embarrassment of an Amateur Sinologist   14
   2. The Legacy of Previous Translations   23
   3. Overcoming the Anxiety of Influence   27
   4. The Temptations of Etymographic Interpretation   29
   5. Imposing Ideological Consistency   37

2 Confucianism and Pound's Rethinking of Language
   1. *Zheng Ming*: The Politics of Naming   45
   2. Poetic Precision: A Modernist Paradigm   55
   3. Poets as the Guardian of Language   64
   4. *Cheng*: The Epistemological Basis of Language   70
   5. The Political Economy of Verbal Precision   77

3 Confucianism and Pound's Political Polemic
   1. Supporting the Self or Subduing the Self?   84
   2. The 'Divine Rights' of the Individual   91
   3. Social Responsibility and the Elite Individual   109
   4. The Heroic Self in Adversity   128

4 Confucianism and Pound's Spiritual Beliefs
   1. The 'Rebellious Protestant'   135
   2. The 'Four Beginnings' of Human Nature   147
   3. 'Man and Earth: Two Halves of the Tally'   158
   4. *Dao*: The Tensile Light from Heaven   169

Conclusion: Poundian-Confucian Humanism at the Crossroads   183

Abbreviations   199
Notes   199
Bibliography   225
Index   237

Acknowledgments

In a letter to Ezra Pound dated 30 March 1957, now preserved in the archives of the Beinecke Library at Yale University, Carson Chang (Zhang Junmai), one of China's premier Confucian thinkers in the twentieth century, expressed his admiration for the American writer: 'The Chinese owe you a great deal for spreading the Confucian ideas in the West.' As a scholar originally from China, I too wrote this book while inspired by Pound's contribution to promoting greater Western understanding of Chinese culture, as so aptly summarized by Carson Chang.

The present volume grows out of the doctoral dissertation that I completed at the University of Notre Dame in 1997. To all my professors at Notre Dame, I owe years of intellectual guidance and mentorship. I am grateful to John Matthias, Dian Murray, and Henry Weinfield for their sustained encouragement and advice during the research and writing of my dissertation. Most of all I feel deeply indebted to Stephen Fredman, who embodies the best that a doctoral student can hope for in an adviser; his support and insights have accompanied my professional growth well beyond my graduate school years.

My colleagues in the Department of Modern Languages at the Florida State University have provided me with an academically stimulating environment wherein I have been able to complete several significant revisions of this work. I thank former and current department chairs, Mark Pietralunga and Peggy Sharpe, for their consistent support and valuable suggestions. I am especially grateful to Bill Cloonan and Joe Ree for their critical comments on the drafts of this book, as well as their wisdom and friendship, which have been blessings for me and my family. I am also grateful to the Winthrop-King Institute and the College of Arts and Science at the Florida State University for their generous funds in aiding the completion of this project.

I thank all those who offered inspiring feedback to my presentations at academic conferences over the past several years, and especially Tu Wei-ming and Huang Wansheng for inviting me to give a talk at the Confucian Studies Seminar at the Harvard-Yenching Institute. The perceptive comments I received from the Harvard-Yenching fellows, Xu Xinjian in particular, have been gratefully incorporated into my revision of the book. I have benefited as well from the insightful reviews by the anonymous readers of the University of Toronto Press. To Jill McConkey, my editor at the University of Toronto Press, I will be forever thankful, as her support and professional efficiency have been instrumental in bringing this work to its present state.

During the early years of this project, many friends gave my family and me various kinds of help that allowed me to concentrate on my work. I am especially indebted to Charles and Simone Parnell, Barth and Helen Pollak, for their intellectual companionship, unfailing friendship, and warmth of heart.

I preserve my deepest gratitude and love for my family: to my wife, Duo, who has never lost confidence in me; to Baolu, daughter, Yalie, and always the first reader of my writings, who 'unfortunately' shares with me the same passion for *belles-lettres*; and to Juliet, my younger daughter, who has grown up alongside the making of this book.

Grateful acknowledgment is given to New Directions Publishing Corporation for permission to use brief excerpts from the copyrighted works by Ezra Pound: *The Cantos of Ezra Pound*, copyright © 1934, 1937, 1940, 1948, 1956, 1959, 1962, 1963, 1966, and 1968 by Ezra Pound; *Collected Early Poems*, copyright © 1976 by The Ezra Pound Literary Property Trust; *Confucius*, copyright © 1947, 1950 by Ezra Pound; *Ezra Pound and Dorothy Shakespear, Their Letters: 1909–1914*, copyright © 1976, 1984 by the Trustees of the Ezra Pound Literary Property Trust; *Guide to Kulchur*, copyright © 1970 by Ezra Pound; *The Literary Essays of Ezra Pound*, copyright © 1935 by Ezra Pound; *Pavannes & Divagations*, copyright © 1958 by New Directions Publishing Corp.; *Selected Prose 1909–1965*, copyright © 1973 by The Estate of Ezra Pound; *The Spirit of Romance*, copyright © 1968 by Ezra Pound. Quotations from unpublished letters by Achilles Fang and Carson Chang are from the Ezra Pound Papers in the Yale Collection of American Literature, Beinecke Rare Book and Manuscript Library. An earlier version of chapter 1, section 4 of this book appeared in *Paideuma: A Journal Devoted to Ezra Pound Scholarship* 30.3 (2001).

A Note on Romanization

The transliteration system of Pinyin is used throughout the book for Chinese names, titles of Chinese works, as well as original Chinese expressions cited for discussion. Pound's romanized spellings of Chinese characters, which are based primarily on transliterations by previous sinologists, in particular Guillaume Pauthier and de Moyriac de Mailla, are preserved only in quotations from his works. All translations are mine unless noted otherwise.

EZRA POUND AND CONFUCIANISM

Introduction
Keeping Confucian 'Blossoms' from Falling

In the summer of 1923, Ezra Pound (1885–1972), the American poet then self-exiled in Paris, wrote a poem dedicated to the Chinese sage Confucius (c. 551–479 BCE). The poem, now known to Pound's readers as the Confucian canto, ends with three memorable lines that encapsulate Pound's almost lifelong commitment to Confucianism:

> The blossoms of the apricot
>   blow from the east to the west,
> And I have tried to keep them from falling. (XIII/60)

The apricot orchard alluded to here, the site of the famed Apricot Platform in the Confucian Temple in Qufu, Shandong Province, China, is the legendary place where Confucius delivered lectures to his disciples. Thus, the apricot 'blossoms' symbolize the ancient master's teachings. Although in the poem these lines seem to be articulated through the voice of 'Master Kung,' they are more relevant to Pound himself than to Confucius. Through the voice of the poetic persona with whom he identifies, Pound is proclaiming his self-ordained mission of transmitting the legacy of Confucius from the East to the West, a mission that constitutes a major focus of his ideological engagement throughout his career as a poet, critic, and translator.

Pound's dealings with Confucianism evolved through three phases, which can be characterized successively as imitative, creative, and comprehensive. His early approach to Confucian ideas was imitative in the sense that it was enabled by his reading of previous Western translations of Confucian works. Pound's first encounter with Confucius went back to his early twenties. According to his biographer Noel Stock, Pound 'had read a little Confucius as early as July 1907' under the influence of his parents, who were interested in the work of some Christian missionaries to China.[1] In September 1913, at the instigation of Allen Upward, friend and author of *The Sayings of K'ung the Master* (1904), Pound began to read Guillaume Pauthier's French translation of the Confucian Four Books, *Confucius et Mencius: Les quatre livres de philosophie morale et politique de la Chine*.[2] Pound must have found his Confucian reading engrossing, for he soon told Dorothy Shakespear in a letter dated 2 October 1913: 'I'm stocked up with K'ung fu Tsze [Confucius], and Men Tsze [Mencius], etc. I suppose they'll keep me calm for a week or so.'[3] Noticeably, it was the same time when Pound met with the widow of Ernest Fenollosa; through her Pound obtained Fenollosa's notebooks on Chinese poetry, which led to the creation of Pound's famous *Cathay* (1915). In other words, Pound's interest in Confucianism developed side by side with his interest in Chinese poetry, even though the former interest was overshadowed by the latter owing to Pound's much-publicized enthusiasm for, as well as his obvious success in, translating Chinese poetry.[4] Still, from the mid-1910s to the late 1920s, Pound's admiration for the Confucian tradition was strong enough for him to make frequent references to Confucius and create extensive commentaries on Confucian ideas in his writing. His Confucian dedication in the first stage culminated in the 1928 *Ta Hio*, his first English translation of the Confucian work *Da xue* or *The Great Learning*, faithfully rendered from Pauthier's French version.

Despite his reliance on previous translations, Pound's grasp of Confucian ideas in this early stage still displayed a certain degree of depth. In 'The Words of Ming Mao "Least among the Disciples of Kung-Fu-Tse,"' his first article on Confucius published in 1914, Pound took issue with sinologist William Loftus Hare on this question: which one of the two ancient Chinese thinkers, Yang Zhu (Yang Chu, 440?–360? BCE) or Confucius, could serve modern Western 'egoists' as a reliable source of inspiration? He argued that in contrast to Yang Zhu's hedonist philosophy, which Pound believed only worked to entrap a person in a sterile life of sensuous gratifications, Confucius possessed a correct understanding of human nature and thus demonstrated a genuine concern with the agency of the human subject, for the master taught us to seek the fulfilment of life in the beautiful creations of the human mind rather than in 'the shilly-shally of circumstance.'[5] Pound's forceful argument concerning the essential difference between the two Chinese philosophers, as well as the confident way in which he drew from

Confucius's life to support his argument, shows that he was more conversant with Confucian works in this stage than has been recognized.

The second, creative phase of his relationship with Confucianism spanned from the early 1930s to the end of the Second World War. During this period, Pound's 'conversion' to Confucianism, so to speak, was firmly established, as indicated by his 1934 declaration that 'I believe the *Ta Hio*,' namely the doctrines about the self, family, and social order advocated in the Confucian work *Da xue*.[6] Yet what really characterizes Pound's commitment to Confucianism during this period is his increasing effort to *reinterpret* Confucian works in order to bring 'Confucius' formula up-to-date,' as he claimed in a 1936 essay, to help meet the 'immediate need' for social change in the contemporary Western world.[7] For this purpose, Pound even began to learn Chinese in the mid-1930s so as to be able to study the original texts of Confucian scriptures. In addition to an English translation of excerpts of *Lun yu* or *The Analects* (1937), such efforts on Pound's part resulted in a retranslation of *Da xue* into Italian (1941, 1942), and a new Italian translation of another Confucian work, *Zhong yong* or *The Doctrine of the Mean* (1945). The poetry Pound composed during this period, in particular the 'China Cantos,' was saturated with allusions to Confucian ideas. Moreover, besides a number of articles in English and Italian focusing exclusively on Confucianism, Pound's prose writing in this phase – essays, correspondences, radio speeches – was replete with his reinterpretations of Confucian doctrines; and such reinterpretations often appeared as problematic as the political opinions he cherished during this period of time.

With the end of the Second World War, Pound's Confucian exploration entered yet another period, which I have termed his comprehensive phase. His virtual incarceration after the war, which cut him off from the bustling world as well as his previous controversial political life, seemed to create a new space wherein he was able to contemplate Confucian teachings with the tranquil intuition of a poet and the energetic perceptiveness of a man of letters, rather than with the utilitarian mentality of a self-styled political reformer. Unlike his poetry during the 1930s and early 1940s, which was often charged with explicit and monotonous political contentions, Pound's postwar cantos were characterized by an arduous spiritual quest sustained by, among other things, his extensive quotations from Confucian texts and his intensified inscription of a Confucian anthropocosmic vision. Interestingly, in contrast to the incoherent and fragmentary reflections on Confucianism in his postwar poetry, his prose translation of Confucian works into English during this period was conducted in a steadily systematic and comprehensive manner. During his custody at St Elizabeths Hospital in Washington, DC, Pound published his complete English translations of *Da xue* (*The Great Digest*, 1947), *Zhong yong* (*The Unwobbling Pivot*, 1947), and *Lun yu* (*Confucian Analects*, 1951), the first three of the four quintessential Confucian books. As for the fourth book, *Mengzi* or *The Works of Mencius*, Pound translated four chapters into English from its Book One and published them in 1947. In addition, he rendered *Shi jing* or *The Book of Songs* into English. The poems in *Shi jing* do not necessarily advocate Confucian ideas. However, similar to many Confucian literati in Chinese history, Pound believed that since this poetic collection was allegedly edited by Confucius, familiarity with these ancient Chinese poems was indispensable for the all-around intellectual accomplishment of a Confucian individual; hence the title of his translation, *The Confucian Odes, The Classic Anthology Defined by Confucius* (1954).

In view of the extraordinary magnitude and intensity of Pound's endeavour to reinstate Confucian values in modern Western thought, a thorough understanding of the nature of his commitment, his strategies of fulfilling that commitment, and the results of his efforts to that end is of enormous importance to two fields of intellectual inquiry, namely, Pound scholarship and Confucian scholarship. In the first field, to date, studies of this subject have been far from sufficient and satisfactory. I am not suggesting that Pound's enthusiasm for Confucianism is unknown to Pound scholars. Although Pound scholars unfamiliar with Chinese culture are inclined to avoid dealing with his relationship with Confucianism, major critical works on Pound, such as Hugh Kenner's *The Pound Era*, Donald Davie's *Ezra Pound*, and Michael Bernstein's *The Tale of the Tribe*, contain frequent references to the impact of Confucianism, varying from passing remarks to longer discussions. However, the question of how Confucianism *systematically* shaped Pound's thought has not yet been convincingly answered, much less analysed with insights from a sustained, coherent perspective.[8] Pound scholars knowledgeable in sinology have concentrated primarily on source studies; to their pioneer works I nonetheless pay great respect. However, we cannot remain content with source studies because they tend to let us see only the trees and not the forest. While it is true that Pound's Confucian interpretations may often seem fragmentary, Pound fractured Confucianism in order to reconstruct it in a consistent scheme; whereas researchers on Pound's use of Chinese sources, overwhelmed by his dazzling play with the ideograms in the Confucian texts, fracture Pound's Confucianism without being able to restore it to a cohesive whole.

So far the only extended study on this subject is Mary Cheadle's *Ezra Pound's Confucian Translations*. This work has made a very valuable contribution by elucidating many issues concerning the history of Pound's translations of Confucian classics and the relevance of Pound's translations to his poetry. As a study of 'translations,' however, the persuasiveness of Cheadle's work is seriously undermined by her inability to directly utilize source-language materials and her unfamiliarity with the Chinese tradition of Confucian studies (that is why she disclaims 'a sinological evaluation').[9] Consequently, her investigation is largely limited to the relationship between Pound's translations and those of his English and French predecessors, and fails to illuminate the implications of major Confucian premises significant both to Confucianism and to Pound's reconstruction of a coherent humanist discourse, such as Confucius's teaching about *ji* or self, his concept of *cheng* or sincerity, Mencius's doctrine of *si duan* or four beginnings (of human nature), and his formulation of *xin* or heart/mind.

What appears especially problematic in Pound studies is that those who touch on Pound's relationship with Confucianism often repeat the same points about the ideological identity of Confucianism, evaluating the Confucian influence from a negative perspective informed by stereotypical perceptions. These perceptions have been assumed by the West since Hegel's influential critique of the hegemonic 'state religion' of Confucianism.[10] Such a critical perspective as manifested in Pound studies bears two striking features. First, it regards Confucianism as a system of thought that is hopelessly conservative, anti-humanistic, and reactionary. Second, it views the East and the West as two irreconcilable worlds of values; here, Western civilization as represented by the Greco-Roman tradition signifies positive values, and stands in opposition to the undesirable values represented by the Confucian tradition, which in this case is seen as the epitome of Eastern authoritarianism. The game of binary oppositions is played to the full in Philip Kuberski's observation on the contradiction between Pound's Western or Odyssean origins and his Eastern or Confucian orientation. 'This contradiction,' in Kuberski's words, 'can be renamed in a number of ways,' such as:

Odysseus	Confucius
open work	closed work
alphabetic	ideogrammic[11]

Such a reductionist dichotomy casts Confucianism in an unfavourable light, predisposing critics to attribute Pound's questionable positions to Confucian influence. For instance, according to Alicia Ostriker, Pound was attracted by the patriarchal ideology of Confucianism. 'It is no accident,' Ostriker asserts, 'that Pound's attention turned from Greece, a culture with remnants of Goddess-worship, to the exclusively male-oriented philosophy of Confucian China.'[12] Such a conversion, so it seems, marked the beginning of Pound's antipathy to feminism. Likewise, Confucianism is said to have enforced Pound's attitude of 'religious intolerance'; James Wilhelm, speaking of Pound's 1928 translation of *Da xue*, observes that this Confucian work increased 'Pound's anti-monotheistic tendency.'[13] On the political front, Pound's abandonment of the ideal of a Platonic *Republic* in favour of Confucian politics, as Leon Surette sees it, indicates Pound's turning to a theory that 'legitimates tyranny.'[14] More seriously, some critics even held Confucianism partly responsible for Pound's Fascist stance, suggesting that Confucianism planted the 'seeds of fascism' in his political philosophy,[15] or that his Fascism was a 'hybrid' product derived from, among other things, his 'enthusiasm' for Confucius.[16] What makes such claims particularly questionable is not whether Confucianism contains the 'seeds of fascism' – which I regard as a fallacious question – but rather that none of these claims is based on a direct study of original Confucian works. Such a reductionist approach not only fails to provide a convincing explanation for the influence of Confucianism on Pound, but also fails to cogently account for Pound's career development. It splits the poet's intellectual growth into two unrelated segments: the earlier Pound, who was a liberal-minded artist committed to true humanist values, and the later Pound, who was ideologically contaminated by Confucianism. This problematic approach precludes the possibility of searching in Pound's earlier orientation for valid explanations of his position after the alleged Confucian conversion.

While Pound's commitment to Confucianism has not received sufficient and adequate treatment in Pound studies, it has been consistently ignored by the intellectual community of Confucian studies. In China, owing to the lack of sufficient materials by and about Pound, the American poet is known to Chinese cultural comparatists mostly as a major English translator of Chinese poetry; few of them are aware of Pound's hand in promoting a Western understanding of Confucianism. In American academia, although Confucian experts are not unaware of Pound's Confucian translations, few have taken seriously his commitment to modernizing Confucianism in Western contexts. Wing-tsit Chan is the only major Confucian scholar to have written a short review of Pound's Confucian translations.[17] Tu Wei-ming, the leading New Confucian in America today, pays a kind of passing tribute to Pound in a brief footnote, marvelling at the 'fascinating' and 'insightful observations' displayed in Pound's translations.[18] But Tu's remarks have never attracted attention, nor has Tu himself developed his own points further. In America, Confucian scholars' lack of interest in Pound can be explained in only two ways. First, perhaps because of Pound's well-known controversial views in political and racial affairs, Confucian scholars have been reluctant to associate the Confucian tradition with his notorious positions. Second, Pound's reputation as an 'amateur' sinologist may have caused Confucian scholars to think of his venture into Confucian works as compelled by a Western poet's whimsical curiosity, which might add some exotic decorations to his poetry, but could not produce worthwhile intellectual results.

Pound's Confucian project deserves attention from the circle of Confucian studies for a number of reasons. The first has to do with the disturbing question of whether or not Confucian doctrines are responsible for Pound's controversial political agenda during the Second World War. Pound himself made the matter even worse by misleadingly labelling Confucianism 'totalitarian' and 'fascist.'[19] Yet the truth is that Confucianism, in and of itself, does not hatch a reactionary agenda any more than Aristotelianism or Platonism. It is up to the student of Confucianism, however, to examine Pound's strategies of appropriating Confucian ideas so as to uncover the myths surrounding the problematic relationship between Pound and Confucianism. Secondly, the impact of Pound's mission to popularize Confucianism in the West is far from negligible. In the twentieth century few have done more than Pound to bring Confucius to English readers. His rendering of the first three of the Confucian Four Books remains one of the major Confucian translations in English available in university libraries all over America and consistently attracts readers.[20] While there are other English translations of Confucius that are considered more accurate than Pound's, many ordinary readers still find Pound's translation more readable and memorable.[21]

The third and most important reason for Confucian scholars' investigation of Pound's relationship with Confucianism is that Pound attained an impressive level of seriousness and depth in reclaiming Confucianism to engage issues confronted by the modern world. When

Pound was declaring in the early 1920s his mission of keeping Confucian 'blossoms' from falling, Confucianism in China was losing its traditional authority in social life under an unprecedented damaging attack by the May Fourth new culturalists, then the best minds of China's intelligentsia. In the West, after prominent thinkers like Max Weber discredited it as a backward and irrational value system, Confucianism had largely lost the appeal to Western intellectuals it once enjoyed with the Enlightenment writers. The widespread assumption of the time was that the Confucian tradition was in hopeless decline, or simply 'dying,' as Joseph Levenson described in his study on the 'modern fate' of Confucian China.[22] In such an intellectual environment, it would have taken both courage and perception to profess and maintain a belief in Confucianism. Pound's convictions about Confucian values at this juncture rested on his discovery in Confucianism of precepts that provided new hope for dealing with social issues generated by Western capitalist society. Among these issues were the tension between the modern individual and the cultural tradition, the formation of the nation-state, natural environment, crisis of spiritual beliefs, and so on. These are the same problems that are preoccupying the minds of New Confucians today.[23] The lessons that Pound's exploration has provided, positive or otherwise, need to be examined, for they can shed light on the nature and historical possibilities of Confucianism in our time, as well as on Pound's own agenda.

The present volume examines Pound's Confucian project, which sought to reestablish a Confucian vision of human existence as an alternative to Western capitalist modernity. The study especially focuses on the strategies with which Pound reconstructed Confucianism, transforming it into a systematic modern discourse for addressing the issues he encountered in the spheres of language, politics, and religion. The central thesis of my study is that when confronted with what appeared to him to be a dehumanizing modern world, Pound discovered in Confucianism certain solutions that the Western intellectual tradition as a whole had failed to provide. By integrating Confucian doctrines with received ideas from the Western tradition, Pound developed a new humanist discourse and brought it to bear on the contradictory conditions of his world and time. The term 'humanist' or 'humanism' as it is used here refers to a mode of thinking, a pattern of speech, which proceeds from the human experience and centres on the values and interests of human beings. Pound's humanist discourse is characterized primarily by the following beliefs: the human mind as the source of creation, the individual's moral will as the basis of truth and social order, the human partnership with nature, the self-perfectibility of human beings, and the innate capability of human beings for internal transcendence in spiritual life. In addition, this study regards Pound's formulation not as a passive recitation of Confucian teachings, but rather as an active intervention into contemporary Western cultures, a *counterdiscourse* that generates meaning by engaging in dynamic dialogue with the ideological discourses that Pound opposed in modern Western society. In terms of the methodology, such a recognition requires examining Pound's works in diverse cultural, historical, and intellectual contexts.

Organized into four major chapters in addition to a conclusion, my inquiry concentrates on four areas: (1) Pound's controversial interpretation of the Confucian scriptures, (2) his rethinking of the nature of language, (3) his political theory of the individual and the state, and (4) his formulation of an unorthodox spirituality. In chapter 1, I identify the patterns in Pound's methods of reading Confucius as manifested in his translations of the three major Confucian works. These translations, which are characterized by Pound's 'misreading,' provide revealing illustrations of his interpretive strategies for appropriating Confucianism for his ideological desires. Pound's 'misreadings' fall into five categories, of which the final three are particularly significant. Except for the first type, which resulted from his insufficient knowledge of Chinese, and the second type, which he inherited from previous Confucian translations in French and English, the other three categories of misreadings are purposeful and consistent, and play a decisive role in his revision of Confucianism. These instances of significant misreading demonstrate Pound's determination to resist established readings of Confucius, to use the act of translation as a transformative quest to restore 'original' textual meaning and, most importantly, to incorporate Confucianism into what he believed to be a more universal and stable value system inscribed by some privileged discourses in the Western tradition.

Chapter 2 analyses Pound's theory of 'precise' language, which he postulated by appropriating the Confucian doctrines of *zheng ming* (to rectify names) and *cheng yi* (to make thought sincere). Pound's concern with language began with a sense of linguistic crisis endemic among modernist writers, who feared that language was becoming a disruptive force because it was no longer able to truthfully articulate thoughts and objectively signify the thing it stood for. Pound's revisionary interpretations of the two Confucian doctrines empowered his rethinking of language by asserting the responsibility of humans to create a socially functional language, giving linguistic activities a political structure, and furnishing language with an epistemological and ontological basis. His resultant theory sought a redeemed language not only as the key to social problems but also as the bridge reconnecting the human world with the worlds of nature and eternity, restored poetry's privileged social position by endowing the poet with the duty of safeguarding the efficiency of language, and reaffirmed Pound's own increasingly intense experiments with poetic language.

Chapter 3 examines the impact of Confucianism on Pound's political thought. I assert that despite the changes in his political views corresponding to his social experiences, his fundamental belief that the individual self constituted the sole source of light and energy for personal development and social reform remained unchanged, a belief tremendously reinforced by the Confucian doctrine of self-cultivation and order. In various stages of his career, Pound was able to readjust his political orientation by integrating different aspects of this Confucian doctrine with his radical individualism and cultural elitism. In his early years, he used this doctrine as a weapon with which to defend individual rights against the tyranny of state institutions. From the early 1930s to the mid-1940s, however, as Pound increasingly emphasized the social responsibility of the individual, the doctrine became the justification for an idealized state that would achieve social harmony by unifying diverse interests and purposes in the elite individuals' 'will to order.' In the wake of the Second World War, the notion of the heroic self embedded in the Confucian doctrine provided a consolation for the demoralized Pound and encouraged him to seek refuge in his private vision.

Chapter 4 reflects on Pound's new spiritual beliefs as a consequence of his embrace of Confucianism. Pound's interest in Confucian spirituality coincided with his view that Christianity, already 'contaminated' by 'historical diseases,' could no longer provide a valid vision by which to guide spiritual life. He intended to replace institutionalized Christianity with a belief system that recognized the intrinsic goodness of humanity, human coexistence with a pantheistic nature, and the continuity between humanity and divinity. To that end, Pound tried to recuperate a number of disparate tenets from such Western traditions as European pagan mythology, Neoplatonism, and Enlightenment philosophy. But it was in Confucianism that he found a set of truly empowering doctrines about human nature, the cosmos, and the transcendental. Confucianism also contributed to Pound's new belief system by serving as a totalizing framework, which allowed him to bring together his previously fragmented beliefs, to reinstate their intelligibility, and to offer a coherent explanation of the relationships of humanity with nature and the divinity.

In the concluding chapter, I situate Pound's Confucian reconstruction in broader historical and cultural contexts so as to evaluate its place in history and illuminate its ideological underpinnings. The nature of Pound's Confucian humanism as a counterdiscourse determines its four major characteristics. First, it stands as a dynamic, revisionary discourse that both informs and is informed by Pound's struggles as a poet and a social critic against what he deemed the dehumanizing conditions of the modern world. Second, it represents a unique humanist discourse that not only gives Pound's poetry an ideological coherence and cogency but also enriches the Western tradition of humanism by incorporating Confucian insights. Third, with an agenda opposed to capitalist modernity, Pound's treatment of Confucianism differs from the three representative Western attitudes towards Confucianism that existed prior to his time: the Christian missionary *accommodation* of Confucianism, the Enlightenment *idealization* of Confucianism, and the Hegelian-Weberian *negation* of Confucianism; all three attitudes derived from respective ideologies that participated in enforcing the process of Western modernization. Finally, thanks to its engagement with issues caused by modern conditions, Pound's Confucian project asserts its relevance to the development of Confucianism, a cause that is being advanced by contemporary New Confucian believers in response to the challenges of modernity.

1
Five Types of 'Misreading' in Pound's Confucian Translations

1. The Embarrassment of an Amateur Sinologist

Pound once remarked that like many people he often loathed a 'conscious' act of reading and just wanted to read for no clear purpose.[1] Nevertheless, nobody would doubt that Pound, author of *ABC of Reading*, was acutely aware of the secrets of using reading to achieve consciously sought objectives. A prototypical 'strong reader,' Pound was aggressive, revisionary, and masterful both in English and several other languages. As with his reading of Homer, Propertius, and Dante, Pound read Confucius in a manner that unmistakably reflected his philosophy of reading, which adamantly treated reading as a powerful instrument in the cultural battle for control of the production of meaning. 'Properly, we shd. read for power,' Pound insists in *Guide to Kulchur*, 'man reading shd. be man intensely alive. The book shd. be a ball of light in one's hand' (55). For the sake of exploring how Pound used his reading of Confucius to empower his ideological agenda, there is no better approach than first examining his translations of the three major Confucian works: *Da xue* (The Great Learning), *Zhong yong* (The Doctrine of the Mean), and *Lun yu* (The Confucian Analects). These translations are crucial to an in-depth investigation of Pound's project of reconstructing Confucianism, for by revealing a consistent and perceivable pattern of interpretation they allow us to recover the strategies that Pound depended on for appropriating the Confucian texts. In other words, the way Pound translated Confucius not only provides a clue to his understanding of Confucian doctrines but also sheds light on the way he integrated these doctrines into his own prose and poetry.

Pound's Confucian translations are problematic in a number of aspects.

For one thing, it is not altogether clear whether they should be called prose or poetry.[2] More important, however, is the central question of whether these translations are truly 'Confucian,' that is, whether they reliably transmit Confucian ideas. Pound, of course, never doubted that his Confucian translations were trustworthy because they were the serious works of a true Confucian believer. As he claimed in an undated 1951 letter to his publisher James Laughlin, his English version of the Confucian works stood out as the 'first translation of Confucius (into our language) by a Confucian.'[3] But the 'Confucian' aura is precisely what Pound has been denied by critics conversant with classical Chinese and Confucian studies. Among sinologists, Achilles Fang was perhaps the most sympathetic with Pound, for Fang actually helped Pound with his Chinese translations in the early 1950s. Yet even Fang was often critical of Pound's rendering of Confucius and inclined to value this rendering only in terms of its being 'indispensable to the study of [Pound's] poetry and poetics.'[4] Instead of the virtues of originality and perceptiveness, which in Pound's view distinguished his own Confucian translations, the only credit that Pound's expert readers seem willing to give him as a translator of Confucius is the 'poetic' appeal of his language. 'Unfortunately,' according to the New Confucian philosopher Wing-tsit Chan in a 1954 review, Pound spoiled his Confucian translations by venturing beyond this 'poetic insight.'[5] Chang Yao-xin, a Pound scholar in China, has expressed the same opinion in rather blunt terms: 'We cannot take Pound's version of the *Four Books* seriously as a work introducing the thought system of Confucius. ... He is a failure in his rendition of the Confucian *Four Books*.'[6]

Chang's criticism begs the question: what is it that defines 'Confucian'? This is a crucial question that Pound's critics have not yet answered. Those who dismiss Pound's Confucian translations usually focus their attention on his idiosyncratic approach to the Chinese language, an approach believed to have 'led him astray' from the original texts,[7] without examining the ideological desires behind his translations. Critical views put forth from this perspective, though valid to a considerable extent, are rather oversimplistic. Predicated on the assumption that a translated text can be evaluated only by the extent of its resemblance to the original, such views run the risk of reducing a complex operation of crosscultural production to a simple linguistic act. They cannot help us to understand Pound's revisionary project because they are unable to provide a cogent account of why, and above all how, Pound chose to translate Confucius in the way that he did.

For Pound, translation has a twofold function in cultural production: restorative in relation to past knowledge and critical with regard to present value formations. On the one hand, a capable translator of classical works should be able to restore valuable insights that have been lost in the texts of bygone ages. To do this, the translator may have to adopt unconventional and even violent means to overcome linguistic barriers that have been built up around the 'original' perceptions in the course of history. In the essay on Guido Cavalcanti, responding to criticisms of his problematic translations, Pound argues: 'As to the atrocities of my translation, all that can be said in excuse is that they are, I hope, for the most part intentional, and committed with the aim of driving the reader's perception further into the original than it would without them have penetrated' (*LE*, 172).

At the same time, what the translator has recuperated from the original text is not meant simply to satisfy intellectual curiosity, but rather to serve as a critical force of interventions in the ongoing cultural reconstruction. In 'Date Line,' an essay on the nature of criticism, Pound mentions five 'categories' of criticism, the second of which is 'criticism by translation' (*LE*, 74). In other words, Pound regards translation primarily as a critical discourse by which 'men of letters' can guide and supervise the production of literary writing and, more significantly, exert an influence on social reform. According to Pound, translation has proved to be such a driving force for change that historically 'every new exuberance, every new heave is stimulated by translation, every allegedly great age is an age of translations' (*LE*, 34–5). Pound's view that translation is a special mode of interpretation and, as such, plays a crucial role in social formations rests on premises that have been developed into a major undercurrent of translation theories over the past several decades. Three important premises in these theories are particularly pertinent to our discussion. First is the notion that the transferral of foreign cultural materials enables us to experience and formulate ideas and feelings that have been suppressed in our own societies by the ruling ideologies. Second is the assumption that the act of translingual practice continually stretches the boundaries of the target language, liberating it from the tyranny of conventionality and thus enlarging its referential or expressive field. Third is the assertion that translation is a dynamic dialogue with contemporary thought, subverting opposing ideologies by offering an alternative model that derives its force from the combined power of past wisdom and visionary insight into the future. A translation guided by such premises obviously should not be expected to speak with the singular voice of the 'original' author, nor should it be measured by the simplistic standard of 'faithfulness' or 'objectivity.' Rather, such a translation posits a site of multiple determinations, requiring an approach that incorporates various considerations.

Thus, Pound's conception of the nature of translation immensely informed his controversial practice and was responsible for his 'misreading' of various classical works, including the Confucian scriptures. In this chapter, which consists of five sections, I will analyse five types of Pound's 'misreading' of the original Chinese texts edited by Zhu Xi in order to reconstruct Pound's patterns of interpreting Confucian works. By 'original' I do not mean to imply that there exists an eternal centre of meaning wherein 'authentic' Confucianism safely resides. Nevertheless, there is no denying that with its long history as the established official ideology in China, the Confucian tradition has so effectively institutionalized the Confucian texts that they have retained a relatively stable kernel of meaning enabling these texts to make consistent sense to Chinese readers. Moreover, I do not necessarily use the term 'misreading' in a negative sense. By this term I am referring to Pound's interpretations that diverge from the readings of Confucius generally accepted by Confucian exegetes both in and outside of China. While some of Pound's problematic interpretations can simply be called mistakes, many of them are intentional divergences and are sustained by the translator's own ideological considerations. The fact that I concentrate on Pound's 'misreading' is not to suggest that his translations do not correspond to the original texts in any way. My primary purpose is to characterize the transformational process in which Pound's interpretation of Confucius unfolds, that is, the process by which it acquires its own mode of signification. To a large extent, what energizes Pound's reading of Confucius, giving it a distinct modern status and a meaningful identity, is its marked difference from other readings of Confucius, a difference that derives its force precisely from these intentional misreadings. The majority of such 'significant' misreading, as I will demonstrate in the last three sections of this chapter, plays a pivotal role in Pound's project of restoring what he perceived as the 'original' meaning of Confucianism to its modern efficacy.

The first source of Pound's misreading of the Confucian texts is his insufficient and inadequate knowledge of Chinese. Pound's knowledge of the Chinese language has often been ridiculed by experts in Chinese studies, discrediting his claim to be a serious translator of Chinese classics. The traditional image of the translator, as in John Dryden's classical definition, is one who is a 'master' of both the source and target languages.[8] In addition, as Matthew Arnold famously maintains in 'On Translating Homer,' the translator should possess both the ability of a creative writer and the special knowledge of a 'scholar' because the success of his translation largely depends on the quality of scholarship informing it.[9] Thus it poses a challenge to the established image of a translator that someone with neither special training in Chinese nor years of scholarly preparation in Confucian studies could venture to translate some of the most sacred books of Chinese culture. This is why critics with a sinological background have found Pound's self-ordained role as a Confucian translator hard to accept. In Pound's view, however, the notion that complete mastery of a language is required for understanding a literary text in it is a misconception entertained only by people 'clumsy at languages'; he believed that 'one does not need to learn a whole language in order to understand some one poem or some dozen poems. It is often enough to understand thoroughly the poem, and every one of the few dozen or few hundred words that compose it' (*LE*, 37). For a linguistically gifted person, then, reading a text in a foreign language can be largely an act of intuitive comprehension. One need not learn to speak that language or master its grammar, but only know the meaning of the words used in the specific text with the assistance of a dictionary or other adequate explanation. Such a rationale, reinforced by his unique understanding of the Chinese character, is primarily what encouraged Pound to embark on the adventure of an amateur sinologist with the making of *Cathay* (1915).

Although he may have read an English translation of Confucius as early as 1907, Pound did not encounter Confucius in Chinese until the mid-1930s. His first translation of *Da xue* (His *Ta Hio: The Great Learning*) came out in 1928, but it was based on Guillaume Pauthier's French version of the Four Books. In 1937 Pound obtained a Chinese-English edition of the Four Books published by the Commercial Press of Shanghai. The English translator was the renowned sinologist James Legge, though his identity was not known to Pound until a year later.[10] The Chinese text of the bilingual edition is *Si shu jizhu* (The Four Books with Commentaries), comprising *Da xue*, *Zhong yong*, *Lun yu*, and *Mengzi*. This standard Confucian text was edited by the Song neo-Confucian philosopher Zhu Xi (Chu Hsi, 1130–1200). The bilingual edition, and Pauthier's French version, were the major sources of Pound's translations of Confucius, which he started to produce around 1937. These translations include a condensation of *Lun yu* (*Confucius. Digest of the*

Analects, 1937; his full translation of *Lun yu* was not completed until 1950), an Italian version of *Da xue* (*Confucio, Ta S'eu. Dai Gaku. Studio integrale*, 1942), an Italian version of *Zhong yong* (*Chiung Iung. L'asse che non vacilla*, 1945), and two English translations of *Da xue* and *Zhong yong* (*The Great Digest* and *The Unwobbling Pivot* published in one book in 1947, *Confucius*). By 1951, Pound had obtained an even older Chinese text of Confucian works – the Tang Stone Classic text – from the orientalist W.M. Hawley,[11] which Pound used for his own bilingual edition of *Confucius* published by New Directions in 1951.[12] Still, during the late 1930s and the 1940s, the Chinese text of Confucian works Pound had access to was the one from Legge's bilingual edition. But it remains to be elucidated to what extent Pound was able to take advantage of that access, that is, how much Chinese he could understand in order to approach Confucius *directly*.

Pound's first contact with the Chinese language occurred as a result of his discovery of Ernest Fenollosa's manuscripts on Chinese poetry. Although Pound's translation of *Cathay* issued from this discovery, his initial experience of Chinese did not go beyond Fenollosa's notes on the meaning of certain Chinese characters in a number of Chinese poems. No evidence exists that Pound actually learned Chinese before the early 1930s, though in 1920 he edited Fenollosa's study, *The Chinese Written Character as a Medium of Poetry*, and in 1928 produced his translation of *Ta Hio*. In fact, the mid-1930s, the period when Pound came to re-edit Fenollosa's study on the Chinese character, was a turning point for Pound. James Laughlin, who stayed in Rapallo, Italy during 1934–5 and frequently visited the Pounds there, claimed he 'observed Pound's Chinese studies,' recalling that during his visits he often saw Pound lying on his bed holding a 'huge Chinese dictionary on a pillow on his stomach.'[13] Hugh Kenner also noted that 'by 1936 Pound was studying Chinese characters.'[14] Mary Cheadle documented Pound's 'initial study of the Chinese texts of the Confucian classics in the later summer of 1937.'[15] Over the next twenty years or so, as some Pound scholars have suggested, Pound 'worked hard on Chinese' and by the mid-1950s had learned enough to be able to read in Chinese.[16] Such a suggestion can be corroborated by Pound's correspondence with Achilles Fang, who had a direct knowledge of Pound's Chinese proficiency. In a letter to Pound dated 26 August 1952, Fang critiqued the Christian orientation of the contemporary Chinese writer Hu Shi and illustrated his point by quoting a Chinese passage from Hu's diary. Moreover, in ridiculing Hu's 'experimental poetry,' Fang cited Hu's poem 'Hudie' (Butterfly) in its entirety, and said that Pound would 'laugh at' the poem if he read it. Apparently, Fang had no doubt that Pound was able to understand both quotations in the original, for he did not supply any English translations.[17]

However, since Pound's translations of the three Confucian works were all completed by 1951, the crucial question is how well he actually knew Chinese during the period from the mid-1930s to the late 1940s, the period when his interpretation of Confucian works fell into a distinct pattern. The level of Pound's reading knowledge in Chinese during that time might be gauged on the basis of three factors. Firstly, Pound did not seem to use any regular textbooks or study materials for learning Chinese as a foreign language. Cheadle's investigation so far has provided the most detailed account of Pound's method for learning Chinese during the late 1930s and the 1940s. According to that account, the primary tools Pound used for his study of Chinese, which Cheadle characterizes as 'lexicographic labors,' were a couple of Chinese-English dictionaries: Robert Morrison's *A Dictionary of the Chinese Language* (first published in 1815–22), a compact edition of Herbert Giles's 1912 *Chinese-English Dictionary*, and later, R.H. Mathews's *Chinese-English Dictionary* (first published in 1931).[18] Linguistic genius though Pound might have been, it is nonetheless inconceivable that he could have achieved a sound mastery of so alien a language as Chinese by using just these materials. Secondly, it is a common expectation that a Confucian exegete, be he Chinese or non-Chinese, should be familiar with, and able to utilize, the rich corpus of Confucian scholarship in Chinese. Yet there is no indication that Pound used any scholarly works in Chinese to assist his understanding of Confucius. The reason is probably not that these works were unavailable to him, but rather that he was unable to work directly from Chinese sources during this period. Finally, Pound's professed interest was in Chinese characters (especially in their etymological formations) and foreign language acquisition with such a concentration can hardly go beyond the lexical level. Thus, although Pound probably acquired some knowledge of Chinese from the mid-1930s to the late 1940s, his grasp of this language must have remained limited, because throughout his project of translating Confucius he had to depend on Pauthier and Legge as his guides.

What we know about Pound's Chinese studies, then, illuminates our understanding of the method by which he was able to read Confucius: he could reach Confucius in Zhu Xi's Chinese text, but not before going through the versions of his predecessors, which served as a starting point and framework for interpretation. When Pound had to deal with the Chinese text directly – that is, where Legge and Pauthier seemed ambiguous or unintelligible and thus not of much help, or more significantly, when he thought they were wrong – he could only resort to his bilingual dictionaries, which he felt he could handle comfortably with his lexical knowledge of individual characters. If he did not have a dictionary at hand (as happened in August 1937 when he went into retreat in order to concentrate on the Confucian works but neglected to bring with him a Chinese-English dictionary) Pound would simply rely on an intuitive approach to the characters in question. He tells us in an article what happened during that August when he had problems with Legge's 'crib': 'When I disagreed with the crib or was puzzled by it I had only the look of the characters and the radicals to go from' (*SP*, 82). These 'characters and the radicals' are from the Chinese text, side by side with Legge's 'crib' on the same pages.

Pound's insufficient knowledge of Chinese, compounded by his intuitive approach, inevitably generated semantic and grammatical errors in his readings. In the remainder of this section I will analyse two typical examples of such errors. To highlight Pound's misreading, I will italicize the problematic parts of his translation and underline the corresponding parts in the original character version, which is accompanied by *pinyin*, the modern romanization form of Chinese. The following example reveals Pound's difficulty in grasping words of multiple meanings:

Zi yue: she ze bu <u>xun</u>, jian ze gu; yuqi <u>bu xun</u> ye, ning gu 子曰：奢則不<u>孫</u>，儉則固。與其<u>不孫</u>也，寧固．(*Lun yu* 7.35)[19]

He said: extravagance is not *a pattern for grandsons*; parsimony is pattern of obstinacy; better be obstinate than *break the line to posterity.* (*Con*, 223–4)

The character 孫 is usually used as a noun, pronounced *sun* in Chinese and denoting 'grandchild' or 'offspring.' But in classical Chinese 孫 is also interchangeable with 遜, which is pronounced *xun* and used as an adjective meaning 'humble' or 'modest.' The character 孫 is used in the second sense in the original passage; and as such it is correctly rendered in Arthur Waley's version: 'The Master said, Just as lavishness leads easily to presumption, so does frugality to meanness. But meanness is a far less serious fault than presumption.'[20] In this statement Confucius is comparing two kinds of fault. One is *bu xun* (not being *xun*), which is caused by extravagance (*she*), and the other is *gu* (Pound's 'obstinacy'), which is caused by excessive frugality (*jian*). Although neither tendency is good, *gu* is more acceptable for Confucius, because *bu xun*, resulting from a lifestyle that does not conform to one's social status, involves the danger of disrupting feudal relations. Pound's reading alters this idea by interpreting 孫 according to its main dictionary meaning, which is irrelevant in this case.

Because his philological knowledge of Chinese was limited to individual characters, Pound's attempt to decipher the Chinese text was usually confined to the level of the word. Yet his misreading of individual words may have affected his reading of larger grammatical elements such as a phrase or clause. For example:

Junzi wu <u>zhong shi zhijian</u> wei ren 君子無終食之間違仁 . (*Lun yu* 4.5.3)

A proper man doesn't merely lay off his manhood *after dinner.* (*Con*, 206)

This is a statement in which Confucius stresses the importance of adhering to the utmost human virtue *ren* 仁 ('humaneness'; Pound's 'manhood') in everyday life. The adverbial phrase *zhong shi zhijian* literally means 'the entire time for a meal,' not 'after a meal.' Modified by the negative particle *wu*, the phrase means 'not at any time.' Pound's 'after dinner' results from fragmenting the phrase and reading an out-of-context meaning into the individual character *zhong* 終 (finish). Waley's accurate translation of the same sentence may help us see the inadequacy of Pound's interpretation: 'Never for a moment does a gentleman quit the way of Goodness.'[21]

Such instances of misreading, or simply mistakes, are deplorable, and had Pound known more Chinese, he probably would have avoided them. However, such mistakes can also be seen as 'normal' in the sense that few translators, even the most sophisticated ones, can be completely free from them, especially when it comes to dealing with antique texts in a difficult language. In so far as Pound's Confucian translations are concerned, this type of clearly erroneous misreading is considerably outnumbered by the other types of misreading I will discuss. Furthermore, this kind of blatant misreading, although not without apparent effects on his understanding of the original texts, played a virtually *insubstantial* role in the Poundian transformation of Confucian works.

2. The Legacy of Previous Translations

The second form of Pound's misreading originated with the inadequate or problematic interpretations he inherited from his predecessors. Before 1928, the translation of Confucius by Pauthier, the French classicist and orientalist (1801–1873), had a great deal of influence on Pound's understanding of Confucian doctrines. After Pound obtained Legge's bilingual edition of the Four Books some time during the 1930s, the translation by James Legge (1815–1897), the ex-missionary to China and Oxford's first Professor of Chinese (1876), became another major influence on Pound. In his intensive study of Confucian works during the late 1930s and the 1940s, Pound relied heavily on both predecessors' versions, frequently switching between their texts to seek a better understanding of particular passages. No matter how vigorously Pound tried to assert the originality of his understanding, the Confucius he presented is by and large a mediated one.

Both Legge's and Pauthier's Confucian translations are among the finest that Western Chinese studies has produced. Like all translators, however, Legge and Pauthier also made mistakes in their versions. Such mistakes were mostly beyond Pound's ability to detect, despite his increasing tendency to challenge, and even find fault with, the two masters. Accordingly, Pound sometimes unknowingly followed his predecessors and reproduced their misreadings. Here is an example:

> <u>Housheng</u> ke wei, yan zhi laizhe bu ru jin ye 後生可畏，焉知來者不如今也.
> (*Lun yu* 9.22)
>
> You can respect '*em soon after birth,* how can one know what will come up to present record. (*Con*, 232)

What Confucius is saying in this statement is that 'You (the elder) should treat young people with respect, for how can you know they won't be able to surpass you?' The crux here is *housheng* 後生, a compound word that means 'young people' or 'younger generation.' Confucius further elucidates this idea by the expression *laizhe* 來者 (newcomer), in contrast to *jin* 今, which refers to the 'present or old generation' in this context. Pound's rendering of *housheng* as someone 'soon after birth' derives from Pauthier's version of this passage: 'Dès l'instant qu'un enfant est né, il faut respecter ses facultés.'[22] Pauthier's mistake is that, instead of construing *housheng* 後生 as a compound word composed of two characters, he treats it as a phrase that consists of two separate words, with *hou* 後 meaning 'after' and *sheng* 生 'birth.' But the mistake is not merely in changing a noun into a prepositional phrase: Pauthier's reading, and thus Pound's as well, alters the original statement from a comparison between the younger and elder generations' achievements to a prediction about a new-born baby's potential future against 'son état présent,' or his 'present record,' in Pound's words. And this misreading is carried over into canto XIII by Pound to valorize the imperative for respecting the inborn nature of an individual, even if the individual is only a new-born baby.

When this type of misreading appears in passages containing key terms, it may create profound transformations of Confucian concepts. This is especially true of the early phase in Pound's reading of Confucius, when he depended almost entirely on previous translations. Such a dependence yielded particular readings that reveal a historical pattern of Western interpretation of Confucius. Pound's translation practice, in that sense, further proves that the act of translation is not an isolated individual undertaking, but rather an integral part of the discursive praxis of a cultural community sustained by shared assumptions. In the following I will analyse an example from Pound's translation to illustrate my point:

Da xue zhi dao, zai ming ming de 大學之道，在明明德. (*Da xue* 1.1)

The law of the Great Learning, or of practical philosophy, lies in *developing and making visible that luminous principle of reason which we have received from the sky.* (*TH*, 7)

This is the opening sentence of *Da xue*, which announces the first and foremost goal of the '*Dao* of the Great Learning' (*Da xue zhi dao*). The goal is stated in the phrase *ming ming de*. The first *ming* 明 is a verb that denotes 'make bright' or 'enlighten,' and the second *ming* 明 (bright) is an adjective modifying the noun *de* 德, which refers to 'virtue.' To be sure, *ming ming de* is a complex Confucian concept, but a cautious translation of it should not move too far from the idea of 'illuminating illustrious virtue.'[23] Pound's rendering of *ming ming de* is not based on the original text; it is rather an English duplicate of Pauthier's French version: 'développer et remettre en lumière le principe lumineux de la raison que nous avons reçu du ciel.'[24]

Pauthier's translation, or overtranslation, of *ming ming de* superimposes on the Chinese text the notion of the human capacity of reason derived from a divine origin. In the introduction to his Confucian translation, where he dwells on the importance of reason to the moral philosophy of Confucius, Pauthier upholds reason as one of God's gifts ('dons de Dieu'), identical with the absolute supreme Reason ('la Raison suprême absolue'), and maintains that reason guides human beings in the search for social harmony and stability.[25] Pauthier's notion of reason, with its Christian flavour, reflects his grounding in the tradition of Enlightenment rationalism. By translating the Confucian *ming de* into 'le principe lumineux de la raison,' Pauthier is reinstating a rationalistic value established by his Enlightenment forerunners. Central to Enlightenment philosophy, apart from the vision of a rationally ordered universe, is the idea that only through the power of reason can human beings understand the universe and improve their conditions. On the other hand, by attributing human reason to a transcendental source, Pauthier seeks to make it a permanent and universal virtue. It is from this perspective that Pauthier finds in the Confucian works the perfect expression of reason and the luminous doctrine of reinvigorating the rational nature of humanity.

Historically, the Enlightenment tradition in which Pauthier wrote derived much of its inspiration from the Confucianism introduced to Europe by earlier Christian missionaries to China. The first major Western translation of Confucius was the product of team effort by two generations of Jesuit priests engaged in a mission to China from the late sixteenth century to the seventeenth century. The strategies of these missionaries rested on the so-called accommodationist policy, by which they sought to reinforce their mission by creating a Chinese-Christian synthesis in order to accommodate Christian teachings to mainstream Chinese moral and social conventions. To translate Confucius into Latin was an important part of that project, for the Jesuits viewed the accommodation of Confucianism as the key to the success of their mission. In an attempt to rescue Confucianism from what they believed to be the heresy of ancestor-worship and frame it in such a way that it could be explained in terms of Christian theology, the Jesuits categorized it as a natural religion, namely a religion based on human reason, thus making it compatible with Christianity, the revealed religion of God. The intention of these missionaries was manifested in their translation of Confucius, a translation which, according to David Mungello, 'over-rationalized' Confucianism.[26] This Latin version of Confucius was published in Paris in 1687, and is usually referred to as 'Couplet's *Confucius*

Sinarum Philosophus' after its chief editor, Father Philippe Couplet (1622–1693).

The impact of the Jesuit translation of Confucius on the Enlightenment writers' conception of a rationalized Confucian China cannot be overemphasized. Conceivably, this monumental translation must have held a strong appeal to Pauthier, who was familiar with works about China by earlier missionaries, including Couplet.[27] The effect of Couplet's *Confucius Sinarum Philosophus* on Pauthier's translation is discernible, especially with regard to the notion of the heaven-endowed rational nature of humanity, as exemplified by the following version of the same *ming ming de* passage from *Confucius Sinarum Philosophus*:

> Moreover, the purpose of learning of great men consists in *refining or improving a rational nature that I may draw down from heaven*, so that certainly, as a most transparent mirror, by means of wiping away a blemish of deformed appetites, may be returned to its pristine clarity.[28]

This paragraph is what caught Voltaire's attention in the eighteenth century. And Voltaire echoed the Jesuits' interpretation in his praise of a Confucian rationalism: 'Confucius begins his book by saying that whoever is destined to rule over a nation ought "to purify that reason which he has received from heaven, in the same manner as we cleanse a mirror when it is soiled."'[29] This same version of Confucian rationality was later reinscribed by Pauthier. Although Couplet's version is more of a paraphrase than a translation, we still can easily perceive the idea of human rationality bestowed from above, an idea that resurfaced in Pauthier's translation first published in 1841.

Eighty-seven years after Pauthier's translation the same idea found its way into Pound's reading of Confucius. However, Pound's emphasis on reason or rationality carries overtones that are distinct from Pauthier's Enlightenment orientation, and will be examined at length in my discussion of his spiritual beliefs in chapter 4. Suffice it to say here that Pauthier's rationalistic approach enormously stimulated Pound's interest in Confucius, because such an approach incorporated Confucianism into an intellectual framework that was familiar and appealing to Pound. In a note commenting on Pauthier's translation of a Confucian term from *Lun yu* 2.5, Pound states: 'P[authier] expands the single word *wei* to mean: *s'opposer aux principes de la raison*, making the sentence equivalent to Gilson's statement of Erigena: Authority comes from right reason' (*Con*, 198). Clearly, in Pauthier's doctrine of reason Pound discerned a means to a possible integration of Confucianism with Western discourses such as Neoplatonism. It was just such a new Chinese-Western synthesis that Pound strove to establish through his Confucian translations as well as creative writing.

3. Overcoming the Anxiety of Influence

While the instances of Pound's misreading that I have just discussed result from the powerful influence of his predecessors, a large number of misinterpretations in his translations derive from a persistent resistance to that influence. Pound's reading of Confucius is also characterized by a tension between a strong desire to 'read for power' and the self-consciousness of an inadequately equipped sinologist, his sense of disadvantage exacerbated by the fact that, as a late-comer in the enterprise of Confucian translation, he was entering a territory already occupied by 'giants' like James Legge. For Pound, dependence on previous translations had to be tolerated only in so far as it added to his interpretive power, his ability to rewrite cultural history. But the pleasure he took in this power diminished in proportion to the extent to which his dependence on his predecessors increased. From the early 1940s on, Pound's awareness of this necessary reliance on previous translations drove him to take a more and more defiant stance in relation to his predecessors. In a letter to Mrs Virgil Jordan on 3 November 1941, Pound asserted that 'I am ... making a real translation of Confucius' Ta S'eu (wrongly spelled Ta Hio, by the frogs whom I followed in earlier edtns.'[30] Those 'frogs' certainly included Pauthier. Yet the truth is, because Pound admired his predecessors, he also feared being overshadowed by them. It was thus necessary for him to challenge and replace them in order to obtain a confidence in locating his own origin. This confidence would allow Pound to claim that what he had accomplished was 'the first translation of Confucius' in English by a true Confucian believer.

In other words, Pound's reading of Confucius was profoundly informed by his determination to look for expressions that could differentiate his translations from those of his predecessors. Such a consciously sought difference engendered a special type of misreading in Pound's translations, one that can hardly be described in terms of translational 'errors' because it is intentional and well calculated. Though a misinterpretation of this kind might make little sense when compared with the original text, it can be intertextually meaningful when construed with reference to a previous translation that Pound consulted.

This type of wilful misreading is often relatively easy to ascertain, for it is marked by an explicit superimposition of additional meaning on top of a previous version. For example:

Yi yue shi zhi zhe xian yi 以約失之者鮮矣 . (*Lun yu* 4.23)

[Legge]: The cautious seldom err.[31]

[Pound]: *Those who consume their smoke seldom get lost.* The concise seldom err. (*Con,* 208)

Legge's rendering is thoughtful. It not only maintains the conciseness of the original sentence, but also preserves the ambiguity of the Chinese term *yue* 約, which in this case can be interpreted either as 'cautious speech' or as 'cautious spending.' It is not difficult for us to perceive the revision Pound makes on the basis of Legge's version: he substitutes 'concise' for 'cautious' but keeps Legge's sentence structure. However, as if anxious to erase the trace of Legge's presence, Pound adds the sentence about 'consuming one's own smoke,' an addition that has no textual basis in the original.

Sometimes these sorts of revisions by Pound are not as obvious as in the example above, since Pound made a thorough effort to conceal his sources by offering what he believed to be fresh interpretations. Nevertheless, because he had to make use of previous translations it was impossible for him not to betray the sense of anxiety that his indebtedness aroused, not so much because it was hard to eradicate the traces of connections between his interpretations and previous translations as because he tended to overemphasize the freshness of his interpretations by inserting material that diverges from the original.

In order to highlight his originality, Pound liked to make a direct contrast between Legge's and Pauthier's translations and his own. On such occasions, not insignificantly, he graphically reduced the names of Legge and Pauthier to 'L' and 'P' respectively, while displaying their versions in brackets accompanied by unfavourable comments, such as in his rendering of the definition of *junzi* or 'superior man' by Confucius's disciple Zengzi.[32] This strategy, which characterizes Pound's translation of *Lun yu* in particular, vividly illustrates his struggle to diminish the shadow of his masters. In essence, the strategy serves no purpose for

Pound other than to reinforce his contention that he was 'nearer the original meaning' than his masters.[33] Yet Pound's self-assurance at being 'nearer the original meaning' depends largely on those of his interpretations that signify a drastic departure from the original texts as well as from his predecessors' translations.

4. The Temptations of Etymographic Interpretation

Central to Pound's interpretation of Confucius is his unique approach to Chinese characters. The approach, which I will refer to as 'etymographic reading,' is responsible for another type of misreading, the largest and the most polemical group of misreadings in Pound's translations of Confucius. Even though it is undisputedly central to Pound's interpretation of Chinese texts, and especially Confucian works, this unique reading method usually attracts critical attention only in so far as it is seen to account for Pound's misinterpretations of Confucius. In other words, Pound's etymographic reading has only been considered in terms of its contribution to his downfall as a translator and as further indication of his ignorance of the Chinese language rather than as a consistent strategy of interpretation sustained by coherent ideological considerations. The basic premises of Pound's etymographic reading need to be systematically clarified not only because this interpretive strategy proves to be his most productive instrument for appropriating Confucianism to his own concerns, but also because it reveals his deep-rooted aspiration to find the 'origin' of meaning and reinstate the authority of the 'primal' language through experimental translation. Even Pound's misunderstanding of the nature of the Chinese character, on which his reading method rests, is more than a personal idiosyncrasy and should be critiqued from a broad cultural and historical perspective.

The immediate (but not the sole) source of Pound's knowledge of the Chinese language was Fenollosa's study of the ideogram, which Pound edited for publication. Fenollosa's influence on Pound's understanding of language and poetry has been a familiar subject for Pound scholars and East-West comparatists.[34] What I will provide here is only a brief account of Fenollosa's notions about the nature of the Chinese character relevant to my discussion. Fenollosa's conception summarizes three characteristics of the Chinese character. The first is its pictorialness, for the character 'is based,' Fenollosa insists, 'upon a vivid shorthand picture of the operations of nature.'[35] From this visual physicality derives the second characteristic of the Chinese character – its metaphoricity. The formation of the Chinese character epitomizes a natural process of signification from thing to thingness, or, in Fenollosa's words, 'the use of material images to suggest immaterial relations.'[36] Theoretically, this metaphorical process of generating new meaning by combining ideogrammic components can continue endlessly on multiple levels. The third characteristic of the Chinese character lies in its etymological stability. Because 'its etymology is constantly visible,' Fenollosa notes, no matter how many semantic changes a character has gone through in the course of history, all meanings it has acquired 'centre about the graphic symbol' and, more remarkably, the 'lines of metaphoric advance' still remain observable even 'after thousands of years.'[37] For Pound, Fenollosa's notion of the ideogram contained a fertile field for two theories. The first is a theory of writing well known as the 'ideogrammic method' to students of modernist poetry. The second, the concern of this section, is a theory of reading, which I have named 'etymographic reading.'

What appears particularly germinal in Fenollosa's formulation is the idea of the traceableness of the metaphorical process of signification, a retrospective act of understanding that Fenollosa describes as 'feeling back along the ancient lines of advance.'[38] In his editing note, Pound asserts that Fenollosa's conception 'applies in the rendering of ancient texts.'[39] With regard to the interpretation of 'ancient texts,' such an application as Pound proposes suggests that the reader take advantage of the metaphorical nature of language by disassembling the mechanism of signification, or to be more exact, dissecting the sign, in order to uncover the original meaning. In this sense, the application of etymographic reading always points to the desired centre of meaning; it always entertains the vision of a unifying origin whose reality can be recuperated by removing the extraneous ideas accumulated over and around it in the course of history. Even before he started translating Confucius, the ultimate goal of Pound's translation theory had been to reach this radiating source of meaning. 'We test a translation by the feel,' Pound had observed, 'and particularly by the feel of being in contact with the force of a great original' (*LE*, 271). Now, a new method of reading, derived from Fenollosa's formulation of the ideogram and immediately applicable in Pound's Confucian translations, seemed to be opening up an illuminating horizon for Pound and helping him find a new route on his quest for the origin.

For Pound, the 'original' is grounded in the etymological visibility of the ideogram. The pictorial nature of the ideogrammic character inscribes the authenticity and the truthfulness of this kind of sign system, enabling the reader to establish a direct relationship with the source of meaning. 'Without knowing at least the nature of ideogram,' Pound once commented on some Confucian translators, 'I don't think anyone can suspect what is wrong with their current translations' (*SP*, 82). On the same occasion, referring to his own 'experiment' in translation, Pound described how he had relied on the visibility of the Chinese character for an intuitive grasp of the Confucian works: in his search for 'a better idea of the whole and the unity of the doctrine,' he would 'look at the ideograms and try to work out the unfamiliar ones from their bases,' until 'the constants [were] impressed on my eye' (*SP*, 85). Here Pound literally means 'look at,' not 'read.' This is to say one need not 'know' the meaning of the Chinese character, but one must be able to 'see' its meaning. This difference between 'seeing' and 'knowing,' a radical difference between two kinds of cognitive theories, sets Pound apart from his predecessors in translating Confucius.

Under the scrutiny of the etymographic reader, then, almost every ideogram in the Confucian texts can become a deep container of intellectual deposits. From Pound's point of view, however, it is the intrinsic richness of the ideogram, rather than the intent of the reader, that necessitates an etymographic approach. 'The ideogram,' Pound asserted in 1941, 'is a rampart against those who destroy language. The ideogram ... has become a treasury of enduring wisdom and an arsenal of living thoughts.'[40] The term 'ideogram' in Pound's formulation has two meanings. One refers to the individual sign of the signifying system, a historical registering of certain values. The other posits the entire sign system that calls each individual sign into action, or the presence of the eternal mind that gives the absolute values coherence ('The ideogramic mind assumes that what has been, is and will be' [*Con*, 53]). A dynamic strategy of reading, the etymographic approach not only seeks to decipher individual ideograms, but also attempts to recapitulate the way the ideogrammic system operates.

Thus, for Pound, etymographic interpretation must have appeared to represent the ideal tool for serving the twofold function of translating classical works: to restore the lost 'original' perceptions and then bring them to bear on contemporary cultural reconstruction. Such a practice is not translation in the traditional sense, because it does not pursue the conventional goal of textual fidelity. It is not 'original' writing either, because it does acknowledge its origin in a text prior to itself. More importantly, instead of merely showing what is signified, the central task of this kind of translation tends to focus on how it is signified, namely, on the mode of signification that is believed to have enabled the original perception. In a 1941 article Pound discusses how to translate Confucius and specifies the way the ideogram should be rendered: 'The ideogram represents more than just a word; that is, it should be translated into a whole phrase. And in this phrase it should indicate the source, and the bottom of the idea, which has only been "scratched." ... For example, an idea rises from a concept: water, tree, grain, bamboo. An idea rises from a concept like fire or light, or from a concept of a man who runs or who watches with attention. These roots of ideas must be preserved in the translation if we want to understand the nature and the power of the original thought.'[41] In terms of translation practice, what Pound recommends here can be summarized as two guidelines. One is that the translator should break down grammatical boundaries by treating all Chinese characters potentially as verbs or verbal phrases. Such an approach rests on Fenollosa's assumption that all Chinese characters originally signified the active operation of nature. The other is that the translator should treat a Chinese character as a palimpsest – that is, recognize the multiple-layeredness of the word – and aim to penetrate the core of its meaning.

Pound began to apply the etymographic approach to Confucian texts in the late 1920s. At this point, however, he did not often use this reading strategy, which remained crude, more graphical than etymological.[42] Not until the mid-1930s, after a more thorough study of Fenollosa's theory, and especially after the acquisition of some knowledge of the formation of Chinese characters, was Pound able to employ etymographic reading skilfully and extensively in his Confucian interpretations. From that time on, his etymographic reading became the most playful, transformative, and prolific mode of translation he had ever practised. It was especially useful for the purpose of appropriating key Confucian concepts and then enriching them, inflating them, and remaking them so that they came to serve his agenda. Starting in the late 1930s, then, of all the Confucian terms that Pound integrated into his poetry, few had not first been subjected to etymographic interpretation.

With the intention of recovering the original meaning and reinstating the original mode of signification, Pound creates a lot of 'significant misreadings' in his Confucian translations. For example:

Five Types of 'Misreading' in Pound's Confucian Translations 33

Zi yue, <u>wei wei</u> hu, Yu Shun zhi you tianxia ye er bu yu yan 子曰，魏魏乎，舜禹之有天下也而不與焉．(*Lun yu* 8.18)[43]

He said: *lofty as the spirits of the hills and the grain mother,* Shun and Yu held the empire, as if not in a mortar with it. (*Con,* 227)

Actually, Pound's translation of this sentence is problematic in several ways, but in order to illustrate the point I have just made, my analysis will concentrate only on his rendering of the character *wei* 魏. The word 'lofty' is an adequate choice for translating this Chinese character. Obviously, however, Pound is not content merely with reproducing the idea 'lofty'; he wants to restage the metaphorical process through which, he believes, this idea was engendered. Pound does so by adding to the expression the simile, 'as the spirits of the hills and the grain mother.' The simile depends on manipulating the four ideogrammic components of the character *wei* 魏 as if they themselves were autonomous ideograms with their own meanings in this instance: *shan* 山 (mountain), *he* 禾 (grain), *nü* 女 (female), and *gui* 鬼 (ghost or spirit). That is how Pound comes up with the phrase of 'the spirits of the hills and the grain mother.'

No Chinese readers will read the 'spirits of hills and the grain mother' from the character *wei* 魏, because for them the lower part of the character 魏, from which Pound derives 'spirits and grain mother,' functions only as a sound component and has nothing more than phonetic value. But we miss an important point if we invoke a Chinese reader's reaction to this character only to demonstrate Pound's 'ignorance' of Chinese, as some critics do in similar cases where his misinterpretations are meaningfully sustained by his vision of etymographic reading. The fact that Pound is capable of selecting the adequate term 'lofty' in his translation indicates that he was not unaware of the 'normal' reading of this character; even if he were totally ignorant of Chinese, he still could resort to the assistance of Legge's and Pauthier's translations. Pound's resolution to pursue an 'abnormal' reading must have derived from the conviction that staying with the normal reading would mean allowing one's perception to be locked up in the conventionality of language, and that this would prevent one from attaining the origin of meaning. As a translator with valuable access to another language community and a strong interest in its intellectual conditions, Pound found himself in a position to enable his readers to perceive what they could not see when isolated in their own language, especially when imprisoned in their everyday concerns, which foster speech habits that pay attention to the signified at the expense of the disappearance of the signifier. In many ways, Pound's translation practice, empowered by his etymographic reading, resonates with Walter Benjamin's now renowned postulate of the translator-angel who attempts to allow us a glimpse of the 'pure language,' not in one sign system, but rather through both the difference and mutual complementarity of two sign systems. By placing in the foreground the particular mode of signification of the original language, the translator is thus able to 'release in his own language that pure language which is under the spell of another, to liberate that language imprisoned in a work in his re-creation of that work.'[44]

For one thing, Pound's etymographic interpretation helped him achieve a writing practice through which he could reconcile prose and verse, or treat ideas normally suitable for prose in a poetic manner. This is perhaps why some readers would rather see his Confucian translations as original poetry.[45] What characterizes this writing is the extensive use of, in Pound's term, 'interpretive metaphor' – which is to say metaphor that enshrines the idea in the image, thus replacing the abstract by the concrete and the 'untrue' by the eternal.[46] How can one, for instance, define the concept of 'learning' (*xue* 學) in terms of interpretive metaphor? It is 'grinding the corn in the head's mortar to fit it for use' (*Con*, 27). How can one conceive of 'possessing' (*ju* 據) virtues? It is to 'grab at clarity in acting on inwit as a tiger lays hold of a pig' (*Con*, 219). Then, how can one know that one is in the state of 'barbarous tribes' (*di* 狄)? Because it is 'where men and dogs sleep around the camp fire' (*Con*, 125). Such a language as Pound explored in his Confucian translations may have led him to see a dream come true: a language that succeeds in dissolving the separation between philosophy and poetry, thereby bringing about the unity of the universal and the particular.

In the history of Western thought, this is not the first time that an alien language has inspired the dream of a transparent language. A similar phenomenon has been noted in John Irwin's study of the impact of the discovery of Egyptian hieroglyphics on the masters of the 'American Renaissance,' such as Emerson, Thoreau, Poe, and Melville.[47] As we know, that 'Renaissance' provided the intellectual climate in which Fenollosa, Pound's mentor, grew up. Though Irwin does not mention Fenollosa or discuss the Chinese ideogram, some critics have noticed a genealogical connection between Emerson's enchantment with Egyptian hieroglyphics and Fenollosa's fascination with Chinese ideograms, since both thinkers were bent on looking for the grounding of thought and language in the emblems of nature.[48] However, in so far as the mystification of the Chinese language is concerned, we need to look farther back in history to seek more convincing explanations.

If one looks farther back into the Western intellectual tradition, one can find Fenollosa and Pound anticipated much earlier by some of the most celebrated names in that tradition. Three hundred years ago, Gottfried W. Leibniz was known for sharing a then commonly held conception that 'the Chinese script, as is known, was arranged not on the word but on the thing.'[49] And before Leibniz, Francis Bacon, misinformed by returning merchants and missionaries that Chinese characters were understood by different language communities in the Far East, had made some influential though misleading remarks on the Chinese language: 'It is the use of China, and the kingdom of the High Levant, to write in characters real, which express neither letters nor words in gross, but things or notions; insomuch as countries and provinces, which understand not one another's language, can nevertheless read one another's writings, because the characters are accepted more generally than the languages do extend.'[50] The fact that these earlier Western views had articulated an understanding of the Chinese character similar to Pound's demonstrates that his etymographic theory is entrenched in European Orientalism. Historically, misunderstandings about Chinese characters might have originated with the misinformation spread by earlier European merchants who had returned from the Far East. But for such misconceptions to gain a strong hold on European thinkers, they must have had a profound intellectual appeal. In his well-researched study of the Jesuit Mission to China and the 'origins of sinology,' David Mungello offers an explanation for such an appeal. According to Mungello, through inadequate reports by missionaries and merchants, European intellectuals in the seventeenth century came to know Chinese, a language that supposedly still retained such antique characteristics as concrete written signs and relative simplicity. Many European scholars of the time were interested in the 'search' for a universal language.[51] The search was inspired, among other things, by a belief in the existence of a *Lingua Adamica*, lost after Babel, and by the need of the rising science for a universal tool of inquiry. The misunderstood characteristics of the Chinese language were seen by some scholars as meeting the criteria of the language that was being sought, and their tireless efforts to promote such a 'discovery' gave rise to the myth of Chinese as the 'Primitive' and 'Universal' language.

That myth anticipated Pound's conception of Chinese characters as the 'universal elements.'[52] Pound has often been criticized by scholars knowledgeable in Chinese for his heavy, almost exclusive, dependence on an etymological approach to the Confucian texts. This approach tends to privilege only one, actually the most primitive one, of the six structural principles of the formation of Chinese characters, and thus reduces all the characters to mere pictograms. In reality, the overwhelming majority of Chinese characters belong to the picto-phonetic category and cannot be taken as verbal pictures.[53] While I agree with such criticisms, I want to point out what has been significantly disregarded: Pound did not invent this approach (a legacy from the institution of Western studies of Chinese), but only took it to its logical conclusion. Pound used his etymological approach for purposes whose idiosyncrasy drew attention to his employment of a method sanctioned by the basic Orientalist trends of the studies of Chinese.

In the West, serious study of Chinese began in the seventeenth century with the intention of facilitating trade and, more important at the time, of training Christian missionaries. Because of the enormous difficulty posed by the Chinese language, European sinologists tried to find an efficient way to help beginners, particularly missionaries, to learn Chinese in a short time. They believed that what distinguished Chinese from European languages was its pictographic origin, and that the readiest access to this 'exotic' sign system was etymological study. The most famous (or notorious) illustration of all the pedagogical formulations that dominated early European study of the Chinese language was the *Clavis Sinica* (key to deciphering the Chinese language), formulated by the German scholars Andreas Müller and Johann Christian Mentzel in the seventeenth century. This influential formulation was premised exclusively on an etymological approach to the Chinese language. Even in the first half of the twentieth century, 'to pursue the fascinating study of the origin of these symbols' remained popular with pedagogical sinologists, and the etymological approach was 'unhesitatingly adopted,' as confirmed by a sinologist in 1922, 'in the teaching of character writing.'[54] What appears problematic in the etymological approach of sinology is that it tends to concentrate solely on the picturesque dimension of Chinese characters, sustained by the myth that these 'fanciful' symbols can reveal the 'workings of the Chinese mind.'[55] When Fenollosa asserted that the metaphoricity of these 'graphic emblems' was the 'very soil of Chinese life' and inscribed the mode of Chinese thinking, he was merely echoing this myth.[56] And, not surprisingly, when Pound equated the 'ideographic manner' of thought with the 'Chinese manner,' he merely buttressed this myth (*TH*, 12). Thus, it was from the original misconception about the nature of the Chinese language that Pound derived a reading method; with this method, he believed, one could achieve a direct dialogue with the 'original' speaker of an ancient Chinese text by traversing the etymographic space.

5. Imposing Ideological Consistency

To some extent, the instances of Pound's misreading I have discussed so far may leave the impression that his approaches, especially etymographic interpretation, tend to fracture Confucian writing. While there is some truth in this contention, it should also be noted that Pound's strategies are always subordinate to his ultimate goal of reestablishing a system of Confucian values, a system whose unity and cogency were validated for Pound by his own ideological premises. Such an agenda helps to explain a particular group of highly problematic readings in Pound's translations, which cannot be appropriately categorized into the previous groups I have analysed. This group, the fifth type of misreading in Pound's translations, includes the instances that are all generated, despite their variety and complexity, by the same intention to bestow an overarching coherence on Confucian texts and to impose on Confucian doctrines a totalizing structure sustained by certain ideological preferences. This fifth type of misreading, then, plays a crucial role in Pound's revision of Confucianism.

As a strategy for containing Confucian writing within a desired teleological scheme, Pound's deployment of such purposeful divergence operates on two levels. On one level he intended to create a kind of *internal unity*, while on the other level he sought to give his Confucian system an *external unity*, that is, its unity with universal values. In his effort to create an internal unity in his Confucian interpretations, he worked to maintain a consistency of articulation in presenting the image of Confucius and conveying his doctrines. A good illustration of this effort is found in Pound's rendering of Confucius's pessimistic remarks, '*Wu yi yi fu* 吾已矣夫' (*Lun yu* 9.8), which he translates as 'I've only myself to rely on' (*Con*, 229). Pound's subtle revision helps to preserve the consistent image of Confucius as a tireless and courageous cultural hero.[57]

Pound's revisionary reading also reveals his inclination to suppress what he sees as textual ambivalence or ambiguity, something he does not tolerate for fear that it might undercut the coherence and persuasiveness of his Confucian vision. If he chooses a reading for a particular term, or invests the term with a meaning that specifically accords with his ideological position, Pound would exclude, regardless of the context, other possible readings when he encounters the same term again elsewhere in the Confucian texts. Such an inclination can be illustrated by his reductive interpretation of the term *zhi* 止 (stop):

Zi wei Yan Yuan ye: Xi hu! Wu jian qi jin ye, wei jian qi zhi ye 子謂顏淵
曰，惜乎！吾見其進也，未見其止也 . (*Lun yu* 9.20)

He described Yen Yuan: Alas, I see him advance, I never see him *stop (take a position)*. (*Con*, 232)

Yan Yuan (Yen Yuan), who died at an early age, was Confucius's favourite student. When Confucius was once asked which of his students was the most dedicated to learning, the master answered that it was Yan Yuan, and that after Yan Yuan's death, he never saw anyone else so fond of learning (*Lun yu* 6.2). The passage above has been read by Confucius scholars in two slightly different ways. The more common reading, adopted by most contemporary Chinese commentators, construes the passage as expressing the master's sorrow over the death of Yan Yuan and his admiration for the disciple's incessant efforts over the course of his life to pursue knowledge and virtue. Legge's version follows this reading: 'The Master said of Yen Yuan, "Alas! I saw his constant advance. I never saw him stop in his progress."'[58] In the other reading, endorsed by Zhu Xi, Confucius feels sorry that Yan Yuan's commitment to learning was disrupted by his untimely death and consequently that others will never fully know how much he might have accomplished.[59] A number of English translators, like Waley, follow this reading: 'The Master said of Yen Hui, Alas, I saw him go forward, but had no chance to see whither this progress would have led him in the end.'[60] Both readings reaffirm Confucius's positive evaluation of Yan Yuan, an evaluation that Pound's reading negates.

The difference in Pound's interpretation arises from his unique understanding of *zhi* 止 (Pound's *chih*). Pound reads the character as a central Confucian term about one's consciousness of an appropriate ideological orientation, rather than as a simple verb meaning 'to stop.' It is for this reason that Pound utilizes the term at least nine times in *The Cantos*. In his note on the Yan Yuan passage, Pound stresses: 'There is no more important technical term in the Confucian philosophy than this *chih* (3) the hitching post, position, place one is in, and works from' (*Con*, 232). Pound's note informs his interpretation of *zhi* as 'take a position' in the parenthesis in the above translation. According to his understanding, *zhi* does not mean 'to stop moving,' but rather 'to stop in order to take a position.' Pound established such an understanding in his earlier reading of the same character in *Da xue*. In the opening paragraph of *Da xue*, the character *zhi* first appears in association with the third important goal of the Great Learning: '*zhi yu zhi shan* 止於至善.'[61] Pound renders the phrase as: 'Coming to rest, being at ease in perfect equity' (*Con*, 29). In this rendering, *zhi* or 'coming to rest' does not mean to stop acting, but rather to take the action of orienting oneself in an adequate mode of existence, or seeking one's proper ethical standing in the given social relations. Pound's reading of *zhi* in the *Da xue* passage is not wrong, even though he overemphasizes the canonical weight of this single character here.[62] What is problematic, however, is his assumption that *zhi* can be read only in this sense throughout the Confucian texts, an assumption that leads to his application of this same reading of *zhi* to the above Yan Yuan passage. In so doing, Pound thinks that he has maintained the consistent formulation of this Confucian concept. Yet the price of such a consistency is the subversion of commonly recognized interpretations: where Confucius is generally believed to be praising his disciple's achievements in life, Pound makes the master appear to deplore the disciple's failure 'to take a position.'

The second level on which Pound's deployment of intentional divergence operates is in his attempt to give his Confucian system an *external unity*, that is, a narrative consistency with what seems to be a larger, more universal pattern especially codified in the Western values that he privileged. In trying to integrate Confucian writing into a comprehensive and amenable scheme, Pound's translations often superimpose on Confucian terms the ideas he received from the Western tradition. And these ideas, in so far as they serve as a sort of master code by which Pound deciphers Confucian theories, tremendously empower his appropriation of an alien cultural tradition. Pound made no secret of his intention: 'Before we can have any serious discussion of Chinese philosophy we must agree on terminology. We must decide ... which ideograms correspond to what terms of good Latin' (*SP*, 84). Here, 'good Latin' is preferred not so much for its effectiveness as for its symbolic nature, its presence affirming the continuity of a 'sacred' tradition, the pre-Reformation European civilization, in which Pound retained his 'faith.'[63] In practice, however, the 'corresponding' choices at Pound's disposal for replacing Confucian terms are not necessarily confined to Latin; they can be Italian, French, or English, as long as they suggest the continuity of the values of that vanished tradition. Since much of Pound's agenda was aimed at reinvigorating that tradition, interpreting Confucian works in terms of these coded values was not an expediency for Pound, but a necessity.

Most of the key terms in Pound's translations – the representative ones are listed in the 'Terminology' section preceding the text of his *Confucius* – are encoded in received concepts. Sometimes the issue is further complicated because a misinterpretation resulting from this kind of deciphering procedure is itself a mixture of several sources: for instance, Pound's Neoplatonic reading of the otherwise simple term *ming* 明 (bright) as 'tensile light,' and the term *de* 德 (virtue) as 'Reason' and 'Intelligence.' These readings incorporate themes from Pound's spiritual mentors, such as John Scotus Erigena, Robert Grosseteste, Richard of St Victor, and Guido Cavalcanti. Loaded with complex implications, Pound's interpretations of the Confucian terms he considers significant often require the reader to look beyond the Chinese contexts for the truly intended meaning.

Pound's strategy of mastering Confucian terms derives much of its force from his conviction that 'the real classics inter-illuminate each other' (*SP*, 30) and that 'honest' minds think in 'one pattern':

> It is OF the permanence of nature that honest men, even if endowed with no special brilliance, with no talents above those of straightness and honesty, come repeatedly to the same answers in ethics, without need of borrowing each other's ideas.
> Shun and Wan had a thousand years between them and when their wills were compared they were as two halves of a tally stick.
> From Kung to Mencius a century, and to St. Ambrose another six or so hundred years, and a thousand years to St. Antonino and they are as parts of one pattern, as wood of a single tree. (*SP*, 89–90)

Pound's contention that a shared pattern of thought exists for all human beings is, in effect, another way of articulating his notion of the 'universality of the Word,' an idea that presupposes the existence of absolute truth or quintessential meaning prior to the construction of language. In regard to translation, the 'universality of the Word' ensures the transmission of meaning from one language into another, with absolute truth being the common destiny that both the translation and the original utterance endeavour to reach. Therefore, the ultimate oneness of the conditions for human thought and action makes it possible to overcome the separation created by the barriers of cultures, and to bridge the gulf wrought by the passage of time. Pound's confidence in universal cognates undercuts others' doubt about his positive view on the possibility of translation.[64] In an age often characterized as the era 'After Babel,' an age when language is seen by modern theorists like Martin Heidegger as the 'prison house of being' that prevents the 'dialogue from house to house,'[65] Pound's position in favour of translatability is reminiscent of the classical assumption that a set of permanent values constitutes the common foundation of all human civilizations, an assumption especially characteristic of the worldview of the Renaissance and Enlightenment writers in the humanist tradition.

With a strong faith in the universal pattern of the human intellect and an urgent sense of the need to reinstate past wisdom in that 'one pattern,' Pound in his translations integrates strategies that accomplish his ultimate purpose of turning Confucianism into a modern discourse both appealing and accessible to the Western mind. Such strategies not only reinterpret characters and restructure sentences, as we have seen, but also 're-form' the contour of Confucian texts. What follows is an amazing instance of such a textual revision, persuasively demonstrating the degree of radical transformation to which Pound could subject Confucian works while seeking to impose on them a contextual and conceptual consistency. The instance is the abridgment of *Zhong yong* in Pound's translation.

Zhong yong, supposedly authored by Confucius's grandson Zisi (?483–?402 BCE) as an independent work, was handed down as one lengthy chapter in *Li ji* (The Book of Rites). Zhu Xi took the text from *Li ji*, and used it with *Da xue, Lun yu,* and *Mengzi,* to form the quintessential Four Books of Confucian learning. Zhu Xi did not alter the original text, but he redivided it into thirty-three chapters. Since the thirteenth century, the text in Zhu Xi's edition has been accepted as the standard text of *Zhong yong* in China. Pound also used this text. He started translating *Zhong yong* into Italian in several parts during the period from April 1944 to January 1945, and published his version in full in February 1945.[66] He completed the rendering of his Italian version into English in October 1945 and published it in 1947 under the title *The Unwobbling Pivot*. The most striking divergence of Pound's *Unwobbling Pivot* from the Chinese *Zhong yong* is that the Chinese text has thirty-three chapters, whereas Pound's translation includes only the first twenty-six chapters.

Pound never fully clarified why he excluded the last seven chapters. The only relevant explanation he gave is ambiguous: 'Twenty-four centuries ago Tsze Sze [Zisi] needed to continue his comment with a profession of faith, stating what the Confucian idea *would* effect; looking back now over the millennial history of China there is need neither of adjectives nor of comment. And for that reason I end my translation at this point, temporarily at least' (*Con*, 188). Pound's 'temporary' omission turned out to be permanent, for in the years after *The Unwobbling Pivot* was first published, he did not add the excluded chapters to the reprints of his translation. In other words, his omission was not due to a lack of time, but rather involved other considerations. Mary Cheadle has tried to explain Pound's intent. According to Cheadle, the last seven chapters in the original text are about the 'ideal of leadership' exemplified by the Confucian sage and ruler. Representing such an image, Cheadle argues, 'would have seemed tauntingly ironic to Pound,' who at that moment saw in the defeat of Mussolini's Italy the further drifting away of Europe from a Confucian vision.[67] Cheadle's commentary may shed light on Pound's overall mindset when he was translating *Zhong yong* in 1945, but it does not adequately explain his deletion of the last seven chapters. The ideal of sage-kinghood, either in the form of a superior person or an enlightened ruler, is always the central theme of Confucian works and not necessarily the exclusive concern of the last seven chapters of *Zhong yong*. In fact, some previous chapters present even more specific configurations of such sage-kings, for instance, chapters 17 to 20, in which Confucius elaborates at length on the ideal kingship exemplified by rulers from Shun to King Wu. Pound had no desire to restrain his promotion of the ideal of Confucian sage-kinghood. Quite to the contrary, in the cantos written after 1945, he increasingly intensified his advocacy of such idealized leadership as personified by these Confucian sage-kings.

Pound's intent is best understood in terms of his effort to reframe the *Zhong yong* narrative, an endeavour derived perhaps from his ambition to accomplish a work comparable to that of previous great Confucian thinkers, such as Zhu Xi. In his commentaries on *Zhong yong*, Zhu Xi suggests that this work can be read in three parts: the first part (chapters 1–11) on the transcendental origins of the *Dao* or Way; the second part (chapters 12–20) on the inseparability of the *Dao* from human existence; and the third part (chapters 21–33) on the manifestation of the *Dao* of Heaven and the *dao* of humanity. Frankly, Zhu Xi does not make a very compelling case for his textual division, largely because his related commentaries are too brief and lack analytical substance. In a sense, Pound follows Zhu Xi's suggestion, but goes much further, not only explicitly dividing the work into three parts in his translation, but also giving each part a new topical focus in the 'Note' preceding the text: Thus, part 1 (chapters 1–11) is entitled 'Metaphysics,' part 2 (chapters 12–20) 'Politics,' and part 3 (chapters 21–6) 'Ethics.' The interpretive logic Pound provides for this textual division is not unjustifiable. As a matter of fact, in his study of *Zhong yong*, Tu Wei-ming praises Pound's editing 'Note' as 'insightful.'[68] However, it should be mentioned that by using for the subtitles a set of terms that apparently invokes the Aristotelian system of learning, Pound's revised tripartite division bears out his intent to Westernize the thematic structure of the *Zhong yong* text.

The more radical of Pound's revisions is the exclusion of the last seven original chapters, but the exclusion is based on his reading of the entire work from a creatively coherent perspective. In Pound's formulation, part 1 deals with the metaphysical nature of the *Dao*, part 2 illuminates the political efficacy of the *Dao* in organizing social relations, and part 3 should focus on the individual's pursuit of ethical perfection, with an emphasis on the *dao* of humanity (the reason why Pound names this part 'Ethics'). The guiding spirit of the *Dao* is defined in the Confucian term *cheng* 誠 (literally 'sincerity'), the significance of which Pound keenly captures by identifying it with the biblical term 'Word.' For Pound, self-cultivation rests on an individual's pursuit of *cheng* 誠, which starts with self-examination and ends with reaching out to embrace eternal truth. Pound finds this individualist vision of ethics logically mapped out in the *Zhong yong* text from chapter 21 to chapter 26. This portion begins with the definition of *cheng* or 'sincerity,' then explores a number of aspects of human 'sincerity,' and concludes with a celebration of King Wen, the paragon of the most 'sincere' individuals of the human race, who at the end of chapter 26 is seen to be purified in the 'tensile light, the Immaculata' (*Con*, 187). The ending is significant in two ways. First, it asserts that partaking of Heavenly 'sincerity' is the ultimate achievement of an individual's self-perfection, a moment when a superior human being transcends the mundane to attain unity with Heaven. Second, it creates a universally appealing vision by combining the Confucian notion of the Heavenly *Dao* with the Neoplatonic notion of the divine light, implying that the grace of 'the tensile light, the Immaculata' is offered, not just to the Chinese sage-king Wen, but to all who follow the call of the divine light. Accordingly, Pound chooses to end his translation with chapter 26, for it marks the climax of his ethical vision, and he deletes the following seven chapters that must have seemed to him anti-climatic, if not irrelevant or redundant.

To do him justice, by leaving out the last seven chapters of the original work (which are mostly on subjects other than 'sincerity') and incorporating received Western ideas, Pound gives the third part of his translation of *Zhong yong* a thematic unity that does not exist in the Chinese text. His practice, of course, raises serious questions regarding the nature of translation and the boundaries of a translator. But we have to remember that in undertaking the task of Confucian translation, Pound never saw himself merely as a translator in the usual sense of the word. Instead, he deemed himself a true 'Confucian' believer whose mission was to ensure the effective transmission of the master's teachings. If Zhu Xi could re-edit the classical Confucian texts for the China of the Song dynasty (960–1279), Pound must have assumed, then why could he not do what he considered appropriate for fulfilling his mission in the modern Western world? From Pound's point of view, his Confucius acquired the philosophical coherence of a unified system cemented by established Western theoretical categories. Before working on *Zhong yong*, Pound had recognized in *Da xue* a theory of 'Great Learning' that laid the epistemological foundation for Confucianism. Thus, with the three new topical formulations invested in *Zhong yong*, Pound sought to complete the task of reconfiguring Confucian works in order to establish a new system of Confucian learning, a system that could claim to include the following four basic branches: 'Epistemology,' 'Ethics,' 'Politics,' and 'Metaphysics.' This thoughtful restructuring, enabled by the Aristotelian methodology of classification, allowed Pound to *re-present* Confucianism in a way that would satisfy the Western expectation for a complete thought system.

2

Confucianism and Pound's Rethinking of Language

1. *Zheng Ming*: The Politics of Naming

When one opens the Ezra Pound journal *Paideuma*, two large Chinese characters on the inside cover immediately attract one's attention: 正名 (*zheng ming*, Pound's *Ch'ing Ming* or *Cheng Ming*). The two characters refer to a major Confucian doctrine known in English as 'to rectify names' and seem to have been inscribed in the Ezra Pound journal as the poet's Confucian hallmark. Beneath the two characters on the verso is Pound's statement acclaiming *zheng ming* 正名 as the 'new Paideuma,' that is, the root of a 'new civilization.'[1] On the same verso, Pound's version of a celebrated Confucian passage from *Da xue* envisions such a civilization. His revisionary rendering of this *Da xue* passage relates to the doctrine of *zheng ming* because this rendering posits the pivotal agenda of *cheng yi* 誠意: 'to attain precise verbal definitions.' The importance of the doctrine of *cheng yi* is highlighted by Pound through his use of the key character 誠 in a poetic celebration of Confucius:

>   the word is made
> perfect 誠
> better gift can no man make to a nation
>   than the sense of Kung fu Tseu
>   who was called Chung Ni (LXXV/474)

The centrality of the *cheng yi* doctrine to Pound's Confucian orientation explains why the character 誠 has come to occupy a prominent place on the title page of recent printings of *The Cantos* published by New Directions.

Indeed, the two Confucian doctrines of *zheng ming* and *cheng yi* are crucial to Pound's formulation of a new theory of language. The theory holds that language is not an *a priori* given predating human existence but rather a nominative act, the primal performance of the creative intelligence by which human beings prescribe the actuality of things, determine existential conditions, and demarcate the distinctions in sociopolitical relations. It is thus the responsibility of human beings to maintain the utmost possible functionality of language, or linguistic precision as Pound called it, in order to fulfil the universal human wish for intellectual progress, moral perfection, and social stability. At the core of Pound's theory of language is a belief that poetry, at its most authentic, represents the highest degree of linguistic precision, in which lies the hope of a redeemed language. At a time when poetry was suffering an inevitable marginalization in social life, such a theory allowed Pound to reassert poetry's privileged position by endowing upon the poet the duty of safeguarding the efficiency of language and, to a large extent, justified Pound's own increasingly intense experiments with poetic language.

In the five sections that compose this chapter, I will analyse the several aspects of the process by which Pound assimilated the two doctrines of *zheng ming* and *cheng yi* into his rethinking of the nature of language, in particular poetic language. This first section focuses on Pound's revisionist interpretation of *zheng ming* and *cheng yi*. In section 2 I uncover the aesthetic implications of Pound's early notion of poetic precision, which he inserted into the two Confucian doctrines. Section 3 examines the political impact of the *zheng ming* doctrine on Pound's postulate of a new theory about the social function of literature, while section 4 deals with the philosophical dimensions of Pound's theory of language based on the doctrine of *cheng yi*. The last section discusses the theme of linguistic precision in *The Cantos*, through which Pound conveyed his reconsiderations of the value of language from economic and historical perspectives.

The idea of *zheng ming* derives from *Lun yu* 13.3. It is recorded in this work that the disciple Zi Lu one day asked Confucius what his priorities would be if he were invited by the Lord of Wei to head the Wei government. Confucius answered that the first thing he would do would be *zheng ming*. *Zheng* is a verb that means 'to rectify' or 'to correct'; *ming* is a noun literally meaning 'name.' From the beginning, Confucius's notion of *zheng ming* appeared ambiguous: in the *Lun yu* account it immediately confused Zi Lu, who, upon hearing Confucius's reply, wondered what the master could 'rectify' in terms of *ming* and why he wanted to carry out such an agenda before anything else. Confucius explained that if *ming* was not corrected, language could not make sense; as a consequence, laws and rites would not be followed, leading to the collapse of society. Two crucial questions arise here: what exactly does Confucius mean by the notion of *ming*? In what way can *ming* be rectified or corrected? In general, three interpretations of this doctrine have been put forth in the history of Confucian hermeneutics.

According to the first interpretation, Confucius's *ming* 名 refers to the foundational codes concerning the social relations of a feudal hierarchy, such as the codes that stipulate the appropriate relationships between father and son, or between ruler and subject. To rectify *ming* is thus to reinstate the authority of these codes in order to restore the proper operation of the feudal social system. The historian Sima Qian (145?–86? BCE) helped to establish this interpretation by providing a historical context for the conversation about *zheng ming* between Zi Lu and Confucius. In his biographical narrative of Confucius, Sima Qian identified the Lord of Wei mentioned in the conversation as Duke Zhe, the young ruler of the state Wei, where Confucius was then residing. Zhe was in danger of losing the throne to his exiled father, Kuai Kui, whose claim for the dukedom was supported by some powerful lords of other states.[2] Kuai Kui, son of Duke Ling, had fled Wei after a failed plot against Duke Ling's young wife. Four years after Kuai Kui's banishment, Duke Ling died and left the dukedom to Zhe, his grandson and the son of Kuai Kui. Since Zhe's father was still alive, the legitimacy of his ascendance to lordship was seriously questioned by rulers of other states. It was in this context that Zhe sought Confucius's political advice. In providing this historical background, Sima Qian meant to make the case that by demanding *zheng ming* Confucius intended to advise Zhe to obey the obligation of a son and abdicate the sovereign title to his father Kuai Kui.

Over the centuries, most Confucian exegetes followed Sima Qian's historicist approach to the *zheng ming* doctrine. The most influential among them was Zhu Xi. In his commentary on the *zheng ming* passage in *Si shu jizhu*, Zhu Xi specified *ming* as the names of father and son. 'At that time Zhe did not treat his father as father,' Zhu Xi explained, '... and thus the relationship between names and the substance of names was disrupted. That is why Confucius held the rectification of names as the foremost thing to accomplish.'[3] With Zhu Xi's commentary, reading the notion of *zheng ming* in terms of rectifying the feudal codes of social relations became firmly established as the standard interpretation. Such an interpretation has appealed to commentators because it convincingly contextualizes Confucius's concerns.

Confucius lived at a time when the Zhou dynasty (1122-221 BCE), once a prosperous and powerful empire, was rapidly dissolving. Zhou China had been built on a feudal system, the political structure of which paralleled the structure of the extended family. The king ruled his nation like a familial head, providing it with order, authority, and benevolence. The nation consisted of many states, in each of which a prince or a duke presided over his smaller hierarchical society in the same patriarchal capacity. The decline of this system in Confucius's time created social chaos: there were constant wars among the rulers of the states, who fought for the hegemony of overlordship and simply defied the authority of the monarch. Within each state there were treacherous murders and intrigues that undermined the court as well as the family structure. To solve these problems, Confucius suggested restoring the political and ritual system of the earlier Zhou. *Zheng ming*, therefore, constituted an important part of this agenda. Confucius's determination to rectify the *ming*, or 'names,' of feudal relations dominated his political speeches recorded in classical texts. The best-known example is his assertion, in *Lun yu* 12.11, that everyone should live in conformity with what is encoded in his *ming*: the ruler acts like a ruler, the minister like a minister, the father like a father, and the son like a son. Another revealing instance, as related in the classical work *Han shi wai zhuan*, is Confucius's suggestion to replace the word 'borrow' (*jia* 假) with the word 'take' (*qu* 取) in describing a ruler's act of getting something from a subject.[4]

The second interpretation of *zheng ming* was proposed by Zheng Xuan (127-200 CE). He construed *ming* as 'written words,' arguing: '*Zheng ming* means to correct the written words, which were called *ming* in ancient times, but "written words" today. It is said in *Li ji* that "when there are more than one hundred *ming*, they are written down on bamboo slips." Because Confucius noticed the improper education of his time, he wanted to correct the miswritten words.'[5] Though this interpretation was adopted by Confucian commentators in the Han dynasty (206 BCE – 220 CE), during which Zheng Xuan was widely respected as one of the best philologists, it lost a following after the Tang dynasty (618-907) and is now generally regarded as an incorrect interpretation.

The third interpretation was offered by Ma Rong (79-166 CE), also a Han dynasty commentator. In Ma Rong's reading, *zheng ming* was to 'correct the names of hundreds of things.'[6] In the history of Confucian studies, orthodox commentators have consistently dismissed Ma Rong's reading as inadequate on the grounds that it misread Confucius's true intention in that particular context. Hidden behind this dismissal, perhaps, was the fear that Ma Rong's reading might diminish Confucius's grand scheme of political restoration to something like a petty concern with rhetorical matters. It is true that in most recorded instances where Confucius addressed issues about name and substance, he was not so much concerned with the exact referentiality of the word as with the ideological correctness of social practices, that is, not so much interested in the signifier-signified relationship in verbal activities as in the power relations manifested in the use of language. But there were also occasions when Confucius was concerned with the appropriate use of words, whether or not such use directly related to political actions. *Lun yu* 6.24, for example, registers Confucius's remark about a kind of drinking vessel called *gu* 觚. This Chinese character consists of two components, one indicating 'corner' (*jiao* 角) and the other 'gourd' (*gua* 瓜). That is because, before Confucius's time, such a vessel had a cornered shape. When Confucius saw a *gu* without corners, his comment was: how could this vessel be called *gu* if it does not have corners? The recounting of this instance suggests that Ma Rong's reading of *zheng ming* is not entirely unfounded.

Ma Rong's commentary on *zheng ming* has been passed down to us in a rather fragmentary and unsustained form through subsequent editions of *Lun yu*. Its briefness notwithstanding, this commentary posits an alternative reading that turns the attention of the *zheng ming* doctrine from merely political spheres back to language itself, to the issue of signification in its broad philosophical sense. From that perspective, Ma Rong's reading is potentially constructive because it helps to release the concept of *zheng ming* from its restrictive tie with feudal ritualism, and in so doing enlarges the scope of theoretical inquiry. Such a reading might enable the concept of *zheng ming* to serve as the paradigmatic basis of a philosophical theory of language, something that the Confucian tradition has not been able to produce. Throughout history, the philosophical value of Ma Rong's reading was ignored by fundamentalist Confucian exegetes, and it remains unrecognized by mainstream Confucian commentators in modern China. Feng Youlan (Fung Yu-lan), for example, has argued that 'what Confucius's *zheng ming* theory paid attention to was not an epistemological issue, or a logical issue.'[7] So far, Cheng Zhongying (Cheng Chung-ying) of the University of Hawaii is the only prominent contemporary Confucian thinker to call attention to the profound philosophical implications of the *zheng ming* doctrine. In Cheng's view, *zheng ming* lays the foundation for an epistemology centring on the acquisition of true knowledge. 'To put it simply,' he maintains in a 1967 essay devoted to the doctrine, '*zheng ming* means to attain correct knowledge of human beings and things, and then express that knowledge in correct concepts and definitions.'[8] Remarkably, Cheng's view was preceded several decades earlier by Pound's rethinking of *zheng ming*, as well as Pound's practice of this doctrine.

Although it is hard to determine exactly when Pound began to take serious notice of the *zheng ming* doctrine, judging from his application of the doctrine to a discussion of literary language in his 1928 essay 'How to Read,' it is reasonable to assume that his interest in *zheng ming* began around the mid-1920s. His *Digest of the Analects*, excerpts from *Lun yu* published in 1937, included the *zheng ming* passage. A year later, he incorporated these excerpts into the opening section of *Guide to Kulchur*, in which the two Chinese characters for *zheng ming* were inserted to highlight Confucius's remarks: 'To call people and things by their names, that is by the correct denominations, to see that the terminology was exact. 正名' (16). Pound's final, and much more thoughtful, rendering of the *zheng ming* passage, to which Pound scholars usually refer, appears in his 1950 translation of *Lun yu*, as given below in its entirety:

1. Tse-lu said: The lord of Wei is waiting for you to form a government, what are you going to do first?
2. He [Confucius] said: Settle the names (determine a precise terminology).
3. Tse-lu said: How's this, you're divagating, why fix 'em?
4. He said: You bumpkin! Sprout! When a proper man don't know a thing, he shows some reserve.
5. If words (terminology) are not (is not) precise, they cannot be followed out, or completed in action according to specifications.
6. When the services (actions) are not brought to true focus, the ceremonies and music will not prosper; where rites and music do not flourish punishments will be misapplied, not make bullseye, and the people won't know how to move hand or foot (what to lay hand on, or stand on).
7. Therefore the proper man must have terms that can be spoken, and when uttered be carried into effect; the proper man's words must cohere to things, correspond to them (exactly) and no more fuss about it. (*Con*, 249)

Pound's version departs from the standard translation of *zheng ming* in two important respects. First is the rendering of *ming*. In its feudal context, apart from a concern with the specific use of language, the term also refers to non-verbal activities, such as an individual person's exercise of rites, observance of ethical codes, and even performance of arts like music and dance, in accordance with the individual's social status. For English translators, the term *ming* poses a difficulty because there is hardly an equivalent for it in the English language. Thus *ming* is usually translated as 'names' to preserve the original ambiguity and complexity of the concept.[9] In the original passage, *ming* appears three times. In the second paragraph of his translation, Pound first renders *ming* as 'names,' but immediately provides an explanation in a parenthesis designating his 'names' as 'precise terminology.' In the fifth and seventh paragraphs where *ming* appears again, Pound simply uses 'words' and 'terms' to translate it. While Pound's revisionist version of *ming* reduces the feudalistic specificity historically deposited in the Confucian *ming*, it widens the scope of the term's application to ordinary instances of linguistic activity.

The second of Pound's departures in translating *zheng ming* is that, instead of calling for 'the rectification of names' in abstract terms, he clearly prescribes what he believes to be the right way of implementing *zheng ming*, that is, making terminology or words precise. In the last paragraph, Pound goes even further in setting up a specific criterion for such linguistic precision: 'Words must cohere to things, correspond to them (exactly).' This sentence has no textual justification from the Chinese passage: it is Pound's own creation, which carries a strong 'objectivist' overtone familiar to the readers of the Imagist-Vorticist Pound. As far as Pound's understanding is concerned, his 1950 rendering of *zheng ming* is consistent with his 1937 version, however. At the crux of both versions lies the same stress on precise terminology, or exact correspondence between words and things. Certainly, Pound is aware that precise language is only a means, and that the *zheng ming* doctrine is important mainly because its implementation concerns the observance of rites, the flourishing of arts, the efficiency of law, and, in short, the stability and continuity of a civilized society.

In addition, Pound's formulation of a theory of precise language is greatly reinforced by his highly revisionary reading of the concept of *cheng yi* 誠意 (to make thought sincere) from *Da xue*, a reading that demonstrates his determination to *restore* what he perceived to be the lost meaning in the Confucian classic. In the 1928 *Ta Hio*, there is little evidence that Pound connected *cheng yi* directly with the issue of language, or interpreted it in any way that explicitly asserted the idea of verbal precision. But in this translation, what makes his understanding of *cheng yi* notably distinct from Pauthier's is that Pound associates the idea of sincerity with that of clarity of thought. For instance, in *Da xue* 6.1, while Pauthier translates *cheng yi* as 'render ses intentions pures et sincères,'[10] Pound adds the idea of clear expression of intention to his version: 'clarify and render sincere one's own intentions' (*TH*, 19).

Before he started retranslating *Da xue* in the late 1930s, the first explicit linkage Pound made between the concept of *cheng yi* and the issue of language emerged in 'Immediate Need of Confucius,' his major article on Confucianism published in 1937. Pound begins this article with a thesis on the problem of 'the words,' using Dante's ideas to illuminate Confucius's concerns about this issue:

> In considering a value already age-old, and never to end while men are, I prefer not to write 'to the modern world'. The *Ta Hio* stands, and the commentator were better advised to sweep a few leaves from the temple steps. ...
>
> Dante for a reason wrote *De Vulgari Eloquio* – On the Common Tongue – and in each age there is need to write De Vulgari Eloquio, that is, to insist on *seeing* the words in use and to know the why of their usage.
>
> No man has ever known enough about words. The greatest teachers have been content to use a few of them justly.
>
> If my version of the *Ta Hio* is the most valuable I have done in three decades I can only wait for the reader to see it. And for each to discover its 'value' to the 'modern world' for himself. (*SP*, 75)

Here the 'modern world' refers to the 'whole Occident' Pound depicts in the passages that follow, which at the time, according to Pound, was 'bathed in mental sewage' as a consequence of the loss of the 'habit of verbal definition.' And lacking 'verbal distinctions' in the production of knowledge, Pound claims, inevitably leads to all conceivable forms of moral corruption and social chaos (*SP*, 76, 77). This is where he discovers the 'age-old value' of *Da xue*, which he anxiously wants his reader 'to see.' The 'immediate' benefit of this Confucian work is that it points out the way to regain the defining power of language to consolidate the foundation of knowledge, for, as Pound quotes Dante approvingly in the article, 'knowledge of a definite thing comes from a knowledge of

Confucianism and Pound's Rethinking of Language   53

things defined' (*SP,* 76). The revelation that verbal precision is vitally important to efficient knowledge and social order comes from Pound's reinterpretation of the *cheng yi* concept in *Da xue.* In another article published a year later, Pound clearly links *cheng* 誠 with the adequate use of language, maintaining that this term derives from the Confucian postulate of categorizing things 'by their right names' (*SP,* 85).

Now we must take a close look at Pound's rendering of *cheng yi* in his re-translation of *Da xue* in order to elucidate his strategy of linking the concept of *cheng yi* with the idea of linguistic precision:

> The men of old wanting to clarify and diffuse throughout the empire that light which comes from looking straight into the heart and then acting, first set up good government in their own states; wanting good government in their states, they first established order in their own families; wanting order in the home, they first disciplined themselves; desiring self-discipline, they rectified their hearts; and wanting to rectify their hearts, they *sought precise verbal definitions of their inarticulate thoughts [the tones given off by the heart]*; wishing to attain precise verbal definitions, they set to extend their knowledge to the utmost. This completion of knowledge is rooted in sorting things into organic categories. (*Con,* 29–31; emphasis mine)

This is one of the most important paragraphs in Confucian works; it crystallizes the Confucian vision of an idealized social order based upon a perfect sage-kinghood. Besides the concern with language, Pound's translation of this oft-quoted paragraph contains a number of ideas instrumental to his political position, ideas that I will deal with in the next chapter. What is specifically pertinent to our discussion here is Pound's translation of *cheng yi*. Standard English translations of the *cheng yi* concept are represented by Legge's version of 'sought to be sincere in their thoughts' and Wing-tsit Chan's version of 'make their wills sincere.'[11] In contrast, Pound's version of *cheng yi,* 'sought precise verbal definition of their inarticulate thoughts,' articulates a strikingly different agenda.

Of the two phrases in Pound's version, 'sought precise verbal definition' and 'inarticulate thoughts,' I will analyse the second phrase first, since it derives from the simpler notion of *yi*. Based on his etymographic assumption, Pound decomposes the character 意 (*yi,* thought or idea) into two elements. The top element is *yin* 音, which means 'sound' or 'music' if used as an individual character. The bottom element is *xin* 心, or 'heart,' when used independently. This is how Pound gets the idea of 'the tones given off by the heart' in the parenthesis. In Pound's philosophy of knowledge, what the heart 'gives off' are merely perceptual or emotional data that have not been defined by language. Hence, 'inarticulate thoughts.'

The Chinese character *cheng* 誠 is commonly rendered as 'sincere' or 'sincerity.' Pound's early conception of sincerity, which was informed by a Romantic perspective that posited this ethical value as the basis for evaluating verbal truth, indeed played a significant role in his initial interest in the Confucian concept of *cheng*. However, in rendering the *cheng yi* passage, Pound feels that the English term 'sincerity' cannot fully express the profound implications about linguistic exertion inscribed by this Chinese character (*SP*, 84). As always, then, he subjects the character 誠 to an etymographic analysis, dissecting it into two meaning units. The left part of the character, 言 signifying 'speech' or 'language,' is that from which Pound derives the idea of 'verbal definition.' As for the right part, 成 meaning 'complete,' he construes it as 'bring to focus.' Such a reading enables him to produce an amazingly creative definition of *cheng*, as given in the list of 'Terminology' preceding the texts of his translations: ' 誠 "Sincerity." The precise definition of the word, pictorially the sun's lance coming to rest on the precise spot verbally' (*Con*, 20). Thus, for Pound, *cheng*, a combination of 'the *word* and the action of fixing or *perfecting*,' comes to signify an active endeavour towards intellectual perfection marked by verbal faithfulness (*SP*, 85).

Pound's deciphering, which invests the concept of *cheng* in *Da xue* with the ideal of verbal integrity, is highly innovative, but not without justification from Confucian classics. In *Yi jing* (the Book of Changes), Confucius himself is recorded to have stated that 'to work on one's words in order to establish *cheng*' (*xiu ci li qi cheng* 修辭立其誠) is essential to the accomplishment of a superior person.[12] There is no evidence, however, that Pound had read *Yi jing* around the mid-1930s, when he began to devote increasing enthusiasm to the passage about *cheng yi* in *Da xue*. His version of *cheng yi* resulted mostly from his unusual, almost instinctive, sensitivity to the etymological construct of the character *cheng* as well as its association with the value of formative linguistic acts in intellectual life. No Confucian exegetes before Pound had interpreted *cheng* from such a perspective; only recently have a few Confucian scholars begun to offer interpretations of *cheng* more or less similar to Pound's. Among contemporary Chinese philosophers, Zhang Dainian has called attention to an 'etymological sense' of *cheng* that indicates that 'the word matches the person and vice versa.'[13] In the American circle of Confucian studies, David Hall and Roger Ames, coauthors of several influential books on Confucian philosophy, put forth an explanation of *cheng* that sounds very much like a restatement of Pound's interpretation. Hall and Ames are interested in the ontological meaning of *cheng*, and such a meaning, according to Hall and Ames, is informed by the etymology of the term: 'The character translated "integrity," *ch'eng* (誠), is etymologically constituted by "to speak" (*yen* 言) and "to complete, to realize" (*ch'eng* 成). Its meaning, then, is "to realize that which is spoken."'[14]

Through his forceful revisionary interpretation, Pound succeeds in transforming the *cheng yi* doctrine in *Da xue* from a basically ethical imperative in the original work to a modern dictum about proper and productive use of language. Moreover, because of its function as a crucial link between idea (acquisition of knowledge) and action (achieving social order), Pound's notion of *cheng yi*, the 'precise definition of the word,' acquires the same weight as *zheng ming* in his formulation of a theory of language. In fact, by interpreting *cheng yi* in terms of the pursuit of linguistic precision, Pound makes this concept a complement to *zheng ming*. While *zheng ming*, a political agenda applied mainly to the public sphere, mandates the superimposition of verbal precision on ordinary people to ensure the ideological correctness of their social behaviour, *cheng yi*, a driving force in the private sphere, aims to promote the individual's consciousness of the important role that verbal precision plays in self-cultivation.

2. Poetic Precision: A Modernist Paradigm

In view of the significance of linguistic precision that Pound attaches to the two Confucian doctrines, the questions we have yet to address are why he puts so much emphasis on the notion of precision and what this notion means within his own system of thought. Pound's idea of linguistic precision defies a dictionary definition and, in fact, is much more complicated than the use of the same term by some of his avant-garde contemporaries in the modernist movement.[15] Before the Confucian doctrines about language attracted his attention, the term 'precision' had gained momentum in Pound's critical vocabulary. Typical of the experience of a fledging poet, Pound's notion of linguistic precision before the 1920s was characterized by his changing concerns. In his pre-Imagist years, Pound's notion referred to a sort of correspondence between poetic vision and its verbal expression; his focus at this point was on the relationship between the mind and language. During his experimental period as an Imagist-Vorticist poet – approximately from 1913 to the end of the decade – the notion mostly referred to a correspondence between the word and the object it signifies, with a focus on the relationship between language and the world of things. Both considerations, though conceived from an aesthetic perspective, derived from an ever-deepening anxiety over the issue of language in the modern society.

The problem of language had been Pound's major concern from the beginning of his poetic career, and was the primary reason for his participation in what he later called the 'revolution of the word' starting in London in 1908 (*PE*, 49). Such a concern was shared by many modernist poets writing in a literary tradition believed to be plagued by the degeneration of language. When T.S. Eliot's Prufrock in 1916 cried out, 'It is impossible to say just what I mean!'[16] he gave a memorable articulation to the sense of linguistic crisis endemic to the modernist movement in which Pound was a major figure.[17] In the essay on 'Cavalcanti,' Pound recalls that when he was a younger poet, the available literary idiom was the 'crust of dead English,' and that in 1910 not only did he lack 'a language to use, but even a language to think in' (*LE*, 193–4).

Pound had begun his creative career by looking into the past for his poetic models. In *The Spirit of Romance*, his first major critical work published in 1910, as well as a series of articles written afterward, he built a literary pantheon inhabited mostly by the Provençal poets of the twelfth century and the Tuscan poets of the thirteenth century. What Pound admired in these poets can be summarized as the power of using precise language to articulate their thoughts: 'In the writers of the duo-cento and early tre-cento we find a precise psychology, embedded in a now almost unintelligible jargon, but there nevertheless' (*LE*, 54). According to Pound, the Provençal Troubadours overwhelmingly preferred 'an extreme precision,' which enabled an individual poet like Arnaut Daniel to find words that could 'convey his exact meaning' (*SR*, 22, 25). Similarly, according to Pound, among the Tuscan poets 'it is in the spirit of this period to be precise,' and consequently, 'the preciseness of the description' in their poetry denoted 'a clarity of imaginative vision' (*SR*, 105, 106). 'In each case,' Pound observed, 'their virtue is a virtue of precision' (*SP*, 31). Pound discovered that this 'preciseness which bewilders one accustomed to nothing more complex than modern civilization' was not available in recent poets (*SR,* 104). For Pound, of all the medieval poets Dante stood out as the most persuasive example of such a verbal virtue: 'Dante's precision both in the *Vita Nuova* and in the *Commedia* comes from the attempt to reproduce exactly the thing which has been clearly seen' (*SR,* 126). In short, in Pound's early evaluations of the medieval poets, precision had already served as a central aesthetic criterion, 'the touchstone and essay of the artist's power, of his honor, his authenticity' (*SR,* 87).

In Pound's early formulation, then, the precision that determines the 'authenticity' of an artist's 'interpretation' of life should include the two essential aspects of artistic creation: the way the artist perceives the world and the way he articulates his findings, or as Pound put it, 'interpretive intention' and 'exactness of presentation' (*SR,* 87). In other words, as the 'touchstone' of an artist's work, precision requires that the artist's perception of the world be authentic and that his presentation of that perception be accurate. I will look into these two aspects separately. Pound's idea of the artist as an inspired interpreter of life incorporates the Romantic notion of the poet as a privileged 'seer' as well as some contemporary influential theories of mysticism celebrating intuition.[18] In Pound's view, the poet 'perceives' the world through a special sense of vision sustained by a combination of sensuous experiences, imagination, and intuition. In the short prose piece 'Religio,' Pound suggests that human beings have two senses of perception, the 'sense of knowledge' and the 'sense of vision' (*SP,* 48). The latter sense, in which lies the power of the arts, plays a very important role in the spiritual life of human beings because it enables them to perceive the 'divine forms' of gods 'by beauty' (*SP,* 47). In the case of the Troubadours, Pound believed that their visionary perception was empowered by a unity of intellect and sensuous energy, a unity that allowed these poets to obtain the essentials of the universe through sensations and instinctive feelings. What the visionary poetic mind captures are the eternal relations, the forms of the 'eternal minds,' as Pound put it (*SP,* 47). Given the Romantic spirit of the early Pound, it is not surprising that his sense of visionary perception is reminiscent of William Blake's similar notion that 'Vision or Imagination is a Representation of what Eternally Exists, Really & Unchangingly.'[19] In both conceptions vision becomes truth. For Pound visionary perception is 'true' or 'real,' not just because it reveals eternal verities, but because the poet has directly experienced it; for instance, 'Dante's vision is real, because he saw it' (*SR,* 178). Pound believed that at the time of the Troubadour and Tuscan poets there existed an overwhelming respect for the 'seeing of visions,' a general sense of confidence in the truthfulness of visionary perceptions. In this cultural climate, Pound felt, a poet was allowed to take 'delight in definite portrayal of his vision' (*SR*, 105).

For Pound, the medieval poets enjoyed a special mode of existence, a kind of unity of being in which flesh and mind, body and soul, were not separated. Here the body, according to Pound, was 'a mechanism rather like an electric appliance,' constantly reaching out to get in touch with the movement of the universe. Such a state of being, the *phantastikon* in Pound's terminology, represented both the desired condition of human existence and a belief cherished by the medieval poets in the strength of this human condition. This belief made the medieval poets highly responsive to the outside world and enabled their minds to reflect the relations of things in a natural manner. Thus, Pound claimed, theirs were the truly poetic minds, not only 'close on the vital universe' but also 'ever at the interpretation of this vital universe' (*SR*, 93). Equipped with this extraordinary capacity, according to Pound, the poetic mind gained credence as a visionary seer, perceiving what otherwise would be invisible 'at greater intensity, and more intimately, than his public' (*SR*, 87).

While precise perception in Pound's view suggests a correspondence between poetic vision and the laws of the 'vital universe,' precise presentation, the other aspect of his early postulate of precision, demands a correspondence between such vision and its verbal expression. Pound once mentioned Guido's work to T.E. Hulme as an example of this type of precision, in which 'the phrases correspond to definite sensations undergone' (*LE*, 162). From its inception, Pound's concept of precision posited an expressionist theory of language, which assumed that the eternal verities, or what the visionary mind seizes in intense moments, exist prior to language and thus operate independently of verbal constructs. In this sense, the strong 'interpretive intention' of the visionary mind, although a prerequisite condition, does not automatically lead to precise linguistic expression. Pound regarded precise expression rather as the fruition of strenuous craftsmanship and, most importantly, as the result of technical choice informed by the poet's ideological and moral intentions. 'Technique,' Pound was convinced, 'is the means of conveying an exact impression of exactly what one means in such a way as to exhilarate' (*SP*, 33); therefore the choice of linguistic technique involves the issue of sincerity. This is why Pound insisted: 'I believe in technique as the test of a man's sincerity ... or the precise rendering of the impulse' (*LE*, 9). A sincere articulation is thus identical with a precise presentation, in the sense that both indicate a truthful expression, or a correspondence between the inner thought and its verbal externalization. From this perspective, it is not difficult for us to understand why, two decades later, Pound was to interpret *cheng yi* as seeking 'precise verbal definitions of thoughts.'

Pound received the critical term 'sincerity' from previous writers. In their battle against the challenges engendered by modern science, and especially against the charge that poetry yielded false knowledge and thus was useless, nineteenth-century writers had persistently valorized 'sincerity' as an important literary virtue justifying the value of literature. In some famous theoretical formulations, from William Wordsworth's 'science of feeling' and Matthew Arnold's 'high seriousness' to Henry James's psychological realism, the concept of 'sincerity' was always employed to enforce the same assertion that poetic knowledge does not need to be empirically verified because it is true by virtue of the faithfulness of the poet's verbal expression to his feelings and emotions. In this respect, even the anti-Romantic T.E. Hulme, Pound's contemporary and friend, spoke in the same vein: 'If it is sincere in the accurate sense ... there you seem to me to have the highest verse, even though the subject be trivial and the emotions of the infinite far away.'[20] Hulme's idea that verbal accuracy was indicative of poetic sincerity voiced the same concern as Pound's postulate of verbal precision and sincerity, a postulate that should be evaluated in the context of the modern poet's endeavour both to resist the positivistic trend of science and to reconcile with the appeal of science. What makes Pound's postulate particularly interesting is that it attempts to take over the lustre of science by incorporating the concept of precision that is usually ascribed to scientific discourse. The modern poet can be 'scientific,' Pound thus claimed, 'in that he presents the image of his desire, of his hate, of his indifference as precisely that, as precisely the image of his own desire, hate or indifference. The more precise his record the more lasting and unassailable his work of art' (*LE*, 46). By asserting the poet's capacity for precise presentation Pound sought to restore poetry's credibility as a special mode of knowledge that is as reliable as science.

As Pound's career developed, his preoccupation with language evolved to include new concerns. With his involvement in such avant-garde movements as Imagism and Vorticism, his poetics, now premised on the assumption that 'language is made out of concrete things' (*L*,

49), tended to privilege a language grounded more in its thingness than in its visionary depth. This does not mean that Pound discarded what he had admired in the medieval poets. The fact is that his undertaking to canonize these poets continued along with the formulation of an 'objectivist' theory of Image. Pound's theoretical focus shifted, or, to be more accurate, expanded, from the relationship between language and the mind to the relationship between language and the world of objects. This development not only brought about new formulations with regard to 'Image' and 'Vortex,' but also allowed him to explain some of his previous notions about poetry in a fresh way, one better suited to his concurrent practice as an experimental poet.

Meanwhile, Pound was expanding the concept of verbal precision to emphasize such qualities as 'objectivity,' 'factuality,' and 'naturalness.' For instance, he remarked in 1914 that 'one might learn from Dante himself all that one could learn from Arnaut: precision of statement, particularization' (*LE*, 215). Pound appreciated the poetic virtue of 'particularization' because it constituted the 'anchorage' of objectivity that he found missing from the modern mind; as he argued in another place: 'It is the curse of our contemporary "mentality" that its general concepts have so little anchor in particular and known objects.'[21] Also, regretting the demise of 'realism' in English literature, which he felt had achieved its last exemplification of precision in Laurence Sterne, Pound insisted on reinstating 'the value of writing words that conform precisely with fact' (*LE*, 276). Apart from 'objects' and 'facts,' which constitute the substance of the external world and hence the legitimate content of the word, Pound viewed the naturalness of the writer's language as the quality most reflecting a precise representation of the relations between things, or, in his words, the 'natural order' of the world of things. He brought up the idea of 'natural order,' for instance, in his discussion of Lionel Johnson. He noticed in Johnson's poetry an 'old-fashioned kind of precision,' which he dismissed because it was not 'the sort of precision' that he was promoting. 'Our aim,' Pound maintained, 'is natural speech, the language as spoken. We desire the words of poetry to follow the natural order' (*LE*, 361, 362). Pound, therefore, considered the naturalness of poetic utterance to be an attribute of language characterized by the rhythm of ordinary speech as well as images and symbols informed by concrete objects we encounter in everyday life, in short, a language totally free from mannerism, in which words are supposed to live close to things.

Around this time, Pound summarized his ideas about precision in the first two of his three famous Imagist principles: 'Direct treatment of the "thing" whether subjective or objective' and 'To use absolutely no word that does not contribute to the presentation' (*LE*, 3). These principles reflect the defining feature of Imagist precision, that is, the 'direct treatment of the thing.' One might find it curious that the 'thing' is here divided into two types: while the 'objective thing' may not be difficult to understand, the idea of a 'subjective thing' appears confusing. However, in light of Pound's earlier postulate of visionary perception, it is justifiable to identify 'subjective things' with the internalized experiences of objects and events that are waiting to be externalized in verbal form. Indeed, the direct treatment of the 'subjective thing' recapitulates Pound's early notion of precise rendering of sensations or feelings. His own recollection, in *Gaudier-Brzeska*, of how he wrote the renowned short poem 'In a Station of the Metro' may give us the sense of such a creative moment: 'In a poem of this sort one is trying to record the precise instant when a thing outward and objective transforms itself, or darts into a thing inward and subjective' (*GB*, 89).

The 'direct treatment' of things demands, above all, avoidance of linguistic conventions. As Pound told Harriet Monroe in a letter in January 1915, 'there must be no clichés, set phrase, stereotyped journalese. The only escape from such is by precision, a result of concentrated attention to what is writing.' He made a demand in the same letter: 'Objectivity and again objectivity' (*L*, 49). It should be noted that here Pound is positing 'objectivity' not as an antithesis to 'subjectivity,' but rather as an effective counter to abstract speech. Abstraction, in his view, is the result of cliché and rhetorical ornament; it separates things from words, substance from form, and meaning from intention. 'Precision' is seen to be able to provide an immunity from such a disease of writing by forcing the creative mind of the poet to concentrate on the subject matter rather than on rhetorical ornaments. In other words, 'concentration' enabled by the pursuit of verbal precision constitutes a form of 'direct treatment.'

The distinction between 'direct treatment' of the thing and 'indirect treatment,' in Pound's Imagist conception, can be simplified as the difference between showing and telling, or between presenting and commenting, a difference marking the tension between precision and abstraction. Such an emphasis on the direct treatment of the thing is characteristic of the determination of modernist writers to turn representation into presentation, a strategy Pound discovered in the French 'prose tradition' of Stendhal and Flaubert: 'Flaubert – mot juste, présentation ou constatation' (*L*, 218). In these nineteenth-century realists Pound saw an aesthetics of linguistic economy and objective presentation representing a modern model of precision. He once quoted Stendhal's words to illustrate his expectation of a modern poet: 'Donner une idée claire et précise des mouvements du coeur' (give a clear and precise idea of the movements of the heart [*LE*, 54]). Pound was convinced, with Stendhal, that although clarity and precision had once been poetry's special merits, these qualities had been taken over by modern prose. 'If we cannot get back to these things,' Pound cautioned, 'if the serious artist cannot attain this precision in verse, then he must either take to prose or give up his claim to being a serious artist' (*LE*, 54). It is conceivable that Stendhal's idea would later contribute to Pound's rendering of Confucius's concept of *cheng yi*, that is, 'seeking precise verbal definitions of their inarticulate thought [the tones given off by the heart]' (*Con*, 31).

As is well known, Pound's search for an 'objective' language was immensely energized by Fenollosa's ideas about language. In the preceding chapter, I mentioned Fenollosa's influence on Pound's theory of reading. What is particularly relevant here is Fenollosa's view of the relationship between language and nature. Indeed, in *The Chinese Written Character as a Medium for Poetry*, Fenollosa locates the very origin of language in nature. Nature in Fenollosa's conception works in a way similar to that of a linguistic system: 'The type of sentence in nature is a flash of lighting. It passes between two terms, cloud and the earth.'[22] The protolanguage, nature, provided a model on the basis of which emerged the first human language, a metaphorical and originary language that enjoyed an intimate relation with the primal text, which is either called nature, essence, or the universal law. According to Fenollosa, however, modern languages, and especially Western languages, have unfortunately lost the vital force of that primitive language. Fenollosa ascribes this linguistic degradation to the tyranny of 'European logic,' which turned thought into a game of piling up abstract units or concepts. As a consequence, the use of language has turned into the 'process of abstraction,' in which the word is increasingly removed from the thing it signifies, and signification has become a matter of defining a thing with an abstract label instead of presenting a thing by what it dynamically does. The antidote that Fenollosa prescribes is a return to the primitive language, namely, poetic language. Fenollosa's theory reinforced, if not initiated, some of Pound's beliefs: that the poet is the only person able to revive language, that poetic language follows the course of a dynamic nature rather than obeying artificial rules, and that the efficacy of language derives mostly from the use of concrete images. By equating the natural with the visual in language, the true with the concreteness of images, Pound assigned to poetry the task of bringing words closer to things. Little wonder that Pound was partial to poetry with a high visual quality, for 'in *Phanopaeia* we find the greatest drive toward utter precision of words' (*LE*, 26).

Another major influence on Pound during his Imagist years was the French writer Remy de Gourmont.[23] For our purposes, Gourmont's doctrine of 'dissociation of ideas,' which makes an argument for cleaning language, is of special interest because it showed Pound a way to verbal precision and, more significantly, prepared him for Confucius's doctrine of *zheng ming*. As Pound later confirmed, 'the art of not being exploited begins with "Ch'ing Ming"! and persists invictis, uncrushable on into Gourmont's *Dissociations d'idées*' (*GK*, 244).

In his essay 'La dissociation des idées,' Gourmont analyses two ways of thinking. The first is association, in which the mind accepts current ideas. The second is dissociation, largely a way of dealing with 'old ideas,' which according to Gourmont is rare but characterizes a creative intelligence: 'It is a matter either of conceiving new relationships among old ideas and images; or of separating old ideas, old images united by tradition, and considering them one by one, being free to rework them and arrange them in an infinite number of new couplings – which a new operation will disunite once again until the new ties, always fragile and equivocal, are formed.'[24] What Gourmont intends to convey by the concept of dissociation of ideas is not simply a process of cognition, but rather the way language operates, the condition of language in which the primordial meaning is constantly wrapped in layers of ideas and images. Therefore, a recognition of this condition and an insight into the way it operates, Gourmont believes, allow the creative mind to turn dissociation into a verbal strategy of retrieving or achieving the desired meaning of the word by trimming it of dead ideas (in much the same way as Pound did later in his etymographic reading of Confucian works). This is exactly the strategy that Pound later asserted in *ABC of Economics*: 'Dissociations: Or preliminary clearance of the ground' (*SP,* 233). As Pound saw it, if creative thinking entails an act of clearing the ground of language, it is because words have been obscured by received ideas and even false ideas, and thus efforts must be made to clear the path so that words can return to their original grounding in the things they signify. For Pound, by proposing such a task Gourmont's notion of dissociation affirmed its connection with the 'uncrushable' way of *zheng ming*, the way of 'making words precise' that Pound would find more convincingly laid out in Confucian works.

3. Poets as the Guardian of Language

Although Pound had shown an impressive familiarity with Confucian ideas before the 1920s, it was not until 1928, in the essay 'How to Read,' that he explicitly linked Confucius with the concept of linguistic precision. Focusing on the relationship between the health of language and the health of society, Pound in this essay attempts to valorize a theory of linguistic determinism on behalf of Confucius. Pound states: 'Misquoting Confucius, one might say: It does not matter whether the author desire the good of the race or acts merely from personal vanity. The thing is mechanical in action. In proportion as his work is exact, i.e., true to human consciousness and to the nature of man, as it is exact in formulation of desire, so is it durable and so is it "useful"; I mean it maintains the precision and clarity of thought, not merely for the benefit of a few dilettantes and "lovers of literature," but maintains the health of thought outside literary circles and in non-literary existence, in general individual and communal life' (*LE*, 22). Confucius, of course, never said that the author's intention does not matter. What Pound is driving at is that a correct language is the single most important thing for Confucius, so much so that one could even exaggerate, or 'misquote,' the ancient sage to foreground his overriding concern. In this passage, Pound makes a direct reference to the Confucian doctrines related to the issue of language and tries to present them in his own words. The idea that 'precise thought' is 'true to human consciousness and to the nature of man' resonates with Pound's interpretation of *cheng yi*, but the argument that 'exact' expression amounts to truth is unmistakably a recapitulation of his earlier concerns about poetic language. At the same time, his assertion that an individual writer's word choice has important social consequences seems to be an application of the Confucian concept of *zheng ming*. These ideas sustain the central thesis of the essay, which claims that writers must maintain the efficiency of their language for the health of society. 'How to Read' represents a turning point in Pound's formulation of a theory of language, especially in terms of integrating his concern with poetic language into his political vision. Actually, he soon after developed the major arguments of this essay into a book, *The ABC of Reading* (1934). By mapping out a history of the 'efficient use of language,' the book seeks to convey a modernized version of *zheng ming*, one that maintains that the solidification of society depends on a solid language.²⁵

From the early 1930s to his later years, with a strong belief that 'any precise use of words is bound in the long run to be useful to the state and the world at large' (*J/M*, 74), Pound's observations on language were saturated with 'Confucian' vocabulary, which put unusual emphasis on the social and political significance of a precise 'terminology,' 'term,' or 'definition.' In order to make his Confucian position more visible, Pound also made use in his writings of relevant Chinese characters selected from Confucian texts. The first Chinese character *xin* 信 (faith) appeared at the end of canto XXXIV (1933). Pound interpreted this term as 'fidelity to the given word,' and deemed it one way of practising *cheng* or 'sincerity.' For Pound, *xin* 信 was part of *zheng ming*, and, as such, epitomized the integrity of one's linguistic consciousness. In his early works, Pound had made frequent (but mostly fragmented) remarks on the moral implications of an individual person's verbal life. Now, with what appeared to him to be the time-honoured framework of Confucianism, he wanted to organize his ideas about language into a well-defined 'discipline' of knowledge, incorporating his own moral, political, and linguistic concerns. Pound called such a discipline 'orthology,' the purpose of which was to promote the idea that 'honesty of the word does not permit dishonesty of the matter' (*PE*, 193). This idea was sustained by the Confucian term *xin* 信. The two Chinese characters for *zheng ming*, 正名, appeared in *Guide to Kulchur* in 1938 (16), and shortly afterward entered *The Cantos* (LI/252). Around this time Pound tried to launch a campaign to continue what he called a 'cleaning up of the WORD' (*PE*, 50), a campaign that inveighed above all against the capitalist banking system he decried as usury. 'Usura falls under the main consideration of unjust price,' Pound explained, and 'mankind's fog concerning it comes from NOT defining one's terms. First the clear definition, then the clear articulation' (*GK*, 247–8).

During the Second World War, Pound's sense of urgency for implementing *zheng ming* intensified further. Thus, he maintained: 'Towards order in the state: the definition of the word' (*SP*, 333). Even after the war, after his political vision had been completely shattered, Pound still insisted on the priority of *zheng ming*. As he declared in a later canto: 'Precise terminology is the first implement' (XCIX/731). In fact, seeking precise terminology remained his lifelong commitment. And this commitment, according to Pound in a 1960 article, defined the central agenda of the 'revolution of the word': 'The befouling of terminology should be put an end to. It is a time for clear definition of terms. Immediately, of economic terms, but ultimately of all terms. It is not a revolution of the word but a castigation of the word. And that castigation must precede any reform, (*SP,* 162).

The immediately noticeable impact of the Confucian doctrines of *zheng ming* and *cheng yi* on Pound's theory of language was that these doctrines tremendously reinforced the political assertion of his theory in two ways. On the one hand, Confucian doctrines, especially *zheng ming*, provided a broad and systematic social perspective, one that helped Pound to enlarge his concerns and deepen his inquiry into the political dimensions of the problem of language. With regard to language, Pound in his early stage had devoted his attention primarily to two kinds of relationships: first, the relationship between the word and the mind, and second, the relationship between the word and the world of objects. But now, under the guidance of the *zheng ming* doctrine, he became more and more concerned with issues involving the relationship between the word and society.[26] This change left a notable mark on Pound's concept of precision. In his early theory, precision had been a primarily aesthetic concept applied to the evaluation of the artistic quality of poetry. Under the influence of the doctrine of *zheng ming*, however, Pound's idea of precision swelled to accommodate all social discourses. For instance, in 'A Visiting Card,' written during the Second World War, he asserts: 'Terminology is not science, but every science advances by defining its terminology with greater precision' (*SP,* 323). Pound thus came to see verbal precision as an important indication of a writer's commitment to order and justice, and to identify the use of words with political action. This is why, for Pound, 'cleaning up' words amounted to a movement of social reform that could affect every aspect of human life: 'The WORD built out of perception of COMPONENT parts of its meaning reaches down and through and out into all ethics and politics. Clean the word, clearly define its borders and health pervades the whole human congeries' (*PE,* 52).

In conjunction with this general trend in Pound's thinking, Confucian teachings strengthened his conviction that language can, and must, be redeemed. According to Pound's interpretation, the earthly, pragmatic tenet of *zheng ming* suggests that language plays a role in social and cultural change and hence can be damaged by inappropriate use. Language here is not seen as a divine creation, or as an autonomous force beyond human control; it is a human product, and as such is to be evaluated primarily for its social usefulness, rather than venerated for its sacredness and self-sufficiency. To maintain the efficiency of language, therefore, is inevitably a human responsibility, and failure in this duty not only results in poor thinking and a weakening hold on reality but leads to anti-social conduct and, eventually, self-destruction. Pound issued this warning in 1934: 'As language becomes the most powerful instrument of perfidy, so language alone can riddle and cut through the meshes. Used to control meaning, used to blur meaning, to produce the complete and utter inferno of the past century ... against which, SOLELY a care for language, for accurate registration by language avails. And if men too long neglect it their children will find themselves begging and their offspring betrayed' (*LE,* 77). Thus, Pound came to think of language as the locus of the solution to social problems, the key to power that must be effectively controlled and utilized in order to maintain social order and ensure social progress.

While his acceptance of Confucian teachings contributed to the politicization of his formulations about language, Pound's theory, in a sense, enriched the Confucian doctrines of *zheng ming* and *cheng yi* by aligning them with a number of aesthetic considerations. In my analysis of Pound's translations of *zheng ming* and *cheng yi*, I have noted that he inserted his own notion of verbal precision into these doctrines. It is useful to remember that verbal precision for Pound was first of all a poetic virtue, something that characterized the language of poetry and sustained its unique strength. However, when imposing the idea of verbal precision onto the meanings of *zheng ming* and *cheng yi*, he did not mean to dilute the social and political content of the two Confucian doctrines. Rather, by placing an essentially poetic category into the political framework of Confucianism, Pound sought to formulate a theory that could reestablish the social value of poetry and eventually restore the social position of the increasingly marginalized modern poet. Given the importance of *zheng ming* and *cheng yi* in the Confucian political system, an interpretation of the two concepts in terms of linguistic precision could make a strong case for the power of the poet because, as Pound saw it, the poet is the only member of society who is seriously and persistently committed to the pursuit of precise language. By possessing the secret of verbal precision, the poet is thus seen to possess the solution to the problem of language and hence the key to the proper operation of social apparatus. In Pound's formulations during the 1920s, the Romantic notion of the poet as the 'word-maker,' a notion he had subscribed to early in his career, received a new interpretation in light of Confucian doctrines.

Based on such an understanding of the poet's social role, Pound attempted to redefine the social function of poetry. In 'How to Read,' in response to the question of whether or not literature has a function in human society, Pound confirms: It has.

> And this function is *not* the coercing or emotionally persuading, or bullying or suppressing people into the acceptance of any one set or any six sets of opinions as opposed to any other one set or half-dozen sets of opinions.
>
> It has to do with the clarity and vigor of 'any and every' thought and opinion. It has to do with maintaining the very cleanness of the tools, the health of the very matter of thought itself. Save in the rare and limited instances of invention in the plastic arts, or in mathematics, the individual cannot think and communicate his thought, the governor and the legislator cannot act effectively or frame his laws, without words, and the solidity and validity of these words is in the care of the damned and despised *litterati*. When their work goes rotten – by that I do not mean when they express indecorous thoughts – but when their very medium, the very essence of their work, the application of word to thing goes rotten, i.e., becomes slushy and inexact, or excessive or bloated, the whole machinery of social and of individual thought and order goes to pot. (*LE*, 21)

Whether or not poetry has any social relevance is an issue with which poets have long been concerned. But Pound seems to believe that he has found the solution that conventional theories of poetry could not offer. Conventional theories of poetry can be generally classified into two kinds. The first kind (such as a didactic theory that emphasizes poetry's ethical impact) regards poetry as a form of knowledge that is bound to have a social effect, whereas the second kind (such as an aestheticist theory) denies poetry's social obligation because it views poetry as providing no more than an aesthetic experience derived from the enjoyment of beauty. In the statement above, as he is engaging the question of the social function of literature, Pound intends to address an audience that includes not only those who 'despise' poetry, but also the poets who tend to willingly relinquish poetry's claim to social relevance. Pound disagrees as well with those who use poetry to propagate some 'opinions.' In fact, he believes that it does not matter what the poet says, be it 'indecorous' or not; what justifies poetry's social existence is its unique capability of maintaining the 'very cleanness' of language. This capability, in Pound's view, determines poetry's social commitment and, at the same time, allows it to transcend the conflicts of various sociopolitical 'opinions.'

Among contemporary writers and critics, Pound was not alone in trying to reinstate the social value of poetry by emphasizing its contribution to language instead of its moral impact or aesthetic appeal. For instance, in his well-known essay 'The Social Function of Poetry,' Eliot also argues for a similar theory: 'We may say that the duty of the poet, as poet, is only indirectly to his people: his direct duty is to his *language*, first to preserve, and second to extend and improve.'[27] One might also think of Cleanth Brooks, the New Critic for whom 'the modern poet has the task to rehabilitate a tired and drained language so that it can convey meaning once more with force and exactitude.'[28] Pound's definition of the 'function' of poetry might have influenced these views either directly or indirectly.[29]

Pound's theory of poetry's social function should be evaluated in two ways. On the one hand, there is little doubt that his contention is problematic and vulnerable. For one thing, his demand that poetry not be used for asserting or imposing some 'opinions' would not even be honoured by his own poetic practice, which was often overtly didactic and oriented towards propagating his ideological agenda. On the other hand, Pound's theory is significant as far as his career is concerned, for it helped him to clarify the direction of his creative life as an experimental poet. Until the early 1920s, his vision of the mission of modern poetry had often seemed clouded by a sense of uncertainty, a problem derived from his self-contradictory orientation. From the start, Pound's understanding of the mission of poetry had rested mainly on a mixture of two conflicting views: didacticism and aestheticism. While he had recognized poetry's inherent commitment to the 'interpretation of life,' he had also believed that poetry should pursue a higher goal, that of transcending the unpleasant realities of life through imaginative vision. In other words, for Pound, poetry acquires its value by fulfilling a social purpose, but still remains a self-contained, autonomous entity, with its appeal sustained by the unity and coherence of its linguistic structure. In an earlier essay, while asserting that 'the arts provide data for ethics,' Pound also argued that 'art never asks anybody to do anything, or to think anything, or to be anything. It exists as the tree exists' (*LE*, 46). This juxtaposition of such ideas highlights Pound's self-contradictory argument that the purpose of poetry is to inform ethics and interpret life without exerting any influence on the reader.

Thus, the problem Pound encountered in the early part of his career was how to reconcile, or balance, a poet's social commitment and his aestheticist pursuits. Succumbing to the latter, Pound was keenly aware, would inevitably result in a severe diminishment of the poet's social power, a result he tried to reverse on behalf of the 'despised *litterati.*' Yet, his search for 'le mot juste,' an essentially aestheticist quest for an ideal poetic language modelled on Flaubert, would lead to just the outcome he dreaded. Nowhere is this predicament more clearly evident than in 'Hugh Selwyn Mauberley,' which Pound published in 1920. In this poem, following Flaubert, his 'true Penelope,' Mauberley has embarked on the mission to 'resuscitate the dead art of poetry' by experimenting with poetic language. As a result, he finds himself isolated from 'the march of events' and, more chillingly, forgotten by society.[30] Mauberley shows no intention of abandoning his 'Penelope.' But to remain committed to his Flaubertian mission without at the same time suffering an alienation from social attention, Mauberley needs a theory that can convince his audience as well as himself that his pursuit of a redeemed language has important social consequences and will eventually benefit society as a whole. Though Mauberley does not come up with such a theory, Pound eventually did, with the help of the doctrines of *zheng ming* and *cheng yi*. By linking verbal precision with the health of society, Pound revised Confucian doctrines to effectively endorse his own pursuit.

4. *Cheng*: The Epistemological Basis of Language

In addition to drawing from the sociopolitical implications of the *zheng ming* doctrine, Pound also elaborated extensively on the concept of *cheng* derived from the *cheng yi* doctrine to reinforce the philosophical foundation of his theory of language. This concept, which occupies an important place in Confucian metaphysics as well as ethics, constitutes a major thesis in *Zhong yong*. Pound persistently applied his reading of *cheng* in *Da xue* to his reading of *cheng* in *Zhong yong*. To be sure, he was aware that *cheng* in Confucianism was first of all an ethical category, but he thought that such an ethical principle must be predicated on verbal integrity. Not surprisingly, in his translation of *Zhong yong*, Pound renders *cheng* in most cases as seeking precise definition of thought. Sometimes, though, he follows Legge by translating *cheng* as 'sincerity.' Even in such instances, Pound's 'sincerity' cannot be relegated to the same Christian ethics as inscribed in Legge's version; rather, the term unequivocally signifies, as Pound asserts in a parenthetical note, the 'activity which defines words with precision' (*Con*, 173). In other words, sincerity and linguistic precision are synonymous terms throughout Pound's version of *Zhong yong*.

In a sense, Pound's revisionary reading of *cheng* in *Zhong yong* does not necessarily contradict interpretations of this concept by major Confucian exegetes ever since neo-Confucianism, who have without exception rejected reading the concept in merely moralistic terms.[31] For instance, Zhu Xi interpreted *cheng* as 'reality, truth, and freedom from error.'[32] Among modern commentators, Wing-tsit Chan has observed that *cheng* is 'at once psychological, metaphysical, and religious,' and thus can be construed not only as 'sincerity' but also as 'truth or reality.'[33] Tu Weiming has read *cheng* in the same way, conceiving it as 'a principle of subjectivity' by which a person can become 'true' to himself and 'form a unity with Heaven.'[34] With them Pound shared the recognition that *cheng* refers to a dynamic process whereby the individual mind is able to complete the knowledge of reality. What characterizes Pound's postulate is a conviction that such a process is sustained by the generative power of language rather than by a mystic force. In his reinterpretations of Confucian teachings centred on the concept of *cheng*, we come to see how Pound envisions the role of precise language in relation to three aspects of cognition: reconciling the human mind and the transcendental mind, prescribing the procedure of self-actualization, and clarifying the truth of things obtained from observation of nature.

Underlying Pound's campaign for a 'clean up of the Word' is the presupposition that there exists a model language of transcendental origin whose perennial efficacy contrasts sharply with the deterioration of the human language. In the Poundian-Confucian cosmos, such a transcendental force manifests as 'the highest grade of this clarifying activity' (*Con*, 179), an activity of perpetually generating meaning and thus calling things into being. In other words, the transcendental force functions in a kind of linguistic way. From this perspective, *cheng* or 'sincerity' is what makes the primal discourse accessible: 'Sincerity is the goal of things and their origin, without this sincerity nothing is. On this meridian the man of breed respects, desires sincerity, holds it in honor and defines his terminology' (*Con*, 177–9). 'Sincerity' here has a twofold function. As the 'goal,' it gives things their forms and purposes; as the 'origin,' it is that from which the essence of things discloses. That is, *cheng* or 'sincerity' is not merely a moral or linguistic accomplishment by an individual. It is rather the primordial condition of being, the absolute power of Being that furnishes all kinds of life with meaning. Therefore it points to a higher mode of existence, inspiring in the human heart awe and respect, as well as desire. In Pound's early writing such a force was referred to as the 'eternal state of mind' (*SP,* 47). Now, in the Poundian-Confucian postulate, it is equated with the Way of Heaven: 'Sincerity, this precision of terms is heaven's process' (*Con,* 167).

Pound deems the 'heavenly process' of Sincerity compatible with the Christian Logos because, for him, both identify a similar source of Meaning. The two concepts merge in *The Cantos*: 'In principio verbum / paraclete or the verbum perfectum: sinceritas' ('In the beginning was the Word / the Holy Ghost or the perfect Word: sincerity' [LXXIV/ 447]).[35] The way Pound articulates his idea in these lines is remarkable in the sense that the 'Word,' which manifested 'in the beginning' of the Christian world, is finally replaced by 'Sincerity,' the 'perfect word' from the Confucian world. The substitution of the Confucian *cheng* or 'sincerity' for the Christian 'Word' is theologically significant: at a time when the Christian God is said to be silent, the 'perfect Word' of Confucianism may provide an alternative to fill that absence. Moreover, for a writer who is committed to the revitalization of language, the Confucian Way is obviously more appealing because it does not demand self-sacrifice or deny one's earthliness. Rather, its sole requirement is one's faith in and persistent practice of 'sincerity.' In short, as long as one adheres to verbal precision, one will always be able to partake of the blessing of the divine. Thus, verbal precision becomes that which enables us to cross the void left by the withdrawal of God to reach the eternal realm of the 'perfect Word.'

This process of transcendence, in Pound's reading of *cheng*, is also identical with the process of self-definition and the process of cosmic revelation, for 'he who defines his words with precision will perfect himself and the process of this perfecting is in the process [that is, ... the total process of nature]' (*Con,* 177). Pound's rendering brings up two important ideas about language: the role of verbal precision in self-actualization and the relevance of precise language to the knowledge of nature. When Pound, in the essay on Mencius, identifies *cheng* with the act of 'naming the emotion or condition' (*SP,* 84), he is endowing precise language with the power of prescribing the essence of human inner morality. From the perspective of Confucian ethics, the ultimate purpose of personal fulfilment is to learn to become fully human, and the only way to achieve full human values is through self-cultivation. In the epistemological process of one's self-actualization, *cheng* is often understood as 'truthfulness' or 'realness' because it indicates the moral exertion to organize one's disordered experiences into self-cognizance in agreement with the reality of both the external world and the inner self. In Pound's revision, such a moral exertion becomes almost entirely a linguistic act, by which a person progresses from an uncultivated state of being to the state of being ethically conscious and articulate, a state of recognizing the self-disciplines of remaining true to himself and the outside world. Precise language is thus the indispensable tool that enables one's inner self to become fully actualized in concrete terms shared by the rest of the community. In other words, precise language is what gives the individual his humanity, his sociality, as well as his individuality.

Moreover, by identifying the process of achieving verbal precision with the 'total process of nature,' Pound is bringing into his Confucian interpretation an idea new to Confucianism: that nature, rather than a self-sufficient entity, is a system of signs signifying something other than itself. I will discuss Pound's reflection on nature in greater detail in chapter 4 of this book, but my discussion here specifically concerns his formulation of the relationship between language and nature. In classical Confucianism, nature, or to be more exact, heaven, which Pound sometimes renders as nature, is an entity that is both physical and metaphysical. It combines the material and the spiritual, or phenomenal and noumenal worlds, in such a way that each informs and manifests the other.[36] Thus, it is almost inconceivable for classical Confucianism to envision a nature that points towards something beyond itself. Pound, on the other hand, grew up in a tradition that conceives nature as a result of God's act of naming, therefore as a sort of writing signifying God's will. Further, as Kenner has pointed out, through Fenollosa Pound was influenced by Emerson's conception of nature, which views the world of objects as symbolizing a transcendental Soul.[37]

It is this conception of nature that Pound incorporates into his representation of the worldview of Confucianism. For example, in *The Cantos*, he invokes Mencius's observations on nature:

> 'We have', said Mencius, 'but phenomena.'
> Monumenta. In nature are signatures
>   needing no verbal tradition,
> oak leaf never plane leaf. (LXXXVII/593)

These lines allude to a passage in *Mengzi* 4.2.26.1, in which Mencius discourses on how to grasp the essential property of things by following their natural course. Pound's poetic diction indicates that his source for this passage is from Legge's translation rather than the Chinese text. Legge's version, with an apparent emphasis on presenting the world of things as a phenomenal-noumenal dichotomy not perceivable in the original passage, posits a dualistic approach to the relation between essence and things.[38] Pound not only picks up the dichotomous implications of Legge's interpretation, but adds to it his idea about the 'signatures' in nature. The 'signatures' Pound discovers here are the signatures of the 'eternal states of mind,' the gods whose message he has been looking for. Transcending the 'verbal tradition' of human languages, these signs in the text of nature designate the perfect design of a divine intelligence. Accordingly, verbal precision or the *sinceritas* of nature embodies the order and clarity of the divine plan:

> The bone is in fact constructed,
>   according to trigonometrical whichwhat. Shinbones!
> Which illustrated Speech as a medium,
>   the problem of order. (LXXXVII/594)

In Pound's view, what nature 'illustrates' through natural signs such as plants and the human body is the mathematical precision of the arrangement wrought in the world by the divine intelligence. Nature as the illustrative text ensures the presence of the supreme 'Speaker,' much to the consolation of the modern mind, which would otherwise feel beleaguered by the fear of groundlessness and emptiness.

Thus the human mind can perceive truth by observing nature, whose organization parallels the linguistic structure of human speech, define the result of the observation by means of language, and generate knowledge to make sense of the world and itself. Yet the creative power of the human mind would be seriously reduced without the assistance of precise language modelled on the orderliness, or the thingness, of the natural world. In the Poundian-Confucian epistemology, there is no truth unless authenticated in precise definition; nor is any knowledge acceptable before it is validated in precise language. 'Thought hinges on the definition of words,' Pound believed, and, 'without the definition of words knowledge cannot be transmitted from one man to another'(*SP*, 350, 308). Such an epistemology finds its perfect expression in Pound's revisionary interpretation of the *cheng yi* doctrine. In section 1 of this chapter, I quoted Pound's version of the first half of the *cheng yi* doctrine to demonstrate how he created the notion of 'precise verbal definitions.' Here I would like to bring up the other half of his version to show what this powerful notion can lead to:

> When things had been classified in organic categories, knowledge moved toward fulfillment; given the extreme knowable points, the inarticulate thoughts were defined with precision [the sun's lance coming to rest on the precise spot verbally]. Having attained this precise definition [*aliter*, this sincerity], they then stabilized their hearts, they disciplined themselves; having attained self-discipline, they set their own houses in order; having order in their own homes, they brought good government to their own states; and when their states were well governed, the empire was brought into equilibrium. (*Con*, 31–3)

This is how the ancient sage-kings in China were supposed to attain order under heaven. There can be no better explication than this translation for Pound's epistemology of 'ideas going into action,' in which the starting point of any sensible idea and any worthwhile action is the 'precise verbal definition.'

While by transforming *cheng* into a linguistic exertion Pound tremendously rienforced the philosophical persuasiveness of his theory of precise language, such a transformation nonetheless engendered some problematic issues that he left unsolved. These issues can be detected first in his rendering of the *cheng yi* passage. According to Pound's reading, it takes at least two steps, 'categorizing' and 'defining,' for the mind to produce knowledge. This reading is open to question: what is the exact relationship between the cognitive act of 'classifying things' and the linguistic act of 'attaining precise verbal definitions'? And, what is the relationship between 'organic categories' and 'inarticulate thoughts'? Pound's reading seems to suggest that it is a temporal relationship, with 'categorizing' preceding 'defining.' Such a reading raises another question: how can things be meaningfully 'classified into organic categories' without these categories being first meaningfully defined? In other words, how can the mind produce knowledge prior to its having been linguistically activated? Or, how can there be any knowledge prior to linguistic definition? These issues do not seem to exist in the Chinese text, in which the same process can be summarized as this: obtaining knowledge depends on categorizing things; categorizing things depends on making intention conform to the nature of things;

making intention conform to the nature of things depends on purifying the mind (or ridding it of all distractions) so that it can concentrate on what is being intended, and so on. In transforming *cheng* into a singularly linguistic act, Pound's interpretation divides what is initially a holistic process of cognition into two parts: pre-lingual and lingual.

The same polemic emerges whenever Pound inflexibly substitutes the concept of verbal precision for the Confucian concept of *cheng*, as is illustrated by the following excerpt from Pound's rendering of a passage from *Zhong yong*:

> If, searching inside yourself, you cannot tell yourself the truth in plain words, you will not get on with your relatives; and for attaining this precision of speech with yourself there is a way; he who does not understand what the good is, will not attain a clear precision in defining himself to himself. (*Con*, 167)

The passage concerns the way leading from the achievement of self-knowledge to social harmony. In the original text, *cheng* is used three times, to the effect that if one knows what the good is, he can be 'sincere' to his inner self, and if he is 'sincere' to himself, he knows how to maintain a 'sincere' relationship with others such as his relatives. Pound replaces the three repetitions of *cheng* with the three phrases: 'tell ... the truth in plain words,' 'attaining this precision of speech,' and 'clear precision.' Consequently, his version focuses on conveying the following argument: to inform the self of truth, one should be capable of precise speech; to attain precise speech whereby to define truth, one should be first aware of what the good truly is. Here again is the same Poundian proposition: defining truth is contingent on knowing what is true. That is, before one is able to make sense of truth linguistically, one must already have a sort of knowledge of what is true. This proposition suggests that the production of knowledge, whether knowledge of truth or knowledge of something, consists of two stages: the verbal stage in which truth is inscribed in words and the non-verbal perception of truth.

The concept of precision applied by Pound in his rendering of the Confucian doctrines of *cheng yi* and *zheng ming* retained much of his earlier conception of truth as double correspondence: the correspondence between verbal expression and 'inarticulate thoughts' on one level, and the correspondence between these thoughts and external realities on the other level. But what had been the 'visionary perception' in his early formulations now becomes the 'inarticulate thoughts' or 'the tones given off by the heart' in his revision of the *cheng yi* passage. Since the 'tone' is generated by the heart instead of the mind, it may also be called 'inarticulate thought,' belonging to the domain of pre-linguistic intentions under the charge of intuition, imagination, or even poetic sensibility. Discoveries made on this level remain perceptual. They need to be ordered, revised, and endorsed before being assimilated into the system of conceptual knowledge, that is, 'defined' knowledge as Pound termed it (*SP*, 76). In Pound's postulation, the act of defining is a sort of rational choice that gives the creative mind full and decisive control in linguistic activities. By selecting words to define what has been perceived, the mind leaves its mark on the achieved meaning or knowledge. For Pound, the mind is never a passive receiver, but rather a powerful transmitter. It is able to make either a true or false report of realities, depending on the way it chooses to utilize language – whether to embrace precise words or resist them. Thus, Pound's 'objective' theory of language is one in which the perceiver is so favourably positioned that his subjective intention is often comfortably disguised behind the concreteness and objectiveness of the word-image of the thing it offers.

5. The Political Economy of Verbal Precision

Although often articulated in incoherent lines and images, the recurrent theme of verbal precision in *The Cantos* forms a subtle and important aspect of Pound's perspective on economics and history. The careful reader of Pound's poetry might notice that *zheng* 正 and *ming* 名 are the second and third Chinese characters introduced into *The Cantos* – at the end of canto LI, one of the famous 'Usury' cantos. The fact that Pound chose to end this canto with *zheng ming* indicates that the Poundian-Confucian concept of precision was incorporated into his economic thinking, especially with regard to the problem of the production of value. This is not surprising, since Pound's economic theory is closely related to his strong interest in the adequate mode of representation conceived to be indispensable for stabilizing the value system of society. Pound's theory, as Robert Duncan once noted, reflects 'a basic concern for the good credit of things: both words and money are currencies that must be grounded in the substance of a real wealth if they be virtuous.'[39] In Pound's view, usury is *zheng ming*'s number one enemy, because in the money-lender's linguistic betrayal Pound detected an increasing gap between the signifier and the signified. In the hands of the usurer, Pound believed, money represents only profits instead of the use value of goods and the labour involved in the production of the goods. The divorce between money and value, money and goods, characterizes a modern mercantile culture that nurtures a habit of abstraction, an inclination to separate the word from meaning and, in turn, the word from thing. 'The battle was won by greed,' lamented Pound in 1934, with specific reference to the loss of a linguistic foundation for faith, 'the language of religion became imprecise, just as the language of all forms of modern flim flam, including popular philosophical lectures, has become imprecise.'[40]

The core of Pound's economic thinking is informed by the idea of a land-based economy. Such an economics often shares with classical linguistic theory the conviction in an established identity between the sign and the thing signified.[41] A basic assumption of this land-based economics is that goods are wealth because they spring from land. Their value, measurable in terms of labour in relation to the land, is empirically realizable in circulation, just as words are referentially reliable in communication because of their etymological and semantic connection with things and facts. Pound emphasized revitalizing a system of representation to 'set down things as they are, to find the word that corresponds to the thing' (*ABCR*, 60), a system that can resist the modern mercantile tendency towards abstraction and hence separation. Thus, for Pound, an abstract verbal expression is as bad as a void 'bank cheque' that cannot deliver any real value; a verbal statement is 'valuable only in REFERENCE to the known objects or facts' (*ABCR*, 13). Pound's economic theory, reinforced by the call for *zheng ming*, demands a correspondence between money and value, as well as a solid relationship between the sign and what the sign represents.

The sign that Pound was bent on seeking should have been one that had both a deliverable and unalterable value. Naturally, with the vision of verbal precision anchored in the Confucian 'process of Heaven' and equated with the 'goal and origin of things,' Pound's theory now pointed the way to a language that would serve as the unifying force of society by fixing what appeared to be permanent truths and universally recognized facts. In Pound's formulation, this language has two distinct features: it is monolithic because it accepts only a single source of meaning, and authoritarian because it privileges an authorial voice in the fiercely contested field of interpretation.

In advocating a language sustained by a privileged centre of meaning, Pound revealed the aspect of his conservatism that endorsed the rule of conformity in verbal activities. Apparently, his dread of the 'chaos' of language, a dread typical not only of Pound but also of many of his fellow modernists, nourished his uncanny desire for a homogeneous world marked by a new cult of the 'standards of writing.'[42] In the world Pound dreamed of, words seem to support a univocal interpretation of the world. They constitute a coercive force to suppress difference and opposition, for each word is permitted to mean the only thing claimed to be true or objective. 'Unless a term is left meaning one particular thing,' Pound insisted in a discussion of Cavalcanti's poetry, 'and unless all attempt to unify different things, however small the difference, is clearly abandoned, all metaphysical thought degenerates into a soup' (*LE*, 185).[43] The 'particular,' conceived earlier by Pound as the concrete and the objective in opposition to the abstract, by the late 1920s had become the 'one,' the 'only,' thus the exclusion of the other. Further, Pound also longed for the word that could withstand the passage of time. He was especially concerned with words used in those areas of life in which change, for him, would often mean uncertainty and disorientation, for instance, 'the legal or scientific word which must, at the outset, be defined with the greatest possible precision, and never change its meaning' (*SP*, 321).

In addition to advocating the fixity of meaning, Pound tended to deny interpretation as a universal right. If the word, like money, is supposed to depend for its validity on circulating absolute value, the crucial question one must ask is, who is in the position to determine that value? In this regard, Pound's theory of language reveals an authoritarian ideology that attempts to limit the power of interpretation to a select few. Such a disturbing tendency had surfaced in his early writings, contrary to a recent critical assumption.[44] In 1913, for instance, in mentioning the 'various and complicated sorts' of artistic precision, Pound wrote that 'only the specialist can determine whether certain works of art possess certain sorts of precision' (*LE*, 48). In so far as precision for Pound was identical with truth, his 'specialist' held a position as powerful and intimidating as that of an ancient oracle. The same elitist contentions about language intensified in Pound's works during the 1930s. In *ABC of Reading*, he remarks that 'an abstract or general statement is GOOD if it be ultimately found to correspond with the facts. BUT no layman can tell at sight whether it is good or bad' (12). Not only is the 'layman' blind to truth, but he is also unable to articulate truth. Thus, according to Pound, 'even if the general statement of an ignorant man is 'true,' it leaves his mouth or pen without any great validity. He doesn't KNOW what he is saying' (*ABCR*, 26). There is no doubt that such an open

80   Ezra Pound and Confucianism

claim for an elitist monopolizing of the articulation of truth can be very disturbing, even for those who admire Pound's poetry.[45] According to Pound's theory of language, the only person who has both access to truth and the ability to articulate it is one who has succeeded in situating himself in the 'process of heaven.' That is, this person must possess the virtue of verbal precision, namely *cheng* or 'sincerity,' because by attaining 'absolute sincerity' he becomes something approximating an all-knowing 'numen,' and thus can 'effect changes' by speaking out his discoveries (*Con*, 175–7).

The extent of Pound's desire for an authority in the production of discourses can also be found in his deliberate misreading of the Confucian concept *ci da* 辭達, which means '[to use] words to get ideas across.' The concept comes from *Lun yu* 15.40. In the original passage Confucius makes the point that the primary purpose of words is to convey meaning, rather than to enhance ornamentation. *Ci da* is a relatively unimportant and simple concept in Confucian aesthetics, but it attracted Pound's attention because it is one of the few terms in Confucian texts that directly addresses issues of writing. Fully aware of its contextual meaning, Pound employs the concept as a poetic theme several times in *The Cantos*. For instance:

> the imprint of the intaglio depends
>   in part on what is pressed under it
> the mould must hold what is poured into it
>   in
>   discourse   辭
>   what matters is
> to get it across e poi basta   達 (LXXIX/506)

On the surface, Pound renders *ci da* 辭達 rather literally in the last four lines. Nevertheless, his etymographic hermeneutics also enables him to 'see' in the characters some profound implications that can serve to legitimate his authoritarian poetics. According to Hugh Kenner, Pound once remarked on *ci da* to the effect that the two Chinese characters summed up Confucius's idea about style. When asked what he 'saw' in the first character *ci* 辭 (speech), Pound replied: 'Lead the sheep out to pasture.'[46] In other words, the concept of *ci da*, informed by the biblical allusion in this case, was able to provide Pound with another 'law of discourse,' which glorified the author as the Shepherd leading his flock to the destination. Such a fascinating interpretation of this Confucian concept about style finds an explicit expression in another canto:

> ... to write dialog because there is
> no one to converse with
> to take the sheep out to pasture
> to bring you g. r. to the nutriment
> gentle reader   to the gist of discourse (LXXX/519–20)

The reason why the poet portrays himself as a solitary figure is that he is set apart from the ordinary folks, or the 'gentle reader' who is symbolically reduced to the insignificant 'g.r.'; it is so because the poet alone is charged with the duty to bring the ordinary folks to truth.

Indeed, the entire *Cantos* is largely intended as such a 'discourse' that feeds the 'gentle reader' with the 'gist' or 'nutriment' dictated by the God-like author. Written in the form of an epic, *The Cantos* seeks to present, among other things, a coherent narrative of those illuminating moments of verbal precision that, according to the poet, have sustained the continuity of history. In so far as the theme of verbal precision is concerned, Pound's didactic intention envisions in *The Cantos* a kind of coalition front historically established by his cultural heroes. Their practice in writing is described by Pound as forming a forceful and persistent counter to social vices, especially to usury, 'the perverters of language, / the perverts, who have set money-lust / Before the pleasure of the senses' (XIV/61).

In Pound's view, the founding father of this time-honoured elite legion of anti-imprecision was Confucius, the advocate of 'precise terminology.' To Pound, moreover, Confucius's contribution is not merely theoretical, for the master also edited *The Book of Songs*, the first anthology of poems in recorded human history. In this work we find:

> for Emperors; for the people
> all things are here brought to precisions
> that we shd/ learn our integrity
> that we shd/ attain our integrity (LIX/324)

Then there was Sigismundo Malatesta, the ruler and patron of the arts who 'transmitted' a cultural tradition by 'precise definition' (LXXIV/445). Back in China there appeared another enlightened ruler: Kang Xi (K'ang Hsi, 1662–1723), who restored the prestige of Confucian ethics, and

> qu'ils veillèrent à la pureté du langage
> et qu'on n'employât que des termes propres
> (namely CH'ing ming)
> 正名 (LX/332-3)

In Pound's homeland, President John Adams is said to have inherited the Confucian legacy. As suggested in *The Cantos*, the Confucian *zheng ming* enlightened the way of life in Adams's world. Thus, Adams not only appreciated the accurate use of 'technical terms' (LXIII/352), but made 'true definition' the basis of his legal and political practice (LXVI/382). More significantly, Adams tried to legalize 'the interests of literature' (LXVII/392), insisting that a nation's achievement could be immortalized only in its literary discourses. In this way, Adams came 'to show U.S. the importance of an early attention to language / for ascertaining the language. / 正名 Ching Ming' (LXVIII/400).

The modern paragon of verbal precision, according to Pound, was Mussolini. Pound often displayed a fascination with Mussolini's habit of speech, and claimed that his 'oratory is worth study' (*J/M*, 65). As Peter Nicholls has noted, Pound's sympathy with Fascism was partly due to his belief that the Duce embodied the ideal of linguistic accuracy and that Fascist ideology emphasized a renovated and dynamic language.[47] In *The Cantos*, in order to illustrate Mussolini's precise use of language, Pound makes reference to the 'Program of Verona' the Duce drew up for the Republic of Salò: '"Alla non della," in the Verona statement' (LXXXVI/584). The phrase 'Alla non della' (to, not of) alludes to the Duce's attention to a verbal unit as minute as a preposition in this statement: 'It is a right *to* property not a right *of* property.'[48] Such a commitment to verbal correctness, in Pound's view, was compelling proof of the Duce's commitment to ideological correctness.

Apart from these major figures, who form the backbone of the tradition of linguistic 'rectitude,' in *The Cantos* there are also other minor contributors to the tradition of precise language. Yet it is curious that none of the figures directly associated with the theme of linguistic precision is a poet or a professional writer. This does not mean that at the time of composing *The Cantos* Pound no longer believed in the primacy of literary language or the mission of the poet to safeguard language. The fact that the linguistic achievements of these historical figures are made visible and available only through Pound's verse reaffirms the poet's conviction: poetry contains the 'gists of discourse' which otherwise cannot be obtained. In that sense, *The Cantos* is meant to assert itself as the perfect poetic definition of the author's ideology of precision, or as the best illustration in the modern world of what verbal precision should be. By composing *The Cantos*, Pound hoped, he made himself the true hero in carrying on the Confucian mission of *zheng ming*, that is, to rectify language for the modern world.

3
Confucianism and Pound's Political Polemic

1. Supporting the Self or Subduing the Self?

Ezra Pound's political identity has always been a controversial issue for Pound scholars. Central to that issue is Pound's confusing position on the relationship between the individual and the state. The question that Pound scholars find particularly intriguing is why the radically iconoclastic, liberal, and individualistic Pound began in the early 1930s to embrace a conservative and authoritarian ideology and openly side with a notoriously oppressive regime in Fascist Italy. Since this change seemed to coincide with Pound's increasingly intense devotion to the study of Confucian works, it is only natural for critics to view Confucianism as the major influence in Pound's shift towards authoritarianism. Also contributing to this view (as I pointed out in the Introduction) is a deeply entrenched assumption that the adoption of Confucian orientation must mean a conversion to reactionary politics hostile to individual values. Such an assumption underlies most of the scholarly discussions of Pound's metamorphosis, whether in political agenda or poetic style, in the 1930s. In an analysis of the change in Pound's narrative patterns in the 'China Cantos,' for example, Michael Bernstein argues that 'the ideology of Confucianism rejects the Western principle of individual self-assertion.'[1]

Pound never thought he had changed his fundamental position at all, however. In an interview with Donald Hall in March 1962, he insisted that even though he had made many 'marginal mistakes' in his ideological struggles over the past several decades, he had persistently committed himself to fighting for a noble humanist cause: 'The whole fight is for the conservation of the individual soul. ... What I was right about was the conservation of the individual rights. If, when the executive or any other branch exceeds its legitimate powers, no one protests, you will lose all your liberties. ... The struggle for individual rights is an epic subject.'[2] Pound's claim to have championed the cause of individualism may seem questionable to those who dislike the political and racial agenda he promoted, but there is no denying that his concern with the impact of sociopolitical conditions on the individual remains a constant and dominant theme in all his work over the course of his career.

More importantly, the complex relationship between Pound and Confucianism resists convenient oversimplification. In fact, the character of Pound's controversial politics is complicated by his interpretation of Confucian doctrines, which consistently reveals an intention to reconstruct precisely an ideology of 'individual self-assertion.' Such an intention is especially highlighted in Pound's interpretation of an overarching Confucian doctrine about the relationship between the self and the efficacy of rites established in *Lun yu*. According to one account in this work, the disciple Yan Yuan once asked Confucius what constituted *ren* 仁 (humanity) and how one could achieve it. Confucius replied in a celebrated passage, which Pound turned into a sort of individualist manifesto in English:

> *Ke ji fu li wei ren. Yi ri ke ji fu li, tianxia gui ren yan. Wei ren you ji, er you hu ren zai* 克己復禮爲仁。一日克己復禮，天下歸仁焉。爲仁由己，而由乎人哉？ (*Lun yu* 12.1)
>
> Support oneself and return to the rites, that makes a man. If a man can be adequate to himself for one day and return to the rites, the empire would come home to its manhood. This business of manhood sprouts from oneself, how can it sprout from others?
> (*Con*, 243)

Pound's complete translation of *Lun yu*, from which I quote the above rendering of the passage about *ke ji fu li* 克己復禮, was published in 1951. But he had started translating *Lun yu* in 1937, the year when he published in Milan an English translation of some excerpts from *Lun yu* under the title of *Confucius: Digest of the Analects*. Quite conceivably, the above rendering by Pound must have been a result of years of 'digesting' *Lun yu*, from the late 1930s to the late 1940s. Contrary to oversimplified views that equate Pound's increasing interest in Confucian works during that period with a surrender of the cause of individualism to the temptations of a Confucian authoritarianism, his translation of the Confucian doctrine on the self (*ji* 己) openly requires one to 'support,' and 'be adequate to,' the self in order to rebuild the 'empire' on the basis of 'manhood.' Pound's rendering is all the more remarkable when contrasted with the following 'anti-self' reading of the same passage by James Legge, whose bilingual edition of the Four Books Pound always consulted during that period:

> To subdue one's self and return to propriety, is perfect virtue. If a man can for one day subdue himself and return to propriety, all under heaven will ascribe perfect virtue to him. Is the practice of perfect virtue from a man himself, or is it from others?[3]

In fact, Pound's reading marks a drastic divergence from all major Western translations either before or after him, which in varying degrees accentuate the notion of *subduing the self*. For instance, where Pound discovers the idea of 'support oneself,' Pauthier perceives 'avoir un empire absolu sur soi-même' (have absolute self-control),[4] William Soothill 'the denial of self,'[5] Waley 'himself submit to ritual,'[6] Chan 'master oneself,'[7] Lau 'overcoming the self,'[8] and Roger Ames 'self-discipline.'[9]

The significance of Pound's unusual translation of the *ke ji fu li* doctrine cannot be fully comprehended unless we contextualize it in the exegetical tradition of Confucian scholarship. Because the doctrine occupies a central place in Confucian ideology, over centuries the original passage in *Lun yu* has received the utmost scrutiny. In the original work, the talk between Confucius and Yan Yuan focuses on how to achieve *ren* 仁, a complex notion variously translated as 'humanity,' 'humaneness,' 'benevolence,' 'love,' 'altruism,' 'human-heartedness,' etc. In Confucian moral philosophy, *ren* posits the ultimate form of perfect virtue under which all virtues can be subsumed. In addition to being a moral concept, *ren* also represents an ontological process of person-making, through which the individual attains the totality of being by realizing the essence of humanity in his life and, at the same time, transcends the isolation of individuality by participating in the social practice of universal moral values. The way of achieving *ren*, according to Confucius in this passage, lies in *ke ji fu li*. What often seems problematic is the relationship between *fu li* (to restore rites) and *ke ji*. The problem is caused by the verb *ke* 克, which can mean either 'overcome' or 'enable' in classical Chinese. Thus, the phrase *ke ji fu li* could generate two readings with diametrically opposed implications: first, 'to overcome the self in order to restore the rites'; second, 'to enable the self in order to revitalize the rites.'

Since the Han dynasty, orthodox exegetes in Confucian scholarship have been overwhelmingly in favour of the first reading. To suppress the possible second reading, Huang Kan (388–545 CE) in his edition of *Lun yu* even replaced the original *ke* 克 with another *ke* 剋 that only meant 'defeat' or 'conquer,' thus eliminating the ambiguity of the original passage.[10] Seen in the first reading as what must be 'conquered,' *ji* 己 (self) appears to embody the unhealthy and disruptive dimensions of human nature. Ma Rong was among the earliest to interpret *ji* as the corporal being of the individual that should be 'restrained.'[11] Liu Xuan (546?–613? CE) of the Sui dynasty went further, describing *ji* as that which nourishes insatiable bodily desires, hence something that must be 'disciplined by means of rites.'[12] Such a reading received its most powerful elaboration from Zhu Xi. In Zhu Xi's neo-Confucian formulation, *ren* is the supreme virtue, identical with Heavenly Principle (*Tian Li* 天理), while Rites (*Li* 禮) are the earthly expressions of Heavenly Principle. For Zhu Xi, *ji* or self poses two kinds of threat: as 'private desires' (*si yu* 私欲) *ji* endangers the social efficacy of Rites; as 'human desires' (*ren yu* 人欲) it opposes the authority of Heavenly Principle. Accordingly, in his commentary on the *ke ji fu li* passage, Zhu Xi calls for 'completely eliminating the private self' (*ke jin ji si* 克盡己私) in order to return to Rites.[13] Because of his position as the primary founder of neo-Confucianism, which was endorsed as the state ideology by rulers of subsequent imperial dynasties in China, Zhu Xi's interpretation of the *ke ji fu li* doctrine exerted an enormous impact on the political culture of feudal China.

Zhu Xi's authoritarian reading later encountered some resistance. The second reading of the *ke ji fu li* passage emerged in the late Ming dynasty as revisionist Confucians of the Wang Yangming school came to challenge the hegemony of Zhu Xi's neo-Confucian ritualism. Prominent among them was Li Zhi (1527–1602), the 'arch-individualist' in pre-modern China, according to W.T. de Bary.[14] Li Zhi believed that the true self is a natural and autonomous being empowered by the innate knowledge that Heaven endows on each individual. Thus, according to Li Zhi, there is no need for the individual to learn moral principles from others, not even from Confucius, for 'each person that Heaven gives life to has his own individual usefulness' and should not depend on external sources to 'achieve humanity' (*wei ren* 爲人).[15] In an essay on the *ke ji fu li* passage, Li Zhi redefines the meaning of *li* (rites): '*Li* is what grows from within the heart, not what comes from outside; it is bestowed by Heaven, not given by others.'[16] Therefore, as Li Zhi insists in another essay, 'one should value the self and be proper to himself.'[17] Li Zhi's iconoclastic thought later influenced his admirer Fang Yizhi (1611–1671). In Fang Yizhi's view, the validity of *li* rests on the free development of the mind, which in turn derives from a vigorous self. For Fang Yizhi, therefore, *ke ji* should be interpreted to mean 'enable the self' and 'give full play to the self.'[18] Clearly, such a reading offers a profoundly different approach to the self from that found in the institutionalized Confucian model, and in the enterprise of Confucian exegesis it has always remained a marginalized one.[19]

Pound's translation of *ke ji* as supporting the self resonates with that of Li Zhi and Fang Yizhi. However, there is no evidence that Pound ever read these writers; it appears that he recovered a suppressed reading without knowing of its previous existence. Pound's interpretation is based on his own understanding of Confucian ideas about human nature, especially the notion of *ren* that constitutes the focal point in the *ke ji fu li* passage. Pound's interpretation of *ren* is notably consistent in his Confucian translations, in which *ren* always signifies the totality of innate human qualities. In his 1928 translation of *Da xue*, *ren* is rendered as 'the practice of the humanities' or simply 'humanity' (*TH*, 14, 25). In the opening 'Terminology' of the 1945 *Confucius*, which includes his translation of *Zhong yong* and retranslation of *Da xue*, Pound provides an elaborate definition of *ren*: '*Humanitas*, humanity, in the full sense of the word, "manhood." The man and his full contents' (*Con*, 22). The definition serves three purposes in guiding all his translations of *ren* throughout Confucian texts. First, it releases *ren* from the mysticism of ritual transcendence as conveyed in Zhu Xi's influential interpretation, placing this concept instead in its human orientation. Pound's definition is supported by his understanding of another celebrated saying from *Zhong yong* 20.5, in which *ren* is 'the full contents of man, it is the contents of the full man' (*ren zhe ren ye* 仁者人也 [*Con*, 149]). In this formulation, *ren* 仁 as the essence of being and *ren* 人 as the abstraction of human beings are interchangeable concepts and mutually illuminating. Second, Pound's definition emphasizes the correspondence between *ren* and the self (*ji*). If *ren* is identical with the 'full contents' of 'the man' himself, what needs to be 'supported' is nothing but the self in order to 'make a man.' For this reason, Pound rejects the 'ascetical' reading of *ke ji* represented by Zhu Xi: 'The "support oneself" is fairly literal. It cannot be limited to superficial idea of making a living, but certainly need not be taken ascetically' (*Con*, 243). Third, with a recognition of the fullness of a person's humanness, Pound's definition stresses the self-sufficiency of the individual. Thus, without seeking the substance of *ren* in external sources, the individual only need look within to bring the potential values there to full display. In other words, the process of achieving *ren* is one of self-making. This idea is reinforced by Pound's interpretation of another famous Confucian saying regarding the relationship between *ji* and *ren*: 'Fulfilling himself he attains full manhood' (*cheng ji ren ye* 成己仁也 [*Con*, 179]).

Pound's revisionist reading of *ke ji fu li* helps him to steer away from a dualism of the self, which inheres in the original passage and tends to create a textual inconsistency with regard to the definition of *ji*. When Confucius tells Yan Yuan that the way of attaining *ren* is through *ke ji fu li*, he also points out that the driving force for attaining *ren* comes from *ji* (*wei ren you ji* 爲仁由己). Thus, one cannot help wondering: if *ji* is undesirable and dispensable in the first place, then how could it be relied on as the sole source of strength for pursuing *ren* in the second place? Orthodox interpretations in Confucian scholarship, represented by Zhu Xi's commentary, address this issue by dividing *ji* into two categories. Here, the first *ji* is treated mostly as the sum of bodily dimensions of an individual human life, something that harbours selfish and unhealthy desires and must be suppressed. The second *ji* is construed as the agent of the individual mind, able to serve as the dynamic source of moral perfection because it is enlightened by, and thus has access to, a larger and transcendental mind whose will manifests in the principle of rites. In such interpretations, the two *ji* are virtually irreconcilable, even though both reside within the same individual existence.

In recent years, such a conception of the split self has become a very disturbing issue for contemporary New Confucian thinkers like Tu Wei-ming and W.T. de Bary, who have undertaken to reinstate the 'liberal tradition' of Confucianism by reclaiming its individualist and humanitarian values. It is crucial, then, to the agenda of New Confucians to establish a Confucian subjectivity whose compelling humanity and individuality are sustained by, among other things, a unity of body and mind. To this end, such scholars seek first of all to reinterpret the doctrine of *ke ji fu li*. Tu Wei-ming, for instance, objects to construing *ji* in this doctrine as the bodily dimensions of the self: 'The Confucian idea does not mean that one should engage in a bitter struggle with one's own corporeal desires. It suggests instead that one should fulfill them in an ethical context.'[20] Instead of seeing the self in terms of a dichotomy between body and mind, contemporary Confucian thinkers see the formation of the self as a two-level transformative process from a small self in its uncultivated stage to a large self, or a selfhood-in-social-context. Tu Wei-ming states: 'The "self" in *ke ji fu li* is a private self, or a small self; one must transcend, overcome, and transform this small self in order to return to the "rites" shared by all human beings.'[21] Despite the connection between the two levels of the self, the 'small self' nonetheless remains a negative category, a sort of self-ego embodying 'certain limits' which, according to de Bary, must be overcome in order to 'join one to a moral and spiritual community.'[22] Hence, Tu Wei-ming has to admit that *ke ji* in the Confucian doctrine indeed ought to be understood as 'to conquer oneself,' even though he tries to downplay its 'misleading' association with anything negative.[23] In other words, the tension between the pre-cultivation self and the cultivated self remains unresolved in the formulations of these New Confucian thinkers.

In contrast, such a tension is absent from Pound's reading of the same doctrine, a reading which, albeit controversial, obtains its own theoretical cogency by virtue of its interpretive consistency. From Pound's perspective, the self is always an indivisible whole, consisting of both the thinking subject and his material existence. The self that needs to be cultivated for achieving full 'manhood' is the same as the self that empowers such an endeavour and enlightens the process of cultivation. That is why, in Pound's translation, 'this business of manhood sprouts from oneself' rather than from others. Yet, Pound does not mean to turn this doctrine into a justification for self-indulgence, for in the Confucian context the purpose of 'supporting' the self is identical to that of enabling the 'empire' to return to 'its home of manhood.'

Pound's translation of the *ke ji fu li* doctrine sheds light on his overriding interest in Confucian ideas concerning the individual and society, an interest derived in the course of constructing an alternative theory of the self by combining Confucianism with his radical individualism and cultural elitism. Pound's political agenda may have changed in tandem with his intellectual development, but his fundamental belief that the individual self constitutes the sole source of light and energy for both personal development and social reform remained unchanged. This belief informed his growing concern with different aspects of the problem of the individual in the modern state. In the next three sections of this chapter, I will examine Pound's strategies for incorporating different Confucian ideas into his polemical postulates about the individual's relationship with the state. Each section will focus on one of Pound's three main concerns: the rights-based individual, the social responsibility of the elite individual, and the redemptive power of the solitary hero's private vision in adversity. The discussion follows the order of the three stages in Pound's career generally accepted in Pound scholarship: the early stage that ended roughly in the late 1920s, the second stage punctuated by the end of the Second World War, and the postwar period. This is by no means a clear-cut division, that is, some aspects of a concern that was primary for Pound in one stage might continue in another stage. For this reason we need to explore each stage thoroughly, drawing on the ramifications of the previous stage to more fully understand a later stage. Despite that, in each stage Pound's thinking of the issues surrounding the individual was apparently dominated by a particular concern in correspondence with his experience and understanding of the social conditions of his time. What is more fascinating is that, in different stages, Pound was able to use different Confucian ideas to serve different, even conflicting, needs of ideological formulations. That is, Pound utilized Confucian doctrines in a rather 'opportunistic' manner that characterizes his overall dealings with Confucianism.

2. The 'Divine Rights' of the Individual

Prior to his translation of *Da xue* in 1928, Pound's general understanding of Confucian ideas lacked a systematic perspective. The same is evident in his use of Confucian ideas concerning the individual. The way Pound explored Confucian ideas in the early stage often appeared fragmentary, overly subjective, and self-problematizing. Briefly, what he found particularly attractive in Confucianism were two primary virtues: a strong respect for the natural integrity of the individual and a clear vision of social order based on the recognition of individual autonomy. It is from this perspective that Pound initially saw Confucianism as a liberal discourse supporting the rights of the individual.

Pound's courtship of individualist philosophy began as early as the inception of his career. In *The Spirit of Romance*, he promulgates 'man's divine right to be himself' as the 'only one of the so-called "rights of man"' (176). And, in 'Rendondillas,' a poem published in 1911, he sounds like a Whitmanian Romantic:

I sing of the special case,
   The truth is the individual.
   ...
   The core in the heart of man

Is tougher than any 'system.'
...
The chief god in hell is convention,
   'got by that sturdy sire Stupidity
Upon pale Fear, in some most proper way. (*CEP,* 219, 221)

In his early works Pound often articulates his commitment to the 'rights of the individual' with such inflammatory and zealous rhetoric that his position is categorized as 'radical individualism' by both Michael Levenson and Cary Wolfe, authors of the two studies on Pound's individualist ideology.

Levenson situates Pound's position within the European tradition of egoism. The originator of this tradition was the German philosopher Max Stirner, and its impact fell on Pound via the modern writers with whom he associated in one way or another, such as Remy de Gourmont, T.E. Hulme, Ford Madox Ford, Allen Upward, and Wyndham Lewis. Premised on the tenets that nothing is true except the willing ego and that art is the apotheosis of individuality, the egoistic tradition provided the basic liberal vision for these modernist writers. Levenson further defines Pound's early pursuits as 'aesthetic individualism' and finds its culmination in his involvement in the drafting of the manifesto of Vorticism published in the short-lived *Blast* magazine. Wolfe's work is more concerned with the politico-economic aspects of Pound's individualist thinking, and delves into his American roots. According to Wolfe, Pound's vision is intrinsically connected to Emerson's ideology of individualism, which begins with a radical critique of the capitalist mode of production as well as the social institutions that sustain it. However, Wolfe contends, because Emersonian-Poundian individualism is modelled on the logic and structure of private property, it has to reproduce the contradictions and alienation it sets out to remedy. Such contradictions constitute, Wolfe suggests through the title of his work, 'the limits of American literary ideology.'[24]

Both Levenson's and Wolfe's studies have convincingly uncovered much of the origin of Pound's individualist orientation. To their discoveries I would like to add my view: part of the source of Pound's leanings in this regard may go farther back to the tradition of Italian humanism. In a way, Pound's admiration for the achievements of the Italian Renaissance had to do with his recognition that the Renaissance had laid the foundation for the modern world by educating Europe about, among other things, the dignity and value of the individual human being.

'Modern civilisation comes out of Italy,' Pound asserted in 1917, 'out of renaissance Italy, the first nation which broke away from Aquinian dogmatism, and proclaimed the individual; respected the personality' (*SP,* 199).[25] It was precisely this task of seeking to 'proclaim the individual and respect the personality' that brought Pound to Confucian works.

To a large extent, Pound's early individualist orientation led to his initial interest in Confucian politics and profoundly shaped his understanding of its basic tenets. Such interest emerged as early as 1914 in the article 'The Words of Ming Mao,' which articulated his belief that the 'dependence on self is the core of Confucian philosophy.'[26] Three years later, in a series of essays published under the title 'Provincialism the Enemy,' Pound endorsed Confucianism specifically because it esteemed 'the value of personality' in sharp contrast to the forces of 'provincialism' that always tried 'to control the acts of other people' and to 'coerce others into uniformity' (*SP,* 193, 189). In Pound's observations on Confucianism at this time, the term 'Confucian' had already acquired the lustre of championing the rights of the individual. In an early study on Gourmont (1920), Pound used the term 'Confucian' to commend the French writer, who was then Pound's *de facto* benefactor of the 'right of the individual':

> Gourmont differentiates his characters by the modes of their sensibility, not by sub-degrees of their state of civilization.
> He recognizes the right of individuals to *feel* differently. Confucian, Epicurean, a considerer and entertainer of ideas, this complicated sensuous wisdom is almost the one ubiquitous element, the 'self' which keeps his superficially heterogeneous work vaguely 'unified.' (*LE,* 340–1)

Interestingly, it was around 1920 when Pound made these remarks identifying 'Confucian' with the Western tradition of liberalism. For those conversant with the history of modern China, Pound's project of liberalizing Confucianism would be an incredible phenomenon. It is immensely ironic that as Pound was advocating a liberal Confucianism against the 'oppressive' social institutions of the West, a widespread anti-Confucian campaign – the May Fourth New Culture Movement – was in full swing in China. The principal charge raised by the movement against Confucianism was that it had nourished authoritarian social formations in China that were hostile to individual values and human dignity and that it was responsible for the cultural backwardness and social stagnation of the nation. Participants in the movement turned mainly to Western liberalism as an antidote against the patriarchal ideology of the Confucian order and as a means of finding a weapon that could enable them to emancipate the individual from the feudal ritualism of the Confucian tradition. It would have been surprising to those in the May Fourth New Culture Movement,[27] and for that matter, to many today, to think that Confucianism could be seen as the protector of the 'rights of the individual,' as Pound asserted. We thus need to clarify what rights Pound conceived of on behalf of the individual and in what ways he thought Confucianism sustained such rights.

Pound's individualist agenda rests on the concept of the autonomous or sovereign individual, a notion central to the entire tradition of Western individualism. From this concept derive the three fundamental rights of the individual: freedom, privacy, and self-development. The concept of autonomy regards each individual human being as an end in himself, rejecting the 'claim for the complete subjugation of the individual to an objective which is externally imposed on him,' according to Pound in 'Economic Democracy' (*SP,* 210–11). From this position, the individual exists with given interests or purposes, while society is only an artifice, an instrument for fulfilling independently given individual objectives. Social establishments are evaluated by the degree of their appeal to the rights of the individual and their cooperation in the fulfilment of the individual's interests. 'Our presumption is,' Pound claims in *Patria Mia,* 'that those things are right which give the greatest freedom, the greatest opportunity for individual development to the individual, of whatever age or sex or condition' (54). The crucial point of this statement is that the rights of the individual, which determine the way society should work, generate their own needs and are assumed as 'givens' that predate the context of social arrangements.

The concept of autonomy holds that the individual is the sole agent and judge of his actions and, for that reason, is entitled to freedom of thought and expression, or in Pound's words, 'a free exercise of the will' (*SP,* 207). For Pound, such freedom is the touchstone of a democratic society, wherein 'each man should look after his own sort of affairs, that he should speak of what he knows, that he should in short attend to his own affairs' (*PM,* 41). In this ideal society, each individual is called on to make conscious and critical evaluations, form intentions, and reach practical decisions as the result of independent and rational reflection. Pound's confidence in the individual's ability to 'attend his own affairs' largely derives from the Enlightenment belief in the power of reason.

Confucianism and Pound's Political Polemic 95

According to this belief, a normal individual – a self-determined, thinking subject – is endowed with a capacity of reason that can lead him to happiness and truth. Reason gives the individual not only the ability to define his own interests but also the power to protect them from being infringed on by external forces. This appeal to reason is a recurrent theme in Pound's works. Even during the 1930s, after he had begun to criticize the contemporary liberal tendency to overemphasize the value of the individual, Pound still regarded reason as the basis of true authority, stating in *The Cantos* that 'Authority comes from right reason / never the other way on' (XXXVI/179). With an emphasis on the absolute authority of the individual, the basic position of the early Pound was radically anti-authoritarian, a stance that corresponded to his social experience as a struggling young poet who sought to establish his own voice and chose to look iconoclastic and defiant.

In Pound's view, the threat to the freedom of an autonomous individual came from the 'coercive evil' of social establishments like Christianity, and his early reading of Confucian works convinced him that Confucianism could serve as a counterforce to resist that threat. In part 3 of 'Mr. Villerant's Morning Outburst,' a series of 'imaginary letters' written in 1918, Pound presents a story from *Lun yu* in which Confucius is seen to set up an example of respecting the free spirit of the individual in contrast to the meddlesome Church:

> Christianity as we understand it, i.e., as it is presented to our gaze in the 'occident', has reduced itself to one principle: 'Thou shalt attend to thy neighbor's business in preference to thine own.' It is upon this basis that the churches are organized, it is upon this basis that they flourish. ... Against all of which I have no defence save the eleventh chapter of the Lun-Yu, the 25th section. (*PD*, 71-2)

The section Pound refers to, according to Legge's textual division, is chapter 25, book 11 of *Lun yu*. The section relates a conversation between Confucius and four disciples. During the conversation the master asks his disciples what they would do if they had the opportunity to give full play to their abilities. Zi Lu (Pound's Tseu-lou), the first of the four, replies that he would in three years turn a medium-sized state from chaos to prosperity. The second, Ran Qiu (Yan-yeou), says that he would administer a small state, making its people affluent in three years.[28] Gongxi Hua (Kong-si-hoa), the third, asserts that he would like to serve as an official master of ceremonies to help with sacrificial rites or other important occasions. When it is the turn of Zeng Xi (Thseng-sie), the fourth disciple, he is hesitant to take the floor, for he feels that his aspiration would appear embarrassingly insignificant in comparison with the grandiose plans of the other three. Confucius tells Zeng Xi not to be afraid of being different and encourages him to express his own wishes freely. It turns out that Zeng Xi has no desire to be a statesman; what he really wants is to go out with friends on a spring day to enjoy the beauty of nature.

In traditional Confucian studies, this section of *Lun yu* had not received the close attention Pound gave to it. Pound was so impressed by Confucius's manner of talking with the four disciples that he actually made, in the 'Imaginary Letters,' his first Confucian translation based on Pauthier's version, and several years later, explored the ideas of this section in canto XIII. In Confucian scholarship, this section is usually read as exemplifying Confucius's expectation that a proper statesman should have a modest personality and rule by virtue of rites. In Pound's view, however, the gem in this piece lies in what Confucius says to Zeng Xi: 'Who forbids you to express it? Here each one may say what he likes' (*PD*, 72). For Pound, Confucius's brief remarks must have sounded like a declaration of each individual's right to free speech. The fact that Pound attached unusual significance to these remarks is further attested by his later translation of the same passage, in which the Confucian notion of free speech is associated with his beloved Dantesque notion of free will: 'What harm, let each say what he wants (*directio voluntatis*)' (*Con*, 243). Another important message that this section conveyed to Pound can be found in Confucius's summary of this talk, which Pound rendered as: 'Each one has expressed his own temperament. That is the end of the matter' (*PD*, 73). By characterizing the purpose of the talk as giving each of the disciples the chance to express his own thought, Confucius's observation appeared to Pound to crystallize the essence of truly intelligent discussions. These few remarks by Confucius in this short conversation allowed Pound to view Confucianism as a libertarian discourse, in opposition to the oppressive force that he detected in modern Western society.

The dignity of a human being as an autonomous individual, in Pound's view, depends largely on another fundamental right, namely, the security of a private existence. According to Pound's notion of privacy, there exists a private life within a public world, a space within which the individual should be left alone, doing or thinking whatever he chooses and pursuing his own good in his own way without interference by external forces. The public world should be subordinate to the primacy of individual privacy, instead of manipulating or tyrannizing the individual. 'The *res republica*,' Pound explains in an article on bureaucracy, 'means the public thing, the public convenience. It is not convenient to have one's nose blown by another, and we therefore blow our own nose, after the age of two' (*SP,* 219). Pound considered any intention to intrude into private spheres, be it in the name of public interest or in the name of divine salvation, a serious violation of an inalienable right, and condemned such intentions as 'oppression,' 'tyranny,' or 'coercive evils' – vices that he frequently lashed out against in his early writings. It is in this sense that Henry James, the 'hater of tyranny,' appears in Pound's appraisal as a true modern hero defending 'human liberty, personal liberty, the rights of the individual against all sorts of intangible bondage' (*LE,* 296).

In his early prose, while criticizing 'all sorts of petty tyrannies and petty coercions' in the Western world (*SP,* 195), Pound vehemently praises Confucianism for placing the ethic of 'non-interference' in a social context:

> Confucius' emphasis is on conduct. 'Fraternal deference' is his phrase. If a man have 'fraternal deference' his character and his opinions will not be a nuisance to his friends and a peril to the community.
> It is a statesman's way of thinking. The thought is for the community. Confucius' constant emphasis is on the value of personality, on the outlines of personality, on the man's right to preserve the outlines of his personality, and of his duty not to interfere with the personalities of others. (*SP,* 193)

Here we are offered a Confucian ethics that appreciates individual personality, and opposes any intrusion into the sphere within the 'outline' of a person's personality. The key concept, 'fraternal deference,' asserts the inviolable value of an individual's personality in meaningful social relations. The concept thus suggests a Confucian version of human equality: if one recognizes that the 'character and opinions' of others are as valuable as his own, he will receive the same treatment in return; if he does not interfere with the personality of others, his personality will be secured.

The term 'fraternal deference' derives from the notion of *ti* 悌 (love and respect for one's elder brother), which appears frequently in Confucian works, especially in *Lun yu*.[29] Pound's final translation of this concept is 'brotherliness' (*Con*, 195). Yet his reading of *ti* contains more than what is conveyed in the original context. Although in Confucian works the concept indeed insists on love between brothers, it puts more emphasis on the virtue of respecting and obeying one's elder brother and acknowledging the latter's authority. In other words, the concept of *ti* imposes an awareness of, as well as a submission to, a hierarchical order. This is why Legge translates this concept as 'fraternal submission.'[30] In contrast, Pound's 'fraternal deference,' which advocates love and respect in terms of universal human fraternity, is informed by the fundamental value of equality cherished by Western liberal thinkers since the French Revolution. Such a notion of 'brotherhood,' for instance, is akin to the following assertion by Gourmont, one of Pound's intellectual mentors: 'What is liberty? A mere word. No more morality, then, save aesthetic or social morality: no absolute system of morals but as many separate systems as there are individual intellects. What is truth? Nothing but what appears true to us, what suits our logic. As Stirner said, there is my truth – and yours, my brother.'[31] This brotherhood, or spiritual equality, demands the recognition of, as well as respect for, each individual's right to truth and self-integrity. It is in this sense that Pound's 'fraternal deference' enforces the importance of the security of the individual's private thoughts and feelings.

Closely related to the value of privacy is that of self-development; these two concepts are mutually reinforcing in Pound's conceptualization. One of the major reasons why Pound felt disenchanted with American democracy was its purported loss of due respect for individual privacy, thus forfeiting the protection of the self-development of its members. He argues this point in the short piece 'Prolegomena' (1927): 'The drear horror of American life can be traced to two damnable roots, or perhaps it is only one root: 1. The loss of all distinction between public and private affairs. 2. The tendency to mess into other people's affairs before establishing order in one's own affairs, and in one's own thought. ... The principle of good is enunciated by Confucius; it consists in establishing order within oneself. This order or harmony spreads by a sort of contagion without specific effort. The principle of evil consists in messing into other people's affairs' (*SP,* 216). For Pound, an America that stoops to 'the principle of evil' has already betrayed the democratic values established as part of its national identity by the Founding Fathers. Pound thus offers the Confucian 'principle' as a magical remedy to the problem.

The 'principle of good' that Pound associates with Confucianism in the statement above refers to the important principle of self-development in Western liberalism. According to this principle, an individual person can fully realize his own value as a human being only by obtaining full development of his faculties – intellectual or moral. In addition, he should enhance his social value – his value to other members of society – by cultivating the values inherent in himself. In a discussion about the 'humanist belief' that learning should be oriented towards cultivating the individual's personality, Pound observes: 'A man acquires knowledge in order that he may be a more complete man, a finer individual, a fuller, more able, more interesting companion for other men' (*SP*, 191). Behind this belief is the assumption that each individual is a miniature cosmos that contains the essence of humanity. In the history of Western thought since the Enlightenment, and especially among the Romantics, the principle of self-development acquired the status of an ultimate value. Friedrich Schlegel, for example, celebrated this value: 'It is just his individuality that is the primary and eternal element in man. To make a cult of the formation and development of this individuality would be a kind of divine egotism.'[32]

Pound's claim that Confucianism encourages the self-development of the individual is based mainly on the first chapter of *Da xue*, which presented Pound with a compelling picture of how a person could achieve self-development both as an individual human being and as a member of society. In this picture, the individual starts by acquiring systematic knowledge of what is around himself and then uses that knowledge as the basis to order his heart and mind; only after obtaining self-knowledge and disciplining his own personality can the individual apply the same principle to the ordering of his family and state. This Confucian doctrine taught Pound to reevaluate the agenda of individualism in terms of its social significance. In other words, the doctrine provided a social justification for Pound's egoistic notion of the aggressively self-assertive individual and his Romantic tendency to maintain the integrity of the self by guarding its private existence. Most important of all, the doctrine convinced Pound that full and harmonious development of the individual personality, free from an externally imposed framework of authority, was the essence of humanity and constituted the starting point for cultural development.

Here we should address the question of what the 'self' means to Pound and in Confucian tradition, and what it is that should be developed on the part of the self. Clearly, the self in Pound's formulation, especially in the first stage of his career, is mainly a discrete individual, a sort of self-determined and self-isolated entity. Such an autonomous individual has little place in orthodox Confucianism, where the individual is granted an existence not as a self-contained individual but as one of the many members of society. The Confucian individual is more of a relational being, defined not by self-sufficiency but by social relevance to, and dependence on, others of the community, whether called a family, clan, or state. The individual can live only in specific social relations, either as a son, a daughter, a wife, or a father.

Self-development in the Confucian tradition, then, is intended to reduce and eliminate what makes a person a self-contained entity, and to cultivate the social attributes enabling an individual to share in the universal ethical principles of humanity. This view of self-development differs profoundly from the early individualist agenda in Pound's ideology. In Pound's conception, the individual maintains his humanness by asserting his individuality, which is defined by his absolute difference from other individuals. In 'I Gather the Limbs of Osiris,' Pound observes:

> The soul of each man is composed of all the elements of the cosmos of souls, but in each soul there is some one element which predominates, which is in some peculiar and intense way the quality or *virtù* of the individual; in no two souls is this the same. ... This virtue is not a 'point of view', nor an 'attitude towards life'; nor is it the mental calibre or 'a way of thinking', but something more substantial which influences all these. (*SP*, 28)

Derived largely from the notion of *virtù* (innermost energy) in Italian humanism, Pound's *virtù*, as he argues here, indicates something that is independent of any social context and 'more substantial' than all social attributes of a person. In a sense, this *virtù* that is essential to individuality cannot be cultivated, for it is an inborn quality in the nature of the individual; it can only be 'discovered' within the individual self (*SP*, 29). Therefore, the action of self-development must be a purely introspective process, a retreat into the inner source of the self, rather than an outward movement towards partaking in the shared commonality of a social existence. What is especially peculiar about Pound's concept of individual *virtù* is that it resists identification with the universal self or a transcendental ego. In comparing Villion's self and Whitman's self in *The Spirit of Romance*, Pound makes observations unmistakably in favour of the former. The essential difference, according to Pound, is that in his 'self-absorption' Villion did not pretend to go beyond his own suffering ego, while Whitman, with a 'horrible air of rectitude,' attempted to make his self the embodiment of the race, the self of everyone (168). Pound's fear is that the unique *virtù*, the absolute difference that defines individuality, might be devoured if it is allowed to be invested in the universal sphere. Thus, self-development for Pound is a process of reinforcing the *virtù* that differentiates the individual from others.

So far I have tried to clarify those basic individual rights that Pound found endorsement for in Confucianism, namely, the freedom of thought and expression, the right to engage in valued activities that require a private space, and the primacy of self-development. In order to further understand the implications of Pound's postulates, however, we need to situate his concerns in the particular social context in which his humanist ideology of the individual operated as a counterdiscourse. Pound's radical polemic, the driving force behind his early liberal politics, shaped his perception of the state and led him to oppose any form of political establishment that threatened individual rights. On the one hand, as a professed Jeffersonian, Pound favoured the least involved government, one that 'impinges least upon the peripheries of its citizens' (*SP*, 213). On the other, he recognized the legitimacy of social functions bestowed upon the government in the modern state. However, for Pound, the essential purpose of these functions is to assist and protect the self-development of each member of the society; therefore, employing these functions in ways contradicting that purpose should be considered a serious misuse of human resources. This, as Pound saw it, is one of the main problems with the modern state. 'The "State" forgot the "use" of man;' he deplored, '"scholarship," as a function of the "State," forgot the use of the individual, or at least, mislaid it, secreted it for its own purpose' (*SP*, 196). What Pound means by this criticism is that instead of helping individuals to fulfil their interests, the modern state has become a manipulative instrument for serving the anti-social purposes of a small group of profit-hungry bankers. The term 'scholarship' here should not be understood in its narrow sense; it actually refers to various establishments of 'Kulchur,' such as German philology, American universities, the social sciences, and so on. These institutions, according to Pound, had degraded themselves to the level of 'coercive force' by impeding intellectual freedom rather than enhancing it.

Pound's concern with the individual was also informed by his perception of the politico-economic structure of his time. In this regard, one major influence on Pound during the 1920s was C.H. Douglas's Social Credit theory of political economy. Much of this theory, according to Pound, was intended to ensure a valid and just pursuit of individual interests and to combat the 'subjugation of the individual' (*SP,* 210–11). Among Douglas's ideas, the one that strongly attracted Pound was Douglas's elaboration on the individual will. Pound expounds Douglas's idea in the essay 'Probari Ratio': 'Major Douglas' realism begins with a fundamental denial that man with his moods and hypostases is or can decently ever become a "unit"; in this underlying, implicit and hardly elaborated contention lies the philosophical value of his treatise. He is for a free exercise of the will, and his paragraphs arouse and rearouse one to a sense of how far we have given up our individual wills in all matters of economics' (*SP,* 207). The word 'unit' in his praise of Douglas invokes Pound's quarrel with socialism. As he argued elsewhere, socialism was 'prone to emphasise the idea of man as a unit, society as a thing of "component parts", each capable of an assignable function' (*SP,* 196). Pound viewed the mechanistic idea of 'unit' as anti-human, for he believed that 'humanity is a collection of individuals, not a *whole* divided into segments or units' (*SP,* 200). He was especially opposed to Fabianism, an intellectual 'poison' in his words (*SP,* 210), and repeatedly challenged its major proponents, including George Bernard Shaw and John Galsworthy, whose theories threatened his own vision of an organic society and individual dignity.[33] Much like the moral philosophy of Confucianism, then, Douglas's theory of political economy provided Pound with some much-desired ammunition for his counterdiscourse.

Even more important, one must take into consideration the fact that Pound perceived the world from the point of view of a poet. In fact, his strong objection to the socialist doctrine of 'unit' was closely related to his bitter experience with the mode of literary production in use at the time. 'The system of magazine publication is at bottom opposed to the aims of the serious artist in letters,' Pound remarks in *Patria Mia*: 'The whole matter is that the editor wants what fits the scheme of his number. As the factory owner wants one man to make screws and one man to make wheels and each man in his employ to do some one mechanical thing that he can do almost without the expenditure of thought, so the magazine producer wants one man to provide one element, let us say one sort of story and another articles on Italian cities and above all, nothing personal' (39–40). In Pound's analysis, both the capitalist approach to magazine publication and the socialist state are seen as dehumanizing machines that relentlessly suppress the independence of the individual soul and, as a consequence, crush the intellectual creativity of humanity. Pound's choice of the machine image for depicting such systems suggests the poet's authentic fear of the sinister side of the modern industrial-commercial society.

After all, Pound's overriding concern was with the modern conditions of the artist. To him, individual freedom generally meant the kind of life that enabled original perception, free speech, and energetic creation, a mode of existence that found its ideal manifestation in the artistic life. Pound repeatedly maintains in writing: 'The artist is free. The true artist is the champion of free speech from the beginning. ... He must be free, either by circumstance or by heroism' (*PM*, 78). Such an emphasis on the absolute freedom of the artist always remained the central appeal of what Levenson calls Pound's 'aesthetic individualism,' and it generated the contradictions in his ideology of individuality as well. Further, this polemical aspect of Pound's individualism sheds even more light on his complex relationship with Confucianism.

Pound's aesthetic individualism, from the start, was grounded on the premises of a cultural elitism that deemed art and poetry the highest achievements of individual intelligence and thus endowed artists with a privileged status as a special species of humankind. Like Emerson's famous notion of the 'Seer,' which conferred on the poet the task of holding a light in the darkness of history, Pound's poet was, in his own words, 'the seeing man among the sightless' (*SR*, 87), whose mission was that of a high priest responsible for interpreting life for the uninformed masses. Such an elitism recognized, or at least submitted to, the notion of the inequality of human beings in intellectual activities. In Pound's early works, poets as a class were categorized as the 'aristocracy of emotion' (*SR*, 90). Given Pound's belief that the *virtù* defining an individual's humanness was an inborn quality, the disturbing implication of his cultural politics is that the difference, namely, the intellectual inequality, between the 'seeing man' and 'the sightless' is an inevitable and irreversible reality. Thus, any possibility for eliminating the difference between individuals could exist only within social classes of the same intellectual category. In other words, Pound only recognized equality in the intellectual life of poets and artists. Among individual poets within this class, Pound encouraged differences so that poetry should encompass diverse perspectives and styles, since each poem, the result of an original creation, must bear the mark of the individual *virtù* of its creator. Only in light of this perspective can we understand why Pound invested a self-conflicting agenda in his idealized cultural product: the 'poetry of a democratic aristocracy, which swept into itself, or drew about it, every man with wit or a voice' (*SR*, 39).

The fundamental contradictions in the political implications of Pound's aesthetic individualism are best expressed in his oxymoronic notion of 'democratic aristocracy.' Pound yearned for a society in which individuals could control their own destiny and enjoy unrestricted intellectual development. On the other hand, he unabashedly insisted on the superiority of certain individuals, whose power derived not from wealth or inheritance but from their innate intellectual *virtù*. These extraordinary individuals – 'poets,' 'artists,' 'creators,' as Pound liked to call them – were deemed the authorities over cultural praxis. In fact, Pound deemed them the 'Authors' of 'Kulchur.' He viewed history as nothing more than a chain of visionary moments constructed by the individual performances of these cultural heroes, whose achievements combined to produce what we proudly call civilization. By the same token, he notes in the preface to *The Spirit of Romance*, 'the history of an art is the history of masterwork' and the 'study of literature is hero-worship' (5).

An aesthetic individualism privileging 'masterworks' and advocating 'hero-worship' would never grant the right of intellectual autonomy to all individuals without reservation. Nor would it favour applying the principles of democracy, in the practical sense of the word, to the realm of artistic creation, which appears to be a special territory guarded and contested by the elite egoists. The privilege of controlling the 'interpretation of life' is preserved for the cultural 'aristocracy,' whose social function, Pound maintains, is 'largely to criticise, select, castigate luxury, to reduce the baroque to an elegance.'[34] In essence, Pound's aesthetic individualism was a weapon used to enforce the modernist writer's claim for a share of power in the cultural establishment. At the same time, by emphasizing the uniqueness of artistic creation and its elite nature, such an individualism also served as a theoretical justification for preventing the crowd, the artistically underprivileged, from interfering with the management of cultural production. The masses, Pound argues in an article published in 1914, composed the 'race with brains like those of rabbits' bred by 'modern civilisation.'[35]

Pound entertained a strong aversion to the artistically less-qualified masses. In *Hugh Selwyn Mauberley*, the poetic speaker deplores the artist's alienation from society, while inveighing harshly against mass culture because it is impregnated by modern commercialism and consumerism and only worships fast and utilitarian production. From Mauberley's perspective, mass culture rejects real artworks, the making of which requires painstaking effort as well as a true appreciation of the principles of beauty and the sublime. Such a mass culture, according to Pound, is a primary cause of the deterioration of the creative spirit of the individual artist. Not surprisingly, during this period, as Pound was intoning the creative freedom of the poet, he simultaneously was seeking to reassert the importance of craftsmanship and artistic discipline, including the rule of 'verbal precision.' Similar to the odd combination of 'democracy' and 'aristocracy' in his critical vocabulary, the coexistence of an insistence on creative freedom and a call for an aristocratic order constituted an important feature of Pound's unique conception of cultural production.

After the First World War it had become even clearer to Pound that the special class of elite individuals could hardly exercise their privileged rights without an appropriate social 'order.' Confronted with what seemed to him to be a cultural 'wasteland,' Pound evidenced a deep pessimism in a letter to William Carlos Williams dated 18 March 1922: 'There is no organized or coordinated civilization left, only individual scattered survivors. Aristocracy is gone, its function was to select. Only those of us who know what civilization is, only those of us who want better literature, not more literature, better art, not more art, can be expected to pay for it. No use waiting for the masses to develop a finer taste, they aren't moving that way. ... Darkness and confusion as in Middle Ages; no chance of general order or justice; we can only release an individual here or there' (*L*, 172). For Pound the overriding difficulty was where to find a model for a much-needed new social 'order.' While the dynamic force of such an 'order' should come from the individual's instinctive aspiration for self-development rather than from the artificial apparatus of conventions, it should be sufficiently persuasive to coordinate individual efforts without interfering with each individual's pursuit. According to Pound, this ideal social order certainly did not exist in the Judeo-Christian tradition because the 'order' of this tradition largely rested on the illusion of salvation through a force extraneous to the individual, and its authority depended on a tyrannical monotheism. Nor did Pound find this model in the modern capitalist society, for its commercial culture alienated the individual intellect from real human needs. Instead, Pound brought his polemical vision of social order to Confucianism, together with all the contradictions and difficulties this vision engendered.

Pound's conflicting agenda informs the thematic structure of canto

XIII, the first complete canto on a Chinese subject, composed in 1923. The poem has two major themes, respect for the 'nature' of the individual and an appeal to social order. The two themes create a tension in the poem and, to a considerable extent, sustain its charm as well. The imperative of order occupies the central place in the poem:

> And Kung said, and wrote on the bo leaves:
>   If a man have not order within him
> He can not spread order about him;
> And if a man have not order within him
> His family will not act with due order;
>   And if the prince have not order within him
> He can not put order in his dominions. (XIII/59)

The poeticized Confucian 'order' is in tune with Pound's vision in every conceivable aspect. The ultimate source of such an 'order' lies within the individual rather than in something external. Not relying on static or dogmatic conventions, the formation of the 'order' is a dynamic process that always generates rules and needs true to the nature of the individual and that derives its vitality through the individual's efforts to concentrate on self-cultivation. In a world unified by this social order, the individual constitutes the radiating centre of consciousness, and his concerns extend from the centre to the peripheries, in the order of self, family, and society. Society is not unimportant in this configuration. Rather, the point is that the individual does not have to deliberately sacrifice the self for anything outside. In Pound's version of Confucius, as long as one establishes order within oneself or one's family, the resultant benefits will automatically reach society as a whole.

But the establishment of such an order also depends on the recognition of its value by others who have equally legitimate contentions. In canto XIII, Pound intentionally has Confucius spell out 'order' and 'brotherly deference' together, for only by combining the two concepts can Pound make his vision complete. Thus, the poem is structured in such a way that the lines about 'order' are surrounded by images and events that exemplify the Confucian virtue of 'brotherly deference.' From this visionary perspective, the entire social order can only function as an organic body when all the individual 'orders' coexist in harmony through mutual recognition. Thus the principle of 'brotherly deference' operates as a social contract coordinating all individual activities and maintaining the functionality of the social order as a whole. In light of our earlier discussion of 'fraternal deference' in terms of human equality, the concept of 'brotherly deference' in this poem can clearly be seen to convey two closely related meanings. First, 'brotherly deference' demands a respect for intellectual freedom, as illustrated in Pound's poetic representation of the same *Lun yu* chapter he had elaborated in the prose piece 'Imaginary Letters' several years ago. What makes his allusion to this chapter in the poem particularly interesting, and thus worth revisiting, is his strategy of creating a desired image of Confucius at the expense of the accuracy of the original text. In the poem, after the four disciples have told the master what they each want to pursue:

    And Kung smiled upon all of them equally
And Thseng-sie desired to know:
    'Which had answered correctly?'
And Kung said, 'They have all answered correctly,
'That is to say, each in his nature.' (XIII/58)

Here we have a Confucius who evaluates his disciples each 'in his nature' and is 'equally' pleased with their ideas. The poet has suppressed some important details from the original text, wherein Confucius is not impartial at all. In the original work, after the disciples complete their speeches, Confucius immediately expresses his preference for Zeng Xi's (Thseng-sie) idea, saying: 'I agree with Dian' (another name for Zeng Xi). Nor does the master treat all four disciples 'equally' with a 'smile.' According to the original text, throughout the entire talk Confucius smiles only once, and disapprovingly: he does so because he finds Zi Lu's speech lacking in modesty and thus signals his disagreement with a slight facial expression.[36] Pound sacrifices these details for the purpose of liberalizing Confucius, to the point that the master appears to treat everyone equally and without bias.

Second, in the poem, Pound's 'brotherly deference' posits an ethical criterion for what constitutes adequate respect for the personality of an individual. The hypocritical Yan Rang (Yuan Jang) fails the test of this criterion and, therefore, is not as worthy as a new-born baby, who deserves respect 'from the moment it inhales the clear air' (XIII/59). The criterion also requires that an individual be judged by the true 'nature' of his personality rather than by social attributes, which are largely materialized in something provisional and insubstantial, such as a person's social position or wealth. In this respect, Confucius is said to have set up a personal example, based on two episodes Pound chose to include in the poem. In one instance, Confucius marries his daughter to Gongye Chang (Kong-Tch'ang) because he believes that Gongye Chang is a virtuous person despite the fact that the latter is 'in prison.' In the other instance, Confucius marries his niece to Nan Rong (Nan-Young), a capable man in Confucius's judgment, even though Nan Rong is then 'out of office,' according to Pound's misreading (XIII/59).[37]

Interestingly enough, such elaborations on respect for the true 'nature' of the individual seem to call into question Pound's own vision of a working order of society. The dominating concern for the principle of 'brotherly deference' is that it can protect the absolute value of the individual 'order' because its objectives are deemed identical with those of the community. Pound presents a case of honouring the primacy of the individual based on his understanding of Confucius. Several lines after Confucius articulates the importance of ordering the self, family, and state, he is asked the question: 'If a man commit murder / Should his father protect him, and hide him?' Confucius replies without hesitation: 'He should hide him' (XIII/59). The hidden logic that supports Confucius's perplexing answer, as well as the reason why Pound cites this anecdote, is that the instinct to defend the son is true to the nature of a father, and to be true to one's nature is reasonable. More significantly, the logic rests on the conviction that it is a father's natural duty to protect the family. Not only is the father-son relationship the basis of the family structure but it also serves as the paradigmatic bond of all social relations. Maintaining the integrity of this relationship, hence the unity of the family, thus becomes the priority in Pound's lyrical representation of an imagined Confucian world.[38] This representation, however, is problematic, because of the anti-social implications it reveals in preferring the primacy of individual interest over social justice.

At the time when he wrote canto XIII, Pound was still primarily concerned with the autonomy of the individual, and this focus prevented him from convincingly envisioning the desired 'order' from the perspective of social relations. The assumption that all individual 'orders' deserve an equal evaluation and therefore should be exempt from conflicts is even challenged by his own poem. What Confucius inscribes on the 'bo leaves' in this poem is not only the order of a 'man' but also the order of a 'prince,' two kinds of order that would posit totally different political agendas. Also, the structure of the poem implies a social context in which diverse 'orders' could come into competition, as clearly demonstrated by Confucius's disciples in their visions of the appropriate political order:

> And Tseu-lou said, 'I would put the defences in order,'
> And Khieu said, 'If I were lord of a province
> I would put it in better order than this is.' (XIII/58)

In the original text, Zi Lu (Tseu-lou) and Ran Qiu (Khieu) are talking about their future pursuits without referring to each other. But in Pound's poem, their words are juxtaposed in such a way that their visions appear to vie for their master's endorsement. Confucius may have accepted both 'equally,' as asserted by Pound, but Ran Qiu's contention that his 'order' is a better one would demand an answer from the implied audience in terms of a value judgment and thus would engender a dilemma of choice on the part of those who are confronted with such a comparison.

Pound's poetic construction of a Confucian outlook in canto XIII leaves some fundamental questions unanswered, and thus tends to intensify, rather than ease, the tension between the individual and society. Pound fails to draw compelling boundaries within which the sovereignty of each individual's 'order' can be rightfully maintained. Nor does his interpretation of Confucius clarify the process by which an individual order's transformation moves from moral accomplishment to political praxis. That is, how can an individual order 'be spread' beyond individual spheres and what can be done if in that process a particular 'order' comes into collision with other 'orders'? Another essential issue from which Pound's poetic construction shies away is this: which individual's 'order' deserves more credit and is therefore more worthy of being socially 'spread around'? If there is such an individual, what enables his position? Most important of all, since the value of an individual 'order' derives from within the individual's inner self, how can this 'order' at once claim to be universally valuable and applicable to society on behalf of the collective good? These are the questions that Pound would bring to his project of Confucian reconstruction in the 1930s and 1940s.

3. Social Responsibility and the Elite Individual

From approximately the early 1930s to the mid-1940s, in the face of a world devastated by economic crisis, ideological conflict, and military confrontation, Pound came to rethink the individual's relationship with the state. In this second phase of his career, his concern shifted from a focus on the rights of the individual to the social responsibility of the individual. Corresponding to this fresh perspective was his modified attitude towards Confucianism, which he no longer deemed a force against the 'evil' of coercion, but rather a force against the threat of social chaos. During this period, Pound's reinterpretation of Confucian politics allowed him to re-envision the formation of the state as a new social order that grows out of the self-knowledge of the duty-bound individual and functions by 'coordinating,' instead of asserting, the rights of all individuals. In this new formulation, Pound incorporated a number of specific Confucian concepts in an attempt to reconcile his liberal individualism and cultural elitism, eventually paving the way to a new autocracy, an authoritarian state in which the supreme vision of 'one man' is privileged as the sole legitimate anchorage of social harmony and thus undercuts the necessity of asserting all other individuals' purposes.

During the 1930s, as he more and more self-consciously identified himself as a social reformer in line with the political and economic movement of Fascist Italy, where he was living,[39] rather than as an oppositional intellectual or an artist in opposition to an uncongenial social environment, Pound became increasingly in favour of the authority of the state and, at the same time, more and more critical of liberal individualism. The change in his position in this regard can be accounted for in two ways. On the one hand, such a change had to do with his earlier self-contradictory conception of the individual. Pound's use of the term 'individual' was often inconsistent and thus ambiguous, and this constituted a prominent feature of his writings on political subjects. When Pound, in early formulations, upheld the 'divine rights' of the individual against the 'coercive evil' of social establishments, he was speaking of individual rights in terms of the absolute and universal values considered inalienable from all human beings. But when he proclaimed the individual mind as the creative source of culture, Pound was envisioning a specific group of elite individuals who served as the torch-bearers of civilization, the legitimate guides and authorities in the ethical and cultural life of their own times. To be sure, such conceptual ambiguity with regard to the implications of the individual can be discerned not just in Pound, but in other contemporary writers as well, such as W.B. Yeats and D.H. Lawrence. This intrinsically self-contradictory ideology is not uncharacteristic of the tradition of liberalism, in which the concept of the 'individual' refers to each and every member of society mainly in an abstract sense and is utilized mostly to legitimate the liberal thinker's self-assertion in his struggle on behalf of the majority of humanity. Yet in social practice the appeal of this concept is severely reduced, in part because there are little historical grounds for such a class-transcending individual and in part because in the realities of social existence, the demand for an equal share of political power and a fair distribution of wealth among all individual members of society could not be honoured even by those who claimed to fight in the name of universal human interests.[40] Thus, the profound contradiction contains the seeds for an ideology that can be both liberal and conservative, individualistic and authoritarian.[41] In Pound's case, the contradiction was intensified by the coexistence of a radical individualism and an elitism, and the balance between the two was upset when the former had to be compromised to serve the interest of the latter.[42]

In view of the fact that Pound's notion of the individual contained implications that could cater to the demands of two conflicting positions, we can conceive of his criticism of liberalism not as an abrupt departure from his previous orientation but as its logical ramification. If there was any change in Pound's thought, it was the increasing awareness of the disruptive nature of the unrestricted 'rights' of the individual, especially when the individual meant 'everyone' of the masses. For Pound, the masses, a social force that always remained menacingly shapeless and obscure, posed a danger to his vision of an ordered and enlightened society. When he complained about the current 'overemphasis on the individual' in a dialogue with Eliot in *Guide to Kulchur,* what Pound found disconcerting was that precisely such a danger would jeopardize the transmission of shared cultural values in society (299). Pound came to see liberalism as promoting such unrestricted rights of the individual, bitterly denouncing it as the 'running sore' of society that committed 'acts contrary to general good' (*GK,* 254). At the same time, he began to question the validity of such major premises as 'democracy' and 'liberty' in classical liberalism. 'Democracy,' he remarks scornfully in *Jefferson and/or Mussolini,* 'is composed one-third of peasant pessimism, one-third of *laissez-aller,* of utter indifference' (109). 'Utter indifference' was another term Pound used for 'irresponsibility,' a social vice that he also came to associate with the notion of liberty: 'Liberty became a goddess in the eighteenth century, and had a FORM. That is to say, liberty was "defined" in the *Rights of Man* as the "right to do anything that doesn't hurt someone else." The restricting and highly ethical limiting clause was, within a few decades, REMOVED. The idea of liberty degenerated into meaning merely irresponsibility and the right to be just as pifflingly idiotic as the laziest sub-human pleased, and to exercise almost "any and every" activity utterly regardless of its effect on the commonweal' (*LE*, 59–60). It must be noted that Pound's remarks should not be taken as an indication of his complete rejection of liberal doctrines. In 1941, he was still able to praise the 'definition of liberty' in the *Rights of Man* as 'among the best formulations of principle that mankind has produced' (*SP,* 303). Also, in canto LXIII, we still see him reciting the slogan of 'every man his own monarch' (353). What he feared, however, was that unrestricted rights granted to the individual members of the masses would reduce them to anti-social elements.

Pound's increasingly harsh criticism of liberalism also had to do with his disillusionment with the current socio-economic situation in Europe and the United States. His intensified exploration of economic issues at this time made him realize that the type of individualism viable in an agrarian society was no longer sustainable in an industrial economy. As he observes in *Jefferson and/or Mussolini*, 'the demarcation between public and private affairs shifts with the change in the bases of production. A thousand peasants each growing food on his own fields can exist without trust laws' (45). In Pound's view, the fact that the individual peasant, a Jeffersonian small producer, could take responsibility for his own material well-being figured significantly in the peasant's ability to enjoy the integrity of his private world. Thus Pound saw political freedom as largely depending on self-reliance in economic matters. In the same work, he also ascribes the loss of real individual values to the emergence of the modern welfare state, in which the rights of the individual are sacrificed for material support: 'We have in our time suffered a great clamour from those who asked to be "governed," by which they mean mostly that they want to run yammering to their papa, the state, for jam, biscuits, and persistent help in every small trouble. What do they care about rights? What is liberty, if you can have subsidy?' (*J/M,* 44). In terms of political economy, Pound's harshest criticism was directed at liberalism's betrayal of the lofty humanist vision of the Enlightenment that had culminated in the French Revolution. In 'A Visiting Card,' he bitterly condemns this betrayal: 'The revolution, or the revolution of the nineteenth century, defined the idea of liberty as the right to do anything that does not injure others. But with the decadence of the democratic – or republican – state this definition has been betrayed in the interests of usurers and speculators' (*SP,* 306). Pound saw the modern state, dominated as it was by a capitalist mode of production and distribution, as immoral and unstable because it wrongly valued diversity over synthesis, private desires over communal interests, and unscrupulous competition over social harmony. According to Pound, liberalism already had degraded itself into an instrument of capitalist exploitation in such a state, concealing 'its baneful economics under two pretexts: the freedom of the spoken and written word, and the freedom of the individual' (*SP,* 342). Under the manipulation of money-lenders for selfish gains, in Pound's view, such rights to individual freedom in speech and action could no longer serve the true interests of humankind.

Deeply disenchanted with classical liberalism, Pound sought to reconstruct a model of social formations in which the individual would be able to enjoy what he liked to call *de facto* rights. In a discussion of 'free speech,' he declared in 1935 that 'I prefer a *de facto* freedom to theoretical freedom' (*J/M,* 43). He even wrote an article specifically on 'Freedom *de Facto*' five years later (*SP,* 303–5). Unlike the kind of 'theoretical freedom' that he wanted to abandon, '*de facto* freedom' for Pound was practical and appropriate to a civilized society because it was predicated on the recognition of necessary ethical restrictions for all individuals as well as on the individual's responsible exercise of his rights. More importantly, *de facto* rights would also include the rights of the state. In *ABC of Economics,* first published in 1933, Pound seeks to clarify the boundaries of individual rights in terms of the extent to which they coexist with the rights of the state:

> Personally I favour a home for each individual, in the sense that I think each individual should have a certain amount of cubic space into which he or she can retire and be exempt from any outside interference what so damn ever.
> From that I should build the individual rights, and as they move out from that cubicle or inverted trapezoid they should be modified by balancing and counterpoise of the same-sprung rights of others, up to the rights of the state or the congeries. (*SP,* 253)

Thus, the rights of the individual, with their legitimacy recognized in the enclosed private space, need in Pound's view to be 'modified' in order to sustain a hierarchical structure topped by the 'rights of the state.' Obviously, Pound's notion of 'state' here refers more to the representation of collective interests than to a governmental body or supreme civil power. Such a state, in its idealized form, is 'totalitarian' in that it provides an all-embracing service to the 'congeries.'

For Pound, the 'totalitarian' state was the most humane form of all social systems, for 'a totalitarian state uses the best of its human components' (*SP*, 158).[43] Pound's 'totalitarian state' is supposed to possess two essential features: first, a commitment to the preservation of the interests of all individuals; second, a government administered by a cultural elite who think in terms of collective interests. The first feature can be viewed as both continuing and transcending Pound's previous individualistic agenda. The totalitarian state, while recognizing the rights of each individual, would try to accommodate the rights of all individual members in an all-encompassing structure of relations. In 'A Visiting Card,' Pound uses a candle analogy to characterize the nature of such a state: 'A thousand candles together blaze with intense brightness. No one candle's light damages another's. So is the liberty of the individual in the ideal and fascist state' (*SP*, 306). In this analogy, even though each candle's light may maintain its own completeness, it does not shine in its own category, but rather in conjunction with all other candles. That is to say, Pound's ideal state is one that recognizes the existence of differences but does not permit, let alone encourage, the assertion of differences, for it should function as an organic whole wherein individual elements are expected to be synthesized rather than remain fragmented.

The second feature of Pound's totalitarian state reflects his fundamental elitist underpinnings. He believed that the ideal state derived its power from the authority of the 'best men' of society and, by so doing, fulfilled the expectation of Jeffersonian democracy. In *ABC of Economics*, Pound refers to the 'preconception of democracy' and explains: 'Let us say at its best, democracy as it existed in the minds of Jefferson and Van Buren, is that the best men, kaloikagathoi, etc., WILL TAKE THE TROUBLE to place their ideas and policies before the majority with such clarity and persuasiveness that the majority will accept their guidance, i.e. "be right"' (*SP*, 247). The special status Pound confers on the elite is problematic, to say the least. According to his description in 'Freedom *de Facto*,' while this 'small group' of privileged individuals might establish a value system by which the state can function and social life can be regulated, they are not restrained by any social institutions. 'It appears to me,' Pound notes in this article, 'that the "small number of people" recognise neither church nor state when it comes to a matter of their own personal conduct' (*SP*, 304). Unlike the crowd, who must succumb to the authority of the state power, the cultural elite is endowed with the privilege of nonconformity and thus can enjoy complete autonomy in their ideological pursuits. They form the central subject of Pound's individualist concerns, and appear to be the true beneficiaries of his totalitarian state. In Pound's view, these extraordinary individuals – artists, writers, or 'any kind of constructors' – earn their credit as the social guides of their communities not only because of their intellectual superiority but also because of their selfless commitment. 'That is to say,' Pound argues in *Jefferson and/or Mussolini*, 'they are interested in the WORK being done and the work TO DO, and not in personal considerations. Personal petty vanities and so on' (68).

Pound got considerable inspiration for his vision of an ideal state from Confucianism, which he frequently came to call a 'totalitarian' philosophy. His reading of Confucian works at this time further convinced him that it was imperative to maintain social order by forcibly coordinating diverse human functions and interests and, more importantly, that an orderly society depended on the presence of some strong-willed individuals with a clear sense of responsibility. Pound found the illustration of such 'responsible' individuals in Confucian works. 'Take the whole ambience of the Analects (of Kung fu Tseu),' he maintains in *Guide to Kulchur*, 'you have the main character filled with a sense of responsibility. He and his interlocutors live in a responsible world, they think for the whole social order' (29). In contrast to the 'responsible world' of the Confucian tradition, the Homeric world becomes

> a world of irresponsible gods, a very high society without recognizable morals, the individual responsible to himself.
> Plato's *Republic* notwithstanding, the greek philosophers did not feel communal responsibilities *vide infra*. The sense of coordination, of the individuals in a milieu is not in them. ... The sense of responsibility, the need for coordination of individuals expressed in Kung's teaching differs radically both from early Christian absolutism and from the maritime adventure morals of Odysseus or the loose talk of argumentative greeks. (*GK*, 38)

It is noticeable that, unlike the contrast he made earlier between the 'coercive evil' of certain Western discourses and the counterforce of Confucianism, Pound here is concentrating on the Confucian ethos of responsibility that he finds absent from the entire Western tradition. From Pound's perspective, however, a commitment to social responsibilities need not detract from individuality, but rather can protect the individual from the threat of irrational authorities. 'People with no sense of responsibility,' Pound explains, 'fall under despotism, and they deserve all the possible castigations and afflictions that the worst forms of despotism provide' (*SP,* 238).

Pound saw individuals 'filled with the sense of responsibility' as the cornerstones of the 'Confucian world.' By no means ordinary, such individuals fulfilled Pound's image of the enlightened cultural hero who is simultaneously the maker, safeguard, and guide of the civilized state. What 'Kung's teaching' provided, in light of Pound's reinterpretations of Confucian works, was a sophisticated theory about how the individual transcends egoistic closure by transforming self-knowledge into the dynamics of an ethical order in which diverse social interests and relations are rationally coordinated. Apparently, this was the same theory of 'order' that Pound had briefly touched upon in canto XIII, a theory from the first chapter of *Da xue* delineating a process that moves from achieving self-awareness to social and cosmic equilibrium. During the 1930s, Pound placed more and more weight on this chapter in developing a political theory. In 1937, as he was making a case for the 'immediate need of Confucius' in remedying the rampant disorder of his time and world, he stressed the Western need 'specifically of the *Ta Hio,* and more specifically of the *first chapter* of the *Ta Hio*' (*SP,* 77). During this period, as a result of his new understanding of key concepts in this chapter and his intense study of the four Confucian books, Pound's elaboration on the Confucian theory of order evidenced a more systematic perspective, greater cogency, and richer implications than previously. What's more important, while his early interest in Confucius had mainly focused on the autonomy of the self supposedly posited by the theory of the individual order, his reformulation of this theory during the 1930s and 1940s was concerned more with the ethical and political consequences of the individual life, especially the social relatedness of the self and the individual's ability and determination to participate in social practice. As a reconstruction of the elitist subjectivity, Pound's theorizing on the concept of order consisted of two parts, self-actualization and social commitment; he then was able to find from Confucian works the ideas he needed to reconcile these two otherwise conflicting undertakings.

As manifested in Pound's Confucian translations and writings on Confucianism, the Poundian-Confucian notion of self-actualization addresses three concerns: the process of self-ordering, the ultimate source of self-knowledge, and the purpose of self-making. The first concern, namely the several steps of self-ordering from classifying 'organic categories' to 'self-discipline,' is represented in our discussion of Pound's theory of linguistic precision in chapter 2 of this book as well as our discussion of his poetic elaboration on 'order' in the second section of this chapter. What deserves particular attention here are the other two concerns. Pound never doubted that the self formed the dynamic source of knowledge, as was demonstrated in our analysis of his interpretation of the Confucian doctrine of *ke ji fu li*. That is why, for Pound, social responsibility was first and foremost self-responsibility. The question that remains for us is how the knowledge derived from selfhood can claim to have an epistemological value beyond the self and thus serve the interests of the 'congeries.' In Pound's early formulation, what had defined the self was the individual's unique *virtù*, a concept that he had used because of the ontological basis it could lend to individual personality. As a result of his reinterpretation of Confucius during the 1930s and early 1940s, Pound tremendously enriched the concept of *virtù* by integrating it with an epistemology of the self. In the new formulation, '*virtù*,' now identified with the Confucian concept of *de* 德 (virtue), becomes an action of self-introspection: 'The *virtu*, i.e., the self-knowledge [looking straight into the heart and acting thence] is the root' (*Con*, 73). The Confucian *de* is a much more powerful concept than *virtù* because it signifies the first of the three aims of the Confucian 'great learning,' one that is both self-driven and capable of self-transcendence.

As the first aim in the Confucian philosophy of learning, the importance of *de* is established in the opening sentence of *Da xue*. Pound's translation of it reads:

> The great learning [adult study, grinding the corn in the head's mortar] takes root in clarifying the way wherein *the intelligence* increases *through the process of looking straight into one's own heart and acting on the results.* (*Con*, 27; emphasis mine)

The italicized part is Pound's new reading of the Confucian term *de* 德, and it shows a significant change from his earlier translation of the same term:

> The law of the Great Learning, or of practicable philosophy, lies in developing and making visible *that luminous principle of reason which we have received from the sky.* (*TH*, 7; emphasis mine)

The two translations – both diverging from the original – suggest completely different understandings of the source of knowledge or reason, which Pound deems the essence of humanity. While the earlier translation, based on Pauthier's French version, locates the source in something entirely external to the individual, the new translation finds the source within the individual himself. Pound's new translation is enabled by the kind of etymographic approach discussed in chapter 1. He first breaks the Chinese character 德 (*de*) into several ideogrammic components, including what appear to him to be the components of 'eye' and 'heart,' and then recombines these components to produce this idea: 'The action resultant from this straight gaze into the heart. The "know thyself" carried into action. Said action also serving to clarify the self knowledge' (*Con*, 21). After all, the 'great learning' of Confucianism is actually the learning of the art of government. If the key to such 'learning' is rooted in selfhood, the knowledge obtained from the self can thus turn out to be a valuable access to political wisdom.

In Pound's early formulation, the individual *virtù* had been intrinsically devoid of social considerations. Although the concept might endow a person with the complete content of individuality, it could also generate the unsettling problem of self-imprisonment as a result of its overemphasis on the absolute difference between the self and others. To a large extent, such a problem was resolved as Pound combined his ontological *virtù* and the Confucian ethical *de* to produce a communitarian concept of virtue invested with Pound's own notions of selfhood and self-knowledge. From the Confucian perspective, *de*, at one with the nature of the cosmos, is the constitutive principle of humanity shared by all human beings. Thus, in Poundian Confucianism, what one can expect to achieve by 'looking straight into one's own heart' is more than self-identity; it also includes insights into one's relations with others and a grasp of the essence of the world of objects. As conveyed in Pound's translation of *Zhong yong*, the individual who obtains full knowledge of himself is capable of 'getting to the bottom of natures of men' and 'the nature of things' (*Con*, 173). Consequently, self-knowledge amounts to the knowledge of the entire human race and acquires the attributes of *universal* truth.

Such a nature of self-knowledge determines the aim of ultimate self-transcendence in person-making, a new teleology in which self-construction is no longer self-centred. In his early formulations, Pound had subscribed to the belief that the essential purpose of learning was to enforce the autonomy of the individual so that he could be 'a more complete man, a finer individual' (*SP*, 191). Such a belief was now modified by the enlarged social perspective that Pound had obtained from Confucianism. From this perspective, 'the complete man wants to build up himself in order to build up others; to be intelligent [see through things] in order to make others intelligent' (*Con*, 218). This is Pound's translation of a major Confucian doctrine from *Lun yu* 6.28 about the relationship between *ji* (self) and others, but it bears two typical Poundian fingerprints. First, Pound's notion of the 'complete man,' which he has carried over from his earlier humanist view asserting the attainable fullness of individuality, is evident in his rendering of the Confucian notion of *ren zhe* 仁者, usually translated as 'the man of perfect virtue' or 'a benevolent man.'[44] Second, in his version Pound prioritizes self-building as the action that must precede the task of building others, an interpretation that differs from the original passage's assertion that one must act in the way that is simultaneously beneficial to himself and others. What Pound has gained from his interpretation is a clear vision of the social grounding of self-cultivation, a vision according to which one cannot achieve the 'complete' human content or 'manhood' unless he moves on to bring the values of the self to bear on the situations of others. In other words, self-knowledge cannot stop with the self, and it is fully realized in enlightening others.

This leads us to the second part of the Poundian-Confucian theory of order, namely the individual's commitment to social order, or 'will toward order' as Pound phrased it in his own terms. For one thing, what truly enabled Pound to get rid of his earlier aestheticist tendency towards self-isolation was a participatory philosophy derived from Confucianism, which convinced him that 'the idea is not achieved until it goes into action' (*SP*, 334). It should be noted that Pound's notion of 'will toward order,' despite its associations with the idea of aggressive struggles for political control, was not an echo of Nietzschean self-glorification. Rather, Pound's notion was directly opposed to Nietzsche's 'will to power': 'The "will to power" (admired and touted by the generation before my own) was literatureifyed by an ill-balanced hysterical teutopollak. Nothing more vulgar, in the worst sense of the word, has ever been sprung on a dallying intelligentsia. ... The great man is filled with a very different passion, the will toward *order*' (*J/M*, 99). Perceiving in Nietzsche's theory the threat posed by liberalism to the stability of his totalitarian state, Pound resisted the 'will to power' out of a conviction that the Nietzschean 'power' was something one might abuse for the selfish purpose of dominating or coercing others. According to Pound, a 'will to power' would endanger the common interests of all individuals. Contrary to the power-driven Nietzschean individual, the 'great man' of Poundian Confucianism needed no power other than his determination to actualize self-values by serving the public. Most importantly, Pound believed the authority of a 'great man' did not rest on power but rather on his grasp of truth or 'Reason,' and for Pound the way to truth was identical with the way to order.

In addition to its emphasis on rational action, Pound's notion of 'will toward order' served to highlight the humanist orientation of his Confucian vision, in which the human will, rather than some materialistic apparatus, sustained human life. For Pound, what characterized a 'Confucian faith' was the belief that 'order should start in one's own cerebrum' (*SP*, 66). He states in his 1938 essay on Mencius: 'Anyone who mistakes Kung or Mencius for a materialist is a plain unadulterated idiot. Their philosophy is not in the least materialist, it is volitionist' (*SP*, 94). In this same essay, he dwells on the notion of *shang zhi* 尚志 (to cultivate the noble will) from a passage in *Mengzi* 7.1.33.[45] This *Mengzi* passage relates a conversation in which a prince asks Mencius what should constitute a person's appropriate pursuit. Mencius replies that it is to cultivate the noble will by living a benevolent life and engaging in righteous actions, and that a person with such a noble will can accomplish great deeds. Pound thinks that the Mencian notion of *shang zhi* 'rimes' with Dante's 'Directio voluntatis,' for both hold in high esteem the power of the human will in creating a desired society with enlightened moral standards (*SP*, 84). The Mencian notion of *shang zhi*, coupled with Dante's notion, is a recurrent theme in *The Pisan Cantos*, which I will analyse in the next section.

In Confucianism, the principal method of transforming self-knowledge into political and ethical rules is summarized in the doctrine of *shu* 恕, translated as 'reciprocity' by both Legge and Tu Wei-ming.[46] All three major Confucian classics, *Da xue*, *Zhong yong*, and *Lun yu*, contain passages related to this doctrine. Pound paid attention mainly to the political and metaphysical implications of the doctrine as formulated in the first two classics. In a note preceding his translation of *Zhong yong*, Pound encapsulates the essence of Confucian politics: 'In cutting an axe-handle the model is not far off, in this sense: one holds one axe-handle while chopping the other. Thus one uses men in governing men' (*Con*, 95). The metaphor of the axe-handle comes from chapter 13 of *Zhong yong*, where Confucius cites a poem to illustrate his point about the relationship between the *Dao* or Way as transcendental principles and the *dao* of humanity. According to Confucius, the *Dao* is immanent in human life. Thus a wise ruler does not have to search far for the wisdom of the *Dao*; he only needs to look within and around his own life to find the appropriate model for his government, in a manner analogous to the making of one axe-handle modelled on another nearby axe-handle. Using such an approach the ruler can succeed in partaking in the blessings of the *Dao*. Confucius concludes that such an intimate relationship between the *Dao* and human nature is most convincingly manifested in the principle of *shu*. In Pound's translation, Confucius's conclusion reads: 'If a man have good will at his center [sympathy in his midheart] the process is not far from him: Do not to another what you would not like to have happen to you' (*Con*, 121). The notion of 'good will at his center' is Pound's etymographic interpretation imposed on the Confucian message to highlight its 'volitionist' dimension. The second half of the sentence following the colon, which is a fairly faithful translation of the original, presents Confucius's famous definition of *shu* or 'reciprocity.' Sustained by one's 'good will' to order, *shu* thus enables one to attain to the Heavenly 'process' (Pound's characteristic rendering of the Confucian concept of *Dao*).

The practical application of *shu* as a method for harmonizing social relationships is fully developed in chapters 8 and 9 of *Da xue*, the two chapters instructing an enlightened ruler how to achieve an organic unity in his family and state. The method, which can be summarized as ruling by means of personal example, functions in two ways. It first requires the ruler to use personal excellence to elicit the pursuit of excellence by others. Hence, 'the prince must have in himself not one but all of the qualities that he requires from others, and must himself be empty of what he does not want from others in reflex' (*Con*, 61). On the other hand, the method allows the ruler to use what he himself desires in his immediate relationships as the model for promoting and organizing larger social relationships. For instance, as conveyed in Pound's rendering:

> If those in high place respect the aged, the people will bring filial piety to a high level; if those in high place show deference to their elders, the people will bring their fraternal deference to a high level; if those in high place pity orphans, the people will not do otherwise; it is by this that the great gentlemen have a guide to conduct, a compass and square of the process.
>
> If you hate something in your superiors, do not practice it on

those below you; if you hate a thing in those below you, do not do it when working for those over you. (*Con*, 65–7)

Such a reciprocal process, always starting with a self-reflexive condition and extending to include others into considerations, serves both as the basis for the establishment of an interactive relationship with others and as the basis for self-actualization. Thus, cardinal human relationships based on the constructive principle of *shu*, such as that between father and son or between brothers, are enhanced with ethical persuasiveness. These familial relationships can be taken a step further to serve as structural paradigms for the state in which people can find their proper relational roles, either as ruler, subordinates, or fellow members of society.

The Confucian ideal of a harmonious state organized under the principle of *shu* or reciprocity is invoked in Pound's later cantos, especially canto XCIX:

> The whole tribe is from one man's body,
>   What other way can you think of it?
> The surname, and the 9 arts.
>   The father's word is compassion;
>   The son's, filiality.
>   The brother's word: mutuality;
>   The younger's word: deference.
> Small birds sing in chorus,
>   Harmony is in the proportion of the branches
>   as clarity (chao).
>   Compassion, tree's root and water-spring;
>   The state: order, inside a boundary;
>   Law: reciprocity.
> What is statute save reciprocity?
> One village in order,
>   one valley will reach the four seas. (XCIX/728–9)

These lines crystallize the Poundian-Confucian vision of a realized 'will toward order,' a vision that overcomes contradictions by coordinating all relations within the unifying structure of the 'village.' In the tranquil centre of this harmonious world stands the 'one man,' the individual who has succeeded in self-actualization by accomplishing the transformation from ego-self to social organizer with indisputable moral and political authority. In so far as it also propagates the Confucian notion of 'order,' canto XCIX may seem to bear a thematic similarity with canto XIII. A fundamental difference exists between the two poems, however. Canto XIII allows individuals to assert their own orders 'each in his nature' and presents a picture of the coexisting orders of various persons – a common family man, a prince, and several disciples of Confucius. In so doing, this earlier canto demonstrates a recognition of diversity and difference and seeks to solve social conflicts by recommending a mutual respect of brotherhood. In contrast, canto XCIX shows no sign of acknowledging differences between people; it instead celebrates a single dominating 'order' that derives from 'one man' only. In this sense, the law of 'reciprocity,' which by definition is a two-way action, calls itself into question because in Pound's poetic configuration this law points to a single direction, disclosing from one privileged source. Such a political vision can hardly be construed as anything but an open endorsement of autocracy.

The problematic vision manifest in Pound's work brings us to the important question of political feasibility often raised in modern projects to reinstate Confucianism. The question concerns whether or not Confucianism inevitably presupposes an autocratic or authoritarian polity. Since the second half of the last century, that question has been addressed extensively by contemporary New Confucian thinkers represented especially by Mou Zongsan among the older generation and Tu Wei-ming among the younger generation. Contemporary New Confucians are committed to the same goal to which Pound also subscribed: to reclaim the humanist values of Confucianism in order to construct a sociopolitical model that can serve both as an answer to the challenges of Western modernity and as an alternative to it. In their efforts to achieve that goal, New Confucian thinkers have resorted to almost the same basic tenets in Confucian classics as did Pound, and have developed a theory about the self and the state, which in many ways strikes a parallel with Pound's theory of 'will toward order.' Therefore, it may help us to grasp Pound's ideological underpinnings by comparing his theory of 'will toward order' with related formulations by New Confucians.

Contemporary New Confucians are fully aware that the principal appeal of modernity rests on the demand for democracy and that the modern challenge to Confucianism, then, is how this old tradition can reconcile itself with this demand. They argue that anti-Confucian critics are incorrect in equating the Confucian tradition with Confucian China, since for New Confucians the two represent different value systems despite their historical relationship with each other. In the view of New Confucians, the former is a humanist philosophy concerned with permanent values that inform the meaningful existence of humanity, while the latter, contingent and insubstantial, is the historical expression of a feudal ideology characterized by the misuse of Confucian ideas.[47] New Confucians believe that rather than opposing democracy, Confucianism contains 'the seeds' that can foster democratic society in a rational and humane way.[48] Among these New Confucian thinkers, Mou Zongsan perhaps has done the most to revitalize such 'seeds of the democratic spirit' in Confucianism. For Mou, democracy as a political system cannot be transplanted into a society from without. The driving force for democracy must come instead from a conscious awareness of human dignity and sublimity, which grows within each individual's mind-heart and always strives for full actualization by transforming the objective world in keeping with the moral ideal of the conscious subject. According to Mou, Confucianism is a moral idealism; it provides a sophisticated theory that convincingly conceptualizes a path that leads from private moral pursuit to public social development. This theory, summarized in *Da xue* and permeating all Confucian classics, is called *nei sheng wai wang* 內聖外王 (internal sagehood and external kinghood), and is recognized by most New Confucians as the center piece of the political philosophy of Confucianism.

To reinstate the vision of 'internal sagehood and external kinghood,' Mou Zongsan maintains, New Confucians should accomplish three tasks. The first task is to reaffirm the Confucian-Mencian moral tradition, by recognizing that the individual moral conscience is the primordial creative force of life and that self-perfection is the only way to sagehood. The second task is to establish a tradition of learning that is independent of the political power structures of the state and enables the individual to translate his moral instincts into systematic rational knowledge. The third task is to develop a political tradition in which each individual is encouraged to contribute his self-knowledge to the ideal of society, that is, as an active participant in the political process who is keenly aware of his own dynamics and values rather than a passive member of society. The three tasks combine to form the complete procedure by which one passes from internal sagehood to external kinghood, a democratic process in which each individual actualizes his self-values in the fully realized moral, cognitive, and political subjectivity.[49]

Clearly, the New Confucian theory of 'internal sagehood and external kinghood' shares strikingly similar goals with Pound's theory of 'will toward order': both view the self as the sole source of truth and creativity, and treat the self as the starting point, as well as the final evaluative basis, for a political process aimed at social justice and stability. In spite of these similarities, however, Pound's formulation contains two fundamental differences from that of contemporary New Confucians, differences that need to be examined in order to clarify his relationship with the Confucian tradition and its historical development.

The first difference between Pound's views and those of the New Confucians lies in Pound's unyielding embrace of a volitional determinism. To a large extent, Pound was attracted to Confucianism because he saw it as upholding the primacy of the human will in a world that had been corrupted by materialist concerns. On the one hand, Pound's unconditional trust in the will revealed a deep-rooted fear of any social institutions. In his early years, he had often displayed a strong antagonism to the tyranny of a sociopolitical system that could diminish the individual to something like a 'piece of the machine' (*SP,* 192). Such an antagonism remained prevalent in his political thinking in the 1930s, when he denounced the 'abuses of the system' because they disrupted the 'root' of human civilization (*SP,* 96). For Pound, it did not matter what system a state adopted; what mattered, he argued, was that 'there should be a *de facto* government composed of sincere men willing the national good' (*J/M,* 95). On the other hand, he truly believed that the human will could provide the patterns for regulating both private life and social activities. In a comparison between C.H. Douglas and Mussolini, Pound emphasized the centrality of the will: 'Mussolini had achieved more than Douglas, because Douglas has presented his ideas as a greed system, not as a will system' (*SP,* 294). Pound believed that a state based on the 'will system' would be more humane and efficient, guided by the good will of those who truly concerned themselves with human needs and possessed a profound understanding of human history. For Pound, it was the human will, not a political or legal system, that sustained the stability of the state. In other words, the essential element for any state was the commitment of the few individuals 'willing the national good.' If they failed in their responsibility, that is, failed 'to impart the result of their understanding' and 'to translate knowledge into action,' the state would collapse no matter what forms its government was built on (*J/M,* 95).

What appears problematic in Pound's formulation is the notion that the will towards order could permit the enlightened individual to bypass the regulations of the system while letting his self-knowledge directly affect social life. Such a volitional determinism is what New Confucians have sought to critique. It is true that contemporary New Confucians are often accused of failing to provide a compelling model of a social system for their visionary world, and thus can be seen as guilty of moral determinism. Yet New Confucians believe that the successful transformation from the 'sagely' moral ideal to the 'kingly' social praxis depends on the mediation of a system that works not only to balance the moral appeals of all members of society but also to ensure the efficacy of each instance of moral pursuit in actual historical contexts. Mou Zongsan calls this mediating process the 'indirect realization' of political kinghood.[50] For New Confucians, the systemization of a democratic procedure would prevent moral kinghood from being usurped by the individual who just happens to be in power but has no sagely moral qualifications.

New Confucians are strongly opposed to endorsing the moral superiority of the privileged minority in society. Herein lies a more fundamental difference separating them from Pound. The lesson that New Confucians have learned from Chinese history is that Confucianism failed as a convincing moral idealism whenever it was manipulated to serve the interests of the privileged minority. Inspired by the Mencian belief that everyone who follows the right path of self-cultivation can achieve the same sagehood as ancient sage-kings, New Confucians maintain that true Confucianism recognizes the equality of individuals and endows all persons with the chance to freely pursue moral perfection. Mou Zongsan states: 'Speaking of the attainment of sagehood, people usually think that the aim is so high, so unreachable, that they feel intimidated. In fact, the aim of moral practice is to assert one's moral individuality. To attain sagehood is precisely to assert one's moral individuality and to develop one's moral character. This is something natural, something close to our life, and thus it should not be feared. Our definition of "internal sagehood" is always clear: the emphasis is on the individual; everyone should establish his moral individuality and assert his moral character through moral practice.'[51] In addition, New Confucians recognize that the results of moral practice vary in real life. In a given society, some individuals may actualize their selfhood more fully than others, hence achieving more 'profound' personalities, to use Tu Wei-ming's term. But this does not mean that these individuals can 'presume to have a privileged access to esoteric truths' or that their self-knowledge is 'necessarily of equal value to others.'[52] To impose a privileged moral pattern, Tu argues, is against human nature because it destroys the 'basis of self-improvement.' He thus cautions: 'It is absolutely impossible to establish a fixed model by which all persons can learn to become profound persons.'[53]

Pound, in contrast, never really gave up his elitist inclinations, which eventually led to his support of political autocracy. As we have seen, even at the most liberal moment of his career, Pound remained adamant in the conviction that culture was created and sustained by 'a small number of people' and that a civilized society depended on the contributions of these privileged individuals. In Pound's view, the achievements of such individuals marked turning points of history and established cultural paradigms followed by the rest of society. Sigismundo Malatesta exemplified such a cultural hero. Upon observing the achievements of Malatesta, Pound wrote: 'It is perhaps the apex of what one man has embodied in the last 1000 years of the occident. A cultural "high" is marked' (*GK*, 159). Pound applied this same reasoning to his explanation of the individual's role in politics. In *Jefferson and/or Mussolini*, making reference to the Duce, Pound says: 'I offer the hypothesis that: When a single mind is sufficiently ahead of the mass a one-party system is bound to *occur as actuality* whatever the details of form in administration' (125).

While Confucianism did not cause Pound's elitism, there is no denying that his reading of Confucian works, informed by his concerns related to his social experiences, did reinforce his elitist orientation. The theory of 'will toward order' was formulated to endorse the legitimacy of the 'small number of people,' be they artists or politicians, who were seen to possess a privileged access to truth and creation. Pound found a compelling conceptualization of such an individual in the description of *junzi* 君子 (usually rendered 'gentleman,' as in Waley's and Lau's translations) in *Da xue*. Pound's translation of the term – 'the man in whom speaks the voice of his forebears,' 'real man,' more frequently 'great gentleman' – highlights the individual's difference from others as well as his privileged position in society, a position that enables this individual to become self-actualized in ways others cannot. Pound's attention to the unique accomplishment of such a 'great gentleman' led him to one particular passage in chapter 9 of *Da xue*, where it is claimed that 'one word will ruin the business, one man can bring the state to an orderly course' (*Con*, 61). The original passage discusses the social consequences of a ruler's life by providing examples of both good and bad ancient emperors in Chinese history. The focal point of the passage is that because of the special position that a ruler occupies in society, whatever he does and says is bound to have a significant social impact. However, the passage in itself does not legitimate, or reject, autocracy. Pound showed unusual interest in this passage because he could stretch its implications to reinforce his radical elitism. For this reason he singled out the idea of 'one man's rule' from this passage, turning it into a recurrent poetic theme in his later cantos, such as in cantos LXXXV, LXXXIX, XCIV, and XCV. In particular, canto LXXXVI makes a graphic contention for this autocratic outlook:

It may depend on one man. (LXXXVI/583)

The four Chinese characters expressing the idea of 'also depend on one man' are typographically arranged to heighten the point that this 'one man' stands out as the pillar of society. But what depends on 'one man' is deliberately made ambiguous by the use of the pronoun 'it,' with the possible implication that 'it' can denote one family, one state, or even the salvation of the entire human race. In this poeticized autocratic vision, Pound's radical individualism and elitism converge with the feudalist memory of a conservative Confucianism. According to this fascinating vision, the attainment of an orderly civil state depends not only on the human will, but on the will of 'one man' only.

4. The Heroic Self in Adversity

Since his first meeting with Mussolini in 1933, Pound had envisaged the emergence of his idealized state in Italy, a state that was characterized not only by the guidance of 'one' enlightened leader and '*de facto* democracy' but also by its cultural achievements and economic prosperity. Pound's dream was shattered by the final outcome of the Second World War. The end of the war came to Pound almost like the end of the world, 'with a bang not with a whimper' (LXXIV/445), leaving him 'as a lone ant from a broken ant-hill / from the wreckage of Europe' (LXVI/478), as he describes it in these famous lines from *The Pisan Cantos*. A prisoner facing the charge of treason at the Disciplinary Training Center (DTC) in Pisa, Pound saw himself as the victim of an unjust war. He bitterly denounced the war by repeatedly citing from Mencius:

'In "The Spring and Autumn" / there / are / no / righteous / wars' (LXXVIII/503).[54] Nevertheless, despite such devastating experience, after the war Pound never abandoned the concerns to which he had committed himself: 'I surrender neither the empire nor the temples / plural / nor the constitution nor yet the city of Dioce' (LXXIV/454). Pound's basic position remained unchanged, except that what had been ostentatiously advocated by the poet-reformer as a public agenda was now withdrawn into the dim corner of its creator's mind, where it was transformed into purely private vision and carefully treasured as the only thing that could sustain his hope for survival in the 'wreckage' of his personal life, his ideal state, and history.

Survive Pound did, both as a poet and a visionary ideologue. He derived much of the strength for his miraculous recovery from Confucian works, and to be more exact, from the Confucian notion of the heroic self, which reinforced his faith in the value of personal integrity and the regenerative power of the individual mind. In a conversation with Angela Palandri, who visited him a number of times at St Elizabeths Hospital in Washington, DC, in 1952, Pound recalled the impact of the bilingual edition of Confucian works that he had brought with him to the DTC in Pisa: 'The little book has been my bible for years, the only thing I could hang onto during those hellish days at Pisa. ... Had it not been for this book, from which I drew my strength, I would *really* have gone insane.'[55] It is not surprising that Confucius provided psychological support for Pound at the most agonizing and humiliating moments of his life. Confucius himself was a political failure, his life being a record of constant struggles under unfavourable circumstances. Pound's familiarity with this particular aspect of Confucius's life manifests itself in his poetic portrayal of the master in canto LIII, in which Confucius is chased around 'like a dog' by hostile soldiers and wanders in the wilderness for 'seven days foodless' (LIII/273). In such a portrait Pound tries to foreground Confucius's ability to maintain an optimistic spirit and to persevere in his undertaking. The Confucian works could have served as Pound's 'bible' because they abound with sayings about individual heroism. Take, for example, Confucius's words from *Lun yu* 9.25: 'The commander of three army corps can be kidnapped, you cannot kidnap a plain man's will' (*Con*, 232). Such sayings can enormously empower the heroic individual in adversity by justifying his efforts to survive as well as encouraging him to preserve his capacity to contribute to society. The Confucian ideal of the heroic self in adversity informed Pound's creation of a captivity narrative, best illustrated by *The Pisan*

Cantos. This narrative primarily conveys two themes consistent with his previous discourse on the individual: self-empowerment through introspection in solitude and the indestructibility of the individual mind.

The strategy of seeking self-protection in seclusion constitutes an important dimension of the Confucian doctrine of self-cultivation. Although Confucianism always requires one to actualize the values within oneself by participating in social construction, it also insists that one may justifiably retreat into solitude if that is the only way to protect the self from being contaminated or harmed by disruptive social forces. In *Lun yu* 15.6, Confucius expresses his admiration for Shiyu and Qu Boyu, two historical personages characterized by the shared ability to preserve personal integrity whether or not the *Dao* or Way prevailed in their respective times. Confucius's remarks in this chapter articulate the doctrine that a principled individual, always 'straightforward like an arrow' under whatever circumstances,[56] should be ready to contribute to society when the government is good and equally ready to withdraw from society when the government is bad. Mencius developed Confucius's idea in a clearer and better-known elaboration (*Mengzi* 7.1.9):

> When the men of antiquity realized their wishes, benefits were conferred by them on the people. If they did not realize their wishes, they cultivated their personal character, and became illustrious in the world. If poor, they attended to their own virtue in solitude; if advanced to dignity, they made the whole kingdom virtuous as well.[57]

For over two thousand years, this Confucian doctrine about when to participate in public life, when to withdraw from it, and why to do so, had been followed as the highest ethical standard by the Confucian literati in China. Pound was familiar with this doctrine. Even before the war started, in the late 1930s, as if he were able to anticipate the ordeal he would endure after the war, he had noted in the article on Mencius that the social responsibility Confucianism assigned to an individual with the will to order also included the individual's willingness and courage to defend his convictions when he was plunged into adverse situations. In this article, he paraphrases Mencius's saying to support his point: 'Mencius' sense of responsibility is omnipresent. It is in man to himself. ... Out of office he attends to his internal order, in office to that of as much of the state as is entrusted to him. But at no moment is he irresponsible' (*SP*, 90). In *The Pisan Cantos* written at the DTC in Pisa, Pound invokes the same doctrine by citing Confucius's words from the above-mentioned passage: 'like an arrow, and under bad government / like an arrow' (LXXVII/488). Here, identifying himself with such Confucian heroes as Shiyu and Qu Boyu, Pound seems to voice his defiance at an outside world that has forced him to seek temporary refuge in the inner world of his moral vision.

In Pound's captivity narrative, the Confucian image of 'arrow' is closely related to the Confucian-Mencian analogy of archery, to which Pound alludes in *The Pisan Cantos*: 'Missing the bull's eye seeks the cause in himself' (LXXVII/488). The idea of archery comes from one passage in *Zhong yong*, which in Pound's translation reads: 'Kung said: there is an analogy between the man of breed and the archer. The archer who misses the bulls-eye turns and seeks the cause of his failure in himself' (*Con*, 127). What we have here is the same teaching that admonishes the Confucian individual to rely on the subjective mind as the stronghold against social changes contradicting his convictions, and to use introspection as a convenient strategy for making sense of a perplexing history. In Mencius's work, the analogy of archery is extensively developed to illustrate the virtue of the 'benevolent' person who is able to properly adjust his moral quest through a sort of self-criticism.[58] Pound calls this analogy a 'parable' and, by using his characteristically provocative and problematic rhetoric, associates this parable with the 'Nordic ethic': 'The ethic of Confucius and Mencius is a Nordic ethic, a Nordic morale, if it has been boggit in *laissez faire* and tropical indolence that cannot be blamed on its shape. It is not quietistic. It is concentrated in the Mencian parable: "An Archer having missed the bullseye does NOT turn round and blame someone else. He seeks the cause in himself"' (*SP*, 96). For Pound, then, this parable does not advocate passive contemplation but calls instead for the individual to recharge the self in the face of outside challenges.

The Confucian-Mencian notion of the heroic self, embodied by the perfect archer, had a profound impact on Pound's poetry, an impact that should be measured dialectically. On the one hand, the introspective tendency inscribed by this doctrine significantly underlies the change in Pound's narrative style in poetry written after the Second World War. While the cantos he wrote during the 1930s and the early 1940s are markedly preoccupied with history and public events, his postwar cantos overwhelmingly contemplate personal feelings and memories, a change too drastic to escape notice. In particular, *The Pisan Cantos*, a poignantly beautiful internalization of the poet's fragmented perceptions of a tumultuous world, faithfully registers his attempt to practise the Confucian theory of self-empowerment through introspection in isolation. The subjectivism derived from the Confucian ethic of self-cultivation immensely informs Pound's poetry; the highly personal worldview in this poetry is justified when the solitary individual feels that he is losing his grip on the reality of the external world.

Yet in valorizing the Confucian-Mencian parable in *The Pisan Cantos*, Pound has no intention of blaming himself for his failed crusade. *The Pisan Cantos* contains little that can 'legitimately be read as self-criticism' on the intellectual level, as noted by Peter Nicholls.[59] It is true that there are lines indicating Pound's regret for his previous lack of sufficient affection for others (LXXVI/480), or lines where he seems to be lamenting his selfish conduct, conduct that led his wife 'to an ill house and there is / no end to the journey' (LXXVIII/497). But even these few instances of self-criticism are directed at some minor mistakes in his domestic life, rather than at his political enterprise. In other words, when he insisted on 'seeking the cause in himself,' Pound meant that he sought to look into the world of his private experience for a redeeming force, rather than to surrender his ideological quest. As a prisoner in the detention camp in Pisa, it was all the more natural that Pound seized the inner world of the self as the only sphere still retaining an appealing reality. Even if he had not been inspired by Confucianism, he might have clung to the self as his only escape from a depressing daily reality. But Confucianism, and in particular the Confucian doctrine of self-cultivation that had long been engraved in his mind, was able to give a strong sense of consistency to Pound as well as an enormous power of persuasion to the kind of captivity narrative that he was creating in *The Pisan Cantos*. Pound's aim in this self-centred narrative was to reassert the validity of his ideological vision by means of the Confucian ritual of self-examination – sorting out and reordering his fragmented experiences so that their meaning could be reinstated in a more 'precise definition' to resist the threat of history.

The other Confucian theme repeatedly promulgated in *The Pisan Cantos* and some later cantos is the belief that the human mind is indestructible and capable of self-regeneration. According to Pound's interpretation of Mencian philosophy, the individual will engendered by a virtuous mind is eternal and able to transcend the physical containment of time and space. Pound cites the example of two ancient Chinese emperors from *Mengzi* 4.2.1:

>   Shun's will and
>   King Wan's will
> were as the two halves of a seal
>   1/2s
>   in the Middle Kingdom
> their aims as one
> directio voluntatis, as lord over the heart 志
>   the two sages united. (LXXVII/487)

Shun is a legendary king living perhaps in the twenty-second century BCE, while King Wan (Wen) lived approximately in the twelfth century BCE. Although the two sage-kings are separated by about one thousand years of history, their wills (*zhi* 志) are seen as having obtained life by taking root in the permanent patterns of human values, and thus transcend history to coexist in a seamless unity.

Moreover, in Pound's Confucian belief, as long as the individual will is true to human nature, it does not perish even after the individual dies. Pound finds individuals with such an inviolable will in Confucian works and enshrines their memory in his poetry: 'Wei, Chi and Pi-kan / Yin had these three men full of humanitas (manhood) / or jên' (LXXXIV/559). Wei (Weizi), Chi (Jizi), and Pi-kan (Bigan) were three virtuous men in the last days of the Shang dynasty (c. 1766–1122 BCE). Because of their opposition to the tyrant Zhou, these men were either persecuted to death or forced to hide in a hermitage, but none of them surrendered his moral ideals. For this reason, Confucius in *Lun yu* 18.1 praises them as the three great men of the Shang dynasty who achieved the virtue of *ren* (Pound's 'jên' or 'manhood'). Pound's celebration of these individuals reflects his strategy of projecting himself into such a Confucian hero whose life is sustained by the consoling conviction that 'nothing matters but the quality / of the affection – / in the end – that has carved the trace in the mind / dove sta memoria' (LXXVI/477).

If the mind is imperishable, nothing except the individual's own will can disrupt his spirit of visionary pursuit and his desire for survival. This is the Confucian-Mencian motto that Pound keeps reminding himself of in *The Pisan Cantos*:

> a man on whom the sun has gone down
> nor shall diamond die in the avalanche
>   be it torn from its setting
> first must destroy himself ere others destroy him. (LXXIV/450)

The first line, which is based on Pound's etymographic reading of the Chinese character 莫 (*mo*, meaning 'no' or 'nothing'), reveals a keen awareness of the devastating situation with which he is confronted. Nevertheless, he is inspired by the Mencian idea to which the fourth line alludes (*Mengzi* 4.1.9): 'A man must first despise himself, and then others will despise him. A family must destroy itself, and then others will destroy it. A State must first smite itself, and then others will smite it.'[60] From the Mencian point of view, while the human mind is responsible for its own destruction, it also possesses the power for its own rebirth. To enhance the universal applicability of this Mencian idea, Pound remarkably blends it with the African myth about Wagadu:

> 4 times was the city rebuilded, Hooo Fasa
>   Cassir, Hooo Fasa   dell' Italia tradita
> now in the mind indestructible, Cassir, Hooo Fasa
> With the four giants at the four corners
> and four gates mid-wall Hooo Fasa
> and a terrace the colour of stars
> pale as the dawn cloud, la luna
>   thin as Demeter's hair
> Hooo Fasa, and in a dance the renewal
>   with two larks in contrappunto
>   at sunset
>   chi'intenerisce (LXXIV/450–1)

According to an African myth, Wagadu is a divine spirit embodied by a splendid city that is destroyed and rebuilt four times. Yet since Wagadu is a spiritual being and lives in human hearts, she reappears as a new city bearing the name Fasa. Pound's Confucian-Mencian conviction is illustrated in his use of this myth: he is convinced that although he is now 'a man on whom the sun has gone down,' as long as he maintains the vitality of his vision of life the city of Dioce, his ideal state, his paradise on earth, will rise up again.

4

Confucianism and Pound's Spiritual Beliefs

1. The 'Rebellious Protestant'

Given the formidable extent of Pound's intellectual interests, what he really believed appears to be a perplexing question to his readers. T.S. Eliot was the first to raise serious questions about Pound's religious propensities. In a 1928 review of Pound's collection of poems, Eliot commented on the 'curious syncretism' that he found characteristic of Pound's writing. According to Eliot, Pound's belief system was essentially a hodgepodge of irreconcilable, 'antiquated' views that included, among other things, medieval mysticism, Yeats's Celtic myths, and 'a steam-roller of Confucian rationalism.'[1] Eliot displayed an especially contemptuous attitude towards Confucianism, which he called 'an inferior religion.' He ended the book review with the famous question: 'What does Mr. Pound believe?'[2]

Eliot intensified his interrogation of Pound's religious beliefs in a series of lectures delivered in 1933 at the University of Virginia, which were soon published in a collection entitled *After Strange Gods: A Primer of Modern Heresy*. Eliot's book initiated a prolonged and heated debate between himself and Pound. The central argument Eliot makes in the book is that the disintegration of Western culture in the modern world results from the decline of Christian orthodoxy, by which Eliot means Catholicism. Based on this thesis, Eliot sets out to criticize the kind of social phenomena that he regards as detrimental to the preservation and reinvigoration of the Western cultural tradition.[3] Among his targets, Eliot takes issue with Pound, Irving Babbitt, and I.A. Richards because of their attempt to find in Confucianism solutions to the social problems of the West. Confucius, Eliot observes, 'has become the philosopher of the rebellious Protestant' and the 'spiritual adviser of the highly educated and fastidious.'[4] Citing linguistic and cultural differences between the East and the West as insurmountable barriers, Eliot seriously questions the ability as well as the intention of these intellectuals to integrate such an alien system of thought as Confucianism with Western culture, and asserts that their efforts will merely make 'matters worse instead of better.' In particular, Eliot attacks Pound's 'powerful and narrow post-Protestant prejudice,' which in his view has caused Pound to neglect the things that gave European culture its significance.[5] Because he recognizes Pound as 'probably the most important living poet in our language,' Eliot appears to feel particularly disappointed with Pound's abandonment of orthodox Christian doctrines. He maintains that such a 'theological twist' – an Eliotic euphemistic expression for 'heresy' – is responsible for Pound's poetic representation of unreal human beings, an empty social environment, and a meaningless Purgatory.[6]

Eliot's critique raised three questions essential to understanding Pound's spiritual quest. Did Pound have a belief system and, if so, what constituted the substance of that system? Why did he rebel against Christianity and what did he particularly oppose in that tradition? How could he reconcile his Protestant upbringing with, in Eliot's words, the 'heresy' of 'strange gods' from alien traditions? Pound responded to Eliot's inquiry in a series of articles in 1934, and his defence over the issues that Eliot raised continued well into the 1940s.[7] Pound's counterargument in this regard contributed enormously to clarifying some of his major concerns with religion, concerns about which he had often talked in an evasive way. More significantly, the debate reinforced his pursuit of, and dependence on, Confucianism as a primary source of inspiration for a new ethical and religious vision. In the first section of this chapter, I will analyse Pound's concerns in light of the three questions posed above. Since the third question has a great deal to do with Pound's Confucian belief, I will continue to address it more extensively in the next three sections. The analysis contained in this section, then, will serve as an introduction to a thorough investigation of Pound's integration of Confucianism into a new belief system.

In their critical dialogue, Pound disagreed with Eliot in reducing all social problems to a religious crisis, and he seemed unwilling to debate in the theological terms set up by Eliot. Nevertheless, Pound was sharply aware that the central issue addressed by Eliot did exist. What separated Pound from Eliot was the difference in their approaches to this issue as well as their proposed solutions to it. The central issue that Eliot endeavoured again and again to bring to the attention of his audience was that the disruption of a shared belief, which had for centuries sustained what he termed the 'European mind,' was turning the Western world into a sort of 'wasteland.' Eliot was not alone, of course, in noting the absence of a desired belief, which he identified with Catholic orthodoxy; Western writers from varied perspectives had long felt confronted with the same crisis. So intense was the perception of a crisis of belief that William James, the American philosopher both Eliot and Pound admired, wrote a book that vehemently asserted the central importance of the 'will to believe.' James made a passionate case for 'belief' despite his recognition that what the will believes cannot be convincingly verified. According to James, the validity of the guiding principles of morality that bind society together depends on the authority of a shared belief in the existence of absolute truth.

This fundamental issue had actually engaged Pound from the beginning of his career when he searched in European mythology for signs of the 'permanent basis in humanity' (*SR*, 92). In spite of his characteristic distrust of religious belief,[8] Pound did believe in the existence of a supreme force of creation. Such a belief can be found, for instance, in the essay 'Axiomata' written in 1921:

(1) The intimate essence of the universe is *not* of the same nature as our own consciousness.
(2) Our own consciousness is incapable of having produced the universe.
(3) God, therefore, exists. That is to say, there is no reason for not applying the term God, *Theos*, to the intimate essence. (*SP,* 49)

The 'intimate essence' is what Pound often referred to as the 'eternal state of mind' or 'permanent truth,' a transcendental entity with divine dimensions. But it is not a univocal, personal Godhead, because, as Pound maintains in the same piece, 'we have no proof that this God, Theos, is one, or is many, or is divisible or indivisible' (*SP,* 49). It is noteworthy that, with regard to religious belief, Pound's early formulation might have engendered more questions than answers; for one thing, the formulation did not recognize a divine immanence and thus separated the 'eternal state of mind' from 'our own consciousness.'

Such an uncertainty about the connection between the human mind and the divine mind disappeared in Pound's debate with Eliot in the

1930s. In 'A Problem of (Specifically) Style,' his seventh review of Eliot's book, Pound talks about the 'usefulness' of religion for those people with truly 'perceptive' minds:

> You might even say they incline toward a belief in the need of a general disposition, toward the Whole, the cosmos, and even toward the consciousness inherent in that cosmos.
>   No man is aware of that consciousness save via his own, but believing in a great telephone central or not or in minor centrals or not, no scientist can deny at least fragmentary portions of consciousness which have a sum, a totality, whether or not they have coherent inter-organisation.
>   The minute a man takes into consideration the totality of this universe, or the sum of this consciousness, he has, whether he wants it or not, a religion. And some phase of that consciousness is his *theos*: whether coherent or non-coherent, labile, intermittent or whatever.[9]

This passage articulates a number of ideas characteristic of Pound's theological considerations. He prefers to use 'general disposition,' rather than established theological terms, to describe religious experience. He sees religious experience as intuitive in nature and informed by the desire of the individual consciousness to become part of the transcendental whole. The real significance of the passage above is that Pound explicitly identifies the individual mind as the only pathway to the transcendental consciousness. At the same time, he recognizes the divine disposition in the individual consciousness, thus setting up the bridge that would allow the individual mind to transcend the finite and reach the eternal. Such a subtle change from his earlier spiritual vision, as I will argue in the next section, may have resulted from his intensive study of Confucian works in the 1930s.

Clearly, Pound was not irreligious; he was only unorthodox in his religious belief. In his formulation, religious belief is a spiritual quest of the individual that follows the summons of the inner heart rather than obeying the dictates of an external authority. Religious experience, then, marks a mysterious moment of being in which the intuitive cognition of the individual mind is enabled to move beyond mundane limitations to obtain a deep connection with the spirit of the omniscient force of creation. From this perspective, religious experience as revelation is not an action, or even an impulse, of negating human existence, but rather a consciousness that reaffirms the divine essence of human nature informed by the divine light of the higher being, which flows like light and water through the universe. As such, religious pursuit approximates artistic activity, for both enable human beings with limited capabilities to partake of the unlimited source of creation.

In a sense, what Pound believed can be best understood in terms of what he opposed in contemporary religious institutions of the West. Pound's bitter disillusionment with the Christian tradition is articulated in the following passage, in which he responds to Eliot's charge that the incorporation of non-Christian ideas will jeopardize the Western tradition. 'The Church had lost its faith anyhow, and mess, unholy and slithering mess, supervened,' Pound contends. 'The Occident has already done its apparent utmost to destroy the best Western perceptions. Official Christianity is a sink. Catholicism reached nadir, let us say, with Antonelli in the eighteen hundred and fifties. It has started a new ascension with the encyclicals, Rerum Novarum and Quadrigesimo Anno. But the whole of Western idealism is a jungle. Christian theology is a jungle' (*SP*, 77–8). The West, in Pound's view, could not be worse off, for the Christian tradition had engendered its own degeneration. Pound's attack on the Christian establishment is launched from three perspectives: ethical, theological, and racio-historical. The first perspective underlies his overriding concern with the validity of religious belief.

Pound held that a valid religion should provide ethical guidance in economic activities. As he argues in his first review of Eliot's *After Strange Gods*: 'In the "Ages of Faith," meaning the Ages of Christian faith, religion in the person of the Church concerned itself with ethics. It concerned itself specifically with economic discrimination.'[10] Pound's notion of 'economic discrimination' refers to what he considers a distinction between a fair loan system and usury. The Church, in Pound's view, should have openly condemned the latter as an unnatural and immoral practice. Pound defines this difference between ethical and unethical money-lending systems in another review of Eliot's book: 'Concurrently: the decline of Christian ethics. The Middle Ages distinguished between SHARING and USURY. In correct theology, as Dante knew it, the usurer is damned with the sodomite.'[11] As Pound saw it, the Church of his time had lost the sense of this important distinction. By giving up its commitment to ethical and economic justice, Christianity had deprived itself of its authority in social life, only to become mired in dogmatic controversies.

For Pound, Christianity also failed to guide modern spiritual life largely because its doctrines, which as a result of the Church's arrested development fostered mere code worship rather than truth worship, were not able to satisfy believers' ever-growing need for convincing knowledge about humanity, the universe, and the divine. Among the Christian tenets, Pound was particularly opposed to the doctrine of Original Sin and the dogmatic insistence on the belief in one God. Eliot was right in noticing the 'disappearance of the idea of Original Sin' from Pound's poetry.[12] As a matter of fact, Pound had no interest at all in propagating this idea, an idea that he later denounced as 'that greatest of fakes Original Sin' in a letter to Wyndham Lewis in March 1951.[13] Pound's rejection of the notion of human beings' predetermined degradation, as we will see, is part of the reason he turned to Confucian humanism. Yet even without the inspiration of Confucian humanism, Pound would have rejected this Christian orthodoxy because it contradicted his Neoplatonic vision that each individual human being possesses a predisposition to follow the divine light.

In the preceding chapter on Pound's politics, I made the point that from the beginning he had been very critical of the coercive nature of Christianity. Much of his criticism in that regard derived from his strong aversion to the Christian 'dogma' of monotheism, because in such a monotheistic religion he saw a monopoly of the access to truth and thus the inevitable oppression of alternative ways to truth. 'The greatest tyrannies,' Pound states in 'Axiomata,' 'have risen from the dogma that the *theos* is one, or that there is a unity above various strata of theos which imposes its will upon the sub-strata, and thence upon human individuals' (*SP*, 51). In contrast, polytheism appealed to Pound for its liberal approach: 'The glory of the polytheistic anschauung is that it never asserted a single and obligatory path for everyone. It never caused the assertion that everyone was fit for initiation and it never caused an attempt to force people into a path alien to their sensibilities' (*SP*, 56).

It is interesting to note that Pound's preference for polytheism has received conflicting critical evaluations from Pound scholars. While Pound apologists may regard his polytheism as a proof of his democratic orientation, unsympathetic critics would interpret his polytheistic scenario as disguising an essentially anti-democratic politics in its exclusion of monotheistic faith from the canon of universal religions.[14] In my view, a fully rounded assessment of Pound's polytheism should be based on a dialectical understanding of his politics. As I have argued, his politics is a mixture of opposing elements, at once radically libertarian and hopelessly authoritarian. Similarly, his theological polemic is often self-contradictory, yet not incomprehensible. For instance, Pound entertained a negative opinion of Protestantism, since he held it responsible for having destroyed an established hierarchy of values in the Western tradition.[15] But he also inherited the individualistic spirit of Protestantism in asserting the individual's right to unmediated truth as well as unmediated relationships with God. Pound's polytheism is liberal only in the sense that, by insisting on diverse forms of divinity, it recognizes various approaches to the divine world, not just the approach sanctioned by the decree of the Church. Nevertheless, calling this theology democratic is misleading because Pound's elitism undercuts the liberal basis of such a theology in practice. Although in theory every individual believer is entitled to a direct relationship with the divine, in Pound's conception the key to God's (or the gods') temple is controlled by the cultural elite because only they are capable of perceiving the legitimate route to the divine kingdom. In other words, the real agenda of Pound's liberal theology is to liberate the favoured cultural elite from any restrictions, conventional or institutional, and to pave the way for the elite to establish a new authority in the arena of ideological struggles.

Above all, Pound's criticism of Christianity cannot be separated from his notorious anti-Semitism. This was especially true during the time from the 1930s to the end of the Second World War, when he fell more and more intensely under the spell of the anti-Semitic frenzy maliciously ignited and manipulated by the Nazi and Fascist propaganda machines. During that period, Pound's remarks on theological matters featured two interrelated tendencies: an increasingly open assertion of the historical impact of Judaism on what he disliked in the current state of Christianity, and a growing contention that Confucianism represented a redemptive force against the influence of Judaism. In the 1938 essay on Mencius, for instance, Pound observes: 'The ethic of Kung and Mencius is not registered in words of irresponsible fanatics. The semitic component in Christianity is anarchic and irresponsible. Take the record on its face value, it is of a sect in rebellious and irresponsible province, and for a kingdom, specifically in the words of its founder, not of this world but the next' (*SP,* 90). In his early writing, such as the 1917 'Provincialism and the Enemy,' Pound had found Christianity guilty of lacking a sense of social order and responsibility; now he specifically linked that guilt to a 'semitic' origin. His assault on the 'anarchic and irresponsible' 'semitic component in Christianity' was typical of some Western intellectuals during the 1930s, who found in racism the means of relieving the burden of their disillusionment with social realities. Frustrated by an overwhelming social chaos, which came in the wake of the First World War and was aggravated by a widespread economic crisis during the 1930s, they resorted to the strategy of scapegoating for a quick explanation. Thus, in an amazingly facile manner, such Western intellectuals attributed the consequences of an undesirable socio-economic process to the influence of the Jews. If the seeds of social anarchy were rooted in Hebrew culture, as asserted by Pound, then blaming the 'semitic component' in Western cultures became an easy way out.

According to the same argument, the doctrines of otherworldliness and salvation, poisonous seeds that Pound believed to have been planted by Judaism, formed a major obstacle to the development of civilization. The contrast that he highlights between 'Confucian ethics' and the 'semitic component' in the passage above illustrates a strategy he employed during this period, a strategy by which 'Confucian' becomes a synonym for anything positive, whereas 'Hebrew' becomes a signifier for everything undesirable. For instance, in the same essay Pound asserts: 'If anyone in calm mind will compare the Four Classics with the greatly publicised Hebrew scriptures he will find that the former are a record of civilised men, the latter the annals of a servile and nomadic tribe that had not evolved into agricultural order' (*SP,* 91). In so far as theological matters are concerned, aside from labelling Hebrew culture 'anarchic and irresponsible,' Pound rested his hostility towards the Jews on two assumptions. First, he persistently dismissed Hebrew culture as 'barbarous,' insisting that such an inferior 'tribal' culture was unable to nourish a 'true religion' that might lay the foundation for a civilized ethics. 'True religion,' Pound contended, 'was from agriculture; the Hebrew religion, on the one hand, with its deity who was a shark and a monopolist, was the religion of the "butchers of lesser cattle."'[16] For Pound the Old Testament showed 'no spiritual elevation' and the Talmud is simply a 'gangster's handbook' (*SP,* 68). Secondly, viewing Hebrew culture as representative of the influence of 'brutal disorder' (*SP,* 150), Pound entertained a groundless and yet strong conviction that Judaism was responsible for the degradation of Christianity starting with the Reformation. Instead of looking directly into that historical moment and analysing the political and economical forces behind the historical change, Pound in *Guide to Kulchur* criticizes the Reformation in harsh, racist terms: 'Nothing cd. be less civil, or more hostile to any degree of polite civilization than the tribal records of the hebrews. There is not a trace of civilization from the first lies of Genesis up to the excised account of Holophernes. The revival of these barbarous texts in the time of Luther and Calvin has been an almost unmitigated curse to the occident' (*GK*, 330). Pound's animus against the 'revival of these barbarous texts' sounds as if he believed in a historical conspiracy in which the Jewish force viciously set the 'Church against Empire, Protestantism against the unity of the Mother Church, always destroying the true religion, destroying its mnemonic and commemorative symbols' (*SP*, 320).

Such a racially biased historical illusion further alienated Pound from the Christian God and reinforced his repugnance to Christian monotheism, which for him expressed the malevolence of a monopolistic, anti-natural, and anti-humanistic tyrant. He characterized Jehovah, the God of the Old Testament, as 'a maniac sadist' who embodied the despicable qualities of an oppressive patriarch whom one would not want to see 'in one's immediate parenthood' (*SP*, 70). For the same reason, Pound disliked John Calvin, who was responsible, according to Pound, for reviving the 'brutal and savage mythology of the Hebrews' (*SP*, 265). The Calvinist Jehovah, in Pound's portrayal, 'is a semitic cuckoo's egg laid in the European nest. He has no connection with Dante's god. That later concept of supreme Love and Intelligence is certainly not derived from the Old Testament' (*SP*, 91). In trying to draw a clear distinction between Dante's benevolent God and Calvin's malicious God, Pound seems to suggest the existence of an authentic European version of divinity that differed from the divinity of biblical origins.

In fact, Pound was never opposed to Christianity in general; what he denounced was the aspect of Christianity – or on a larger scale, the aspect of Western civilization – that had been 'contaminated' by what he called the 'Jewish poison.' In his debate with Eliot, Pound elaborated on the danger of this 'poison that lost no time in seeping into European thought,' and he maintained that one could not even think in the right way unless he consciously 'purges himself of this poison' (*SP*, 320). Pound saw Eliot as 'contaminated' in this way as well, and for this reason ridiculed Eliot's claims on behalf of the orthodox tradition and his vain effort to revitalize the Christian religion. Pound remarked: 'Until he [Eliot] succeeds in detaching the Jewish from the European elements of his peculiar variety of Christianity he will never find the right formula' (*SP*, 320).[17] Pound actually had nothing against Eliot's 'peculiar variety of Christianity,' namely, Catholicism, because he himself often displayed a warm attachment to the Catholic 'Mother Church.' What he found unacceptable was Eliot's attempt to define Christian orthodoxy by imposing the doctrine of Original Sin and a morality on the 'division between the damned and the saved,' which Pound regarded as elements of the 'Jewish poison' carried over from the Old Testament. For Pound, true Catholicism, the genuine tradition of Christianity, derived from the paganism of the Mediterranean basin, not the Judaism of the Near East.[18] In Pound's view, this Catholicism appealed to its believers through the notion of supreme love instead of the punishment of sins, celebrated the 'mystery of fecundity' instead of the 'cult of sterility,' and sustained the 'unity' of the Church rather than creating its 'schism' (*SP,* 317).

Thus, as Pound's deep disappointment with the current state of Christianity led to his persistent search in pagan culture for things by which he could recuperate the origins of Western civilization, his racially prejudiced interpretation of the historical changes in the Judeo-Christian tradition gave him a deluded but compelling justification for that task. The paganism that Pound thought had furnished the 'consciousness' for the 'mind of Europe' (*SP,* 317) mostly consisted of the myths celebrating the cult of Eleusis and the worship of pagan gods and goddesses such as Dionysus, Apollo, and Demeter. In Pound's formulation, myth does not merely represent a primitive mode of artistic experience but rather a 'totalitarian' view of the universe that pursues an 'expression for reality without over-simplification' (*SP,* 87) and thus belongs to the mode of truthful knowledge. Moreover, myth reflects a harmonious relationship between the individual perceiver and the outside world, because the perceiver, when faced with a world beyond his understanding, would never attempt to dominate that world by forcing it into preconceived categories. The perceiver would instead rely on an intuitive and holistic grasp of the perceived object, because the 'mythological exposition,' according to Pound in *Guide to Kulchur,* 'permits an expression of intuition without denting the edges or shaving off the nose and ears of a verity' (127). For Pound, the complex of mythical experiences, such as the fertility cult or the mystery of metamorphosis, offers visionary insights into divinity, insights derived from human sexual energy and the cosmic creative force mirrored in human imaginative thinking. Even more importantly, myth does not simply register an individual's perception; it serves the crucial function of reinforcing the shared belief of a community, which in Pound's words was 'a company of people who could understand each other's nonsense about the gods' (*LE,* 431). Pound had accepted the German anthropologist Leo Frobenius's theory that a civilization cannot survive unless it possesses a core culture, or 'paideuma,' which, as 'the mental formation, the inherited habits of thought, the conditionings,' serves to sustain the continuity of the civilization (*SP,* 148). In Pound's view, the core culture of European civilization resided in the pagan tradition of mythology that had once thrived in the soil of the Mediterranean basin. This culture, according to Pound, was destroyed by alien forces (especially the forces from the Near East) when 'some unpleasing Semite or Parsee or Syrian began to use myths for social propaganda, when the myth was degraded into an allegory or a fable, and that was the beginning of the end' (*LE,* 431). The end of the belief in the authenticity of myth, from Pound's perspective, was not simply a rejection of a way of reading things as signs of the transcendental ideas they embodied. The loss of the pagan tradition meant the disappearance of a shared basis for religious faith and ethics, and the rupture of a narrative framework by which the 'mind of Europe' could define its historical identity. With his particular historical outlook, Pound regarded it as an important part of his mission to recuperate that tradition. Unlike Eliot, who treated the Anglo-Catholic Church as his spiritual home wherein he could take ideological refuge, Pound took a far more radical – and more problematic – position. He resolved to return to the very root of what he believed to be the real Western tradition, the 'Mediterranean sanity,' and to rescue it from the harms inflicted by various historical 'maladies' (*LE,* 154).

The pagan ideologies Pound sought to recover, apart from polytheism, included three main categories: the fertility cult that deemed nature the benevolent embodiment of abundance; the mysterious faith in sensual human life as divine experience; and the solar worship that saw all things as infused and informed by the divine Light. As Pound summarized it: 'Paganism included a certain attitude towards; a certain understanding of, coitus, which is the mysterium. The other rites are the festivals of fecundity of the grain and the sun festivals, without revival of which religion can not return to the hearts of the people' (*SP,* 70). Central to all these pagan mysteries was the glorification of the power of the divine light. With a firm belief that 'a light from Eleusis persisted throughout the middle ages and set beauty in the song of Provence and of Italy' (*SP,* 53), Pound saw a metaphysics of light as what provided a sort of rational basis for pagan mysteries and permitted those who still believed in them to retain the 'Mediterranean sanity,' even after the Church had discarded this pagan faith. In canto XXXVI, he invokes the association of the Albigenses with Scotus Erigena, the pivotal medieval transmitter of the Neoplatonic philosophy of light:

'Called thrones, balascio or topaze'
Eriugina was not understood in his time
'which explains, perhaps, the delay in condemning him'
And they went looking for Manicheans
And found, so far as I can make out, no Manicheans
So they dug for, and damned Scotus Eriugina
'Authority comes from right reason,
    never the other way on'
Hence the delay in condemning him
Aquinas head down in a vacuum,
    Aristotle which way in a vacuum?
Sacrum, sacrum, inluminatio coitu. (XXXVI/179–80)

The light of reason makes sexual love a sacred and illuminative virtue. It is this same light that illuminated Dante's journey, which 'becomes a symbol of mankind's struggle upward out of ignorance into the clear light of philosophy' (*SR*, 127). From Pound's point of view, therefore, the task of restoring the spirit of the pagan tradition largely consisted in reinstating the intelligibility of the metaphysics of light.

Such a task substantiated Pound's call for a return to origins. 'A return to origins invigorates,' he wrote in an article on the tradition, 'because it is a return to nature and reason. The man who returns to origins does so because he wishes to behave in the eternally sensible manner. That is to say, naturally, reasonably, intuitively' (*LE*, 92). Pound's agenda of 'returning to origins' strikes a familiar chord because it reminds us of the return to nature of Romantic writers in the preceding age. This similarity is not surprising, because Western intellectuals, from the time of the Industrial Revolution, had been facing essentially the same ongoing social crisis, generated by the transition of the Western world from an agricultural society to an increasingly industrialized and commercialized modern society. The process of this transition was attended by a profound alienation of human beings from nature and the Creator, and by a shattered faith in the origin of human existence. What differentiated Pound from his predecessors was that, in criticizing the economic, political, and religious systems of his time, he addressed the social crisis in boldly racist terms, under the influence of the contemporary anti-Semitic frenzy. Aside from this anti-Semitic sentiment, Pound was fighting, so to speak, the same war against the same undesirable social process. Inevitably, in his search for 'eternally sensible' origins, he would bring to bear on his concerns a variety of theories that had distinguished his European predecessors, theories that could reassert Europe's lost pagan values using a modern interpretation. Primary among these theories were the Enlightenment definition of reason as a foundational force, the Romantic belief in the natural goodness of humanity, and pantheistic theology, with its view of nature as the embodiment of an omnipresent divinity. In these formulations Pound found the premises for establishing a worldview that could resist the hegemony of the Judeo-Christian tradition. However, what he was facing were some disparate formulations. In order to render these fragmented beliefs into a coherent scheme, he had to resort to the 'totalitarian' framework of Confucianism.

2. The 'Four Beginnings' of Human Nature

In his early years Pound had already recognized the value of Confucianism in spiritual life. Writing from Paris on 16 July 1922, he told Harriet Monroe: 'I consider the Writings of Confucius, and Ovid's *Metamorphoses* the only safe guides in religion' (*L*, 183). Later, responding to questions about his beliefs, Pound in a 1930 article told his readers 'to read Confucius and Ovid' (*SP*, 53). He singled out Ovid because he considered the Roman poet's works representative of the spirit of 'Mediterranean paganism.' Pound believed that Confucianism shared with that pagan tradition some basic premises, such as the resistance to monotheism, the appreciation of earthly life, and the recognition of truth as the dynamic personal experience of divine revelation rather than the passive reception of dogmas. No wonder Pound saw a light running 'between KUNG and ELEUSIS,' as he claims in *The Cantos* (LII/258).

Yet in Pound's project of constructing a new spiritual belief, Confucianism played a more important role because it gave him the synthesizing tools that Western discourses could not supply. For Pound, one particular advantage of Confucianism was its unswerving humanist orientation, which places the human individual, not the Divinity, in the centre of its theological considerations, and allows the individual believer a vast, favourable space for spiritual development. Such a humanist feature of Confucian religiosity has been convincingly captured by Tu Wei-ming. Tu thinks that Confucian metaphysics has strong religious implications. 'However,' he points out, 'the religiousness of Confucianism does not rest on the mysterious atmosphere of a personal God, but rather on the solemnity, transcendence, and infinity of the self-development of the individual.'[19] Self-development in Confucianism is not meant to encourage self-indulgence, but rather to serve as a means for the individual to obtain knowledge of universal humanity and to use that knowledge to benefit society. Such an orientation is consistent with Pound's model of a humanist religion: 'Religion in humanist terms would be valuable in the degree in which it directed a man toward the welfare of humanity.'[20]

The other advantage of Confucianism, from Pound's point of view, was its holistic conceptualization of the relationships in the human world and the universe, something that he found missing from the 'splitting' visions of Western philosophy. 'Confucius offers a way of life,' says Pound in *Guide to Kulchur*, 'an Anschauung or disposition toward nature and man and a system for dealing with both' (24). For Pound, this 'system' was attractive especially because it provided a unifying scheme through which he was able not only to reorganize his fragmented beliefs but also to lend them new meanings. Moreover, Confucianism offered him a set of useful concepts about humanity, nature, and divinity, which enabled him to construct a coherent narrative of human existence by bringing together the human world, the natural world, and the divine world. In the three sections on the following pages, I will examine Pound's exploration of each of these three categories from a Confucian perspective.

With an intense belief in the 'permanent basis of humanity,' as he proclaims in *The Spirit of Romance* (92), Pound started his visionary search as a poet, positioning himself in European humanism, a tradition that had attracted Western intellectuals, particularly Enlightenment philosophers and Romantic writers, since the Renaissance. Essentially, the humanist camp was characterized by its assertions about the natural nobility of and intrinsic potential for self-perfection in human nature. Such a rebellious assertion directly challenged the institutionalized Christian tenet that defined human nature in terms of its natural depravity. There is no doubt that the belief in the good nature of man, an idea famously championed by Jean-Jacques Rousseau, was what initially allowed Pound to align himself with Confucian humanism. And his tireless probing of Confucian ideas about humanity eventually enabled him to celebrate 'man's paradise [in] his good nature' in *The Cantos* (XCIII/643), with stronger spiritual confidence and greater theoretical persuasiveness.

Before looking into Pound's appropriation of Confucian ideas about human nature, we must address this question: from which specific school of thought in the Confucian tradition did he draw his inspiration in this regard? Although Confucianism in general supports the idea of the good nature of humanity, not all Confucian masters held this view. For instance, Xunzi (313?–238? BCE), considered with Confucius and Mencius (372?–289? BCE) as one of the three founders of classical Confucianism, maintained that human nature is innately bad, for human beings are inclined to satisfaction of physical desires, which in turn causes disorder and chaos. Zhu Xi, the leading philosopher of Song-Ming neo-Confucianism, conceived of human nature from virtually the same perspective, even though he did not openly espouse Xunzi's theory. As I noted in my earlier discussion of his interpretation of the *ke ji fu li* doctrine, Zhu Xi's dualism basically negated the physical constitution of human nature as something that should be suppressed, for he found it to pose a threat to the Heavenly Principle (*tian li* 天理). Though the prevalent opinion in Pound studies is that Zhu Xi influenced Pound, or, according to Kenner, 'prepared' Pound's 'mind,'[21] the truth is that Zhu Xi's view of human nature was far from 'congenial' to Pound's mind. Confucius himself established the view that human nature is bestowed by Heaven and is thus intrinsically benevolent; yet this view, scattered in his fragmented remarks, seems to lack the support of sustained formulations. In the Confucian tradition, Mencius developed Confucius's ideas into a systematic theory of human nature, and it was Mencius's theory that significantly shaped Pound's rethinking of this issue.

Mencius's influence on Pound came through two books, *Zhong yong* and *Mengzi*. In his preface to *Zhong yong*, Zhu Xi maintains that Zisi, Confucius's grandson, authored the book to preserve Confucius's thoughts about *xin* 心 (usually rendered 'heart/mind' as a special Confucian term) and then passed his knowledge to Mencius.[22] Zhu Xi's claim reinforced a long-held view since Sima Qian of the Han dynasty that Zisi and Mencius established the so-called *Si-Meng xuepai* (school of Zisi and Mencius), and that one of the major contributions of this school to Confucianism was the learning of heart/mind. The fact that Pound included Zhu Xi's preface in his English translation of *Zhong yong* indicates that he was aware of this genealogy. Such an awareness might have had a significant impact on his reading of *Mengzi*, especially when it came to Mencius's concepts about the relationship between the mind and human nature, for Pound would have interpreted Mencius's ideas in light of the Confucian metaphysics postulated in *Zhong yong*. Pound had a clear sense of where Mencius stood in the Confucian tradition. 'Mencius never has to contradict Confucius,' he noted; 'he carries the Confucian sanity down into particulars, never snared into rivalry by his flatterers' (*Con*, 191). Pound studied *Mengzi* seriously during the 1930s and the 1940s. Aside from an extended essay on the second great master in the Confucian canon (1938) and a translation of some excerpts of *Mengzi* (1947), in *The Cantos* Pound makes frequent references to Mencius and cites amply from his works.

Mencius's view of human nature is forcefully enunciated in the famous argument he made during a debate with a contemporary, the philosopher Gaozi (*Mengzi* 6.1.2). Believing that human nature was essentially neutral, Gaozi maintained that human nature was like running water that could flow either to the east or to the west. In other words, human nature was indifferent to good and evil, just as water made no distinction between the east and west. Mencius eloquently replied:

> Water indeed will flow indifferently to the east and west, but will it flow indifferently up or down? The tendency of man's nature to good is like the tendency of water to flow downwards. There are none but have this tendency to good, just as all water flows downwards.[23]

Mencius pressed his point further by arguing that water could go up only when we applied force to it and, similarly, when man did bad things, there must be an external influence that caused him to do what was against his nature.

Pound elaborates on Mencius's analogy of water and human nature in canto XCIX: 'that man's phallic heart is from heaven / a clear spring of rightness, / Greed turns it awry' (717). Here, human nature is made concrete in the poetic image of a 'phallic heart'; it is good because it is spring water flowing down from heaven. The image of spring water not only alludes to Mencius's analogy but also derives additional meaning from the opening chapter of *Zhong yong*, which dwells on the relationship between human nature and the *Dao* or Way of Heaven. In his editing notes on this chapter Zhu Xi provides a summary of its thesis, in which he mentions the origin of the Heavenly *Dao*. In Pound's etymographic translation of Zhu Xi's note, the idea of this 'origin' becomes 'the root of the process, a fountain of clear water descending from heaven immutable' (*Con*, 99). Thus Pound enriches Mencius's water image by connecting it directly to the Heavenly origin in *Zhong yong*. In his debate with Gaozi, Mencius affirmed that although human beings are born with a natural inclination towards what is good, their good nature can be corrupted by bad social influences. In his poetic lines, Pound specifically identifies such bad influences as 'greed,' the cardinal vice of usury.

Mencius's claim that human nature is good is thoroughly developed in his theory of *si duan* 四端 (four beginnings). Conveyed twice in *Mengzi*, first in his talk with the disciple Gongsun Chou (2.1.6) and then in another talk with the disciple Gongduzi (6.1.6), the theory gives Mencius's conception of the inborn inclination of human beings an ethical and cognitive basis. The notion of *si duan,* or four beginnings, refers to the four ethical predispositions: *ren* (humaneness, benevolence), *yi* (righteousness, justice), *li* (propriety, observance of rites), and *zhi* (wisdom). According to Mencius, these innate capacities are not instilled into us from without, but are part of us when we are born. In their natural state, each of these beginnings (*duan*) is an innate sense constituting the heart/mind (*xin*). *Ren* manifests as the sense of compassion (sympathy with the suffering of others, for instance); *yi* as the sense of shame, *li* as the sense of respect, and *zhi* as the sense of right and wrong. The purpose of self-development is to cultivate these innate senses and bring them to light so that they become consciously practised virtues. As a result of cultivation, compassion becomes the virtue of *ren*, the feeling of shame the virtue of *yi,* respect the virtue of *li*, and the sense of right and wrong the virtue of *zhi.*

The doctrine of *si duan* forms an important theme in *The Cantos.* In this work Pound calls *si duan* the 'four tuan' and makes repeated reference to the four virtues (his 'jen, i, li, chic') starting from the section of Rock-Drill.[24] In his translation of *Zhong yong,* Pound renders *duan* 端 as 'origin' (*Con,* 119). He equates the concept of *duan* with 'foundations' in canto LXXXV (565), and in canto XCIX, he identifies it with 'verity' or truth (720). In the same canto, he gives this doctrine a poetic expression:

> The basis is man,
>   and the rectification of officers
> but the four TUAN
>   are from nature
>   jen, i, li, chih
> Not from descriptions in the school house;
> They are the scholar's job,
>   the gentleman's and the officer's. (XCIX/731)

Pound's idea of 'nature' here refers not so much to the natural world as to the 'inborn nature' of humanity from his translation of the first paragraph of *Zhong yong* (*Con*, 99). The proposition that the four *tuan* are from nature prepares for the argument made in the last several lines: human beings are naturally endowed with these 'original' or 'foundational' attributes, which cannot be obtained from outside sources like school books.

Of the four *duan* or beginnings, *ren* 仁, or the sense of compassion, is the central concept on which Pound elaborates more than the rest in *The Cantos*. In the previous chapter, I dwelt mostly on the ontological dimension of this concept to clarify its role in Pound's reconstruction of an individualist ideology. Here, in *The Cantos*, Pound's poetic treatment of *ren* 仁 gives us a chance to explore the ethical dimension of the concept. In Confucian moral philosophy, the concept *ren*, as the major aspect of the ethical ideal emphasizing affective concern, was established by Confucius himself. It is recorded in *Lun yu* 12.22 that when he was once asked what *ren* 仁 was and how to practise it, Confucius replied: 'Love human beings' (*ai ren* 愛人). Mencius inherited this basic approach to *ren* and developed it further in his theory of *si duan*. In Mencius's formulation, benevolence, or the ability to love derived from one's innate sense of compassion for fellow human beings, constitutes the most important quality of a superior individual. That is why Mencius once asserted: 'The benevolent embrace all in their love.'[25] Pound was keenly aware of this ethical implication of *ren*. In *Guide to Kulchur*, when referring to the Confucian concept of *ren*, he states: 'Humanity? [it] is to love men' (18).

For Mencius, *ren*, or benevolence as a universal attribute inherent in human nature, determines the reciprocal nature of love. From this perspective, self-examination is not only the means of cultivating one's ability to love others but also the way to seek and appreciate the love from others. 'If a man loves others,' Mencius claimed, 'and no *responsive* attachment is shown to him, let him turn inwards and examine his own benevolence' (*Mengzi* 4.1.4).[26] The idea of cultivating the ability to love through introspection informs a self-revealing moment in *The Cantos*:

J'ai eu pitié des autres.
    Pas assez! Pas assez!
For me nothing. But that the child
   walk in peace in her basilica,
The light there almost solid.

力 li
行 hsing
近 chin
乎 hu
仁 jên

holding that energy is near to benevolence. (XCIII/648–9)

The five Chinese characters refer to a clause from *Zhong yong* about how to achieve *ren* (Pound's 'jên'), a clause that Pound translates as 'energy is near to benevolence' (*Con*, 155). These lines seem to assert that one can never have too much 'compassion' for others, as in the case of the poet who, while recalling his daughter, thinks that perhaps he has not done enough in loving others, especially those dear to him. However, if one makes the utmost effort, enacting one's 'energy' as thoroughly as possible, one may get close to 'benevolence' and thus may partake of the universal love of the sacred 'light.'

In canto XCVII (696), Pound creates two poetic lines by using five Chinese characters from a clause about *ren* in *Da xue*. The original clause, *ren qin yi wei bao* 仁親以為寶, is translated by Pound as 'counting his manhood and the love of his relatives the true treasure' (*Con*, 75). The two lines in *The Cantos* thus can be construed as Pound's poetic foregrounding of an important aspect of love that both Confucius and Mencius inscribed. Confucian 'love' is not an abstract notion, but one made very concrete by Confucianism's constant emphasis on defining human nature in terms of social relations. Confucian ethics demands that one first of all love one's family members, and then extend that love to relatives, friends, and eventually those to whom one is politically and socially related. In this instruction we see once again the fundamental Confucian principle that conceives of all social practices in terms derived from the model of family. In other words, according to Confucian ethics, one's love is meaningful only in so far as this love is in conformity with one's specific social position. For instance, one loves his father precisely as a son should; in a larger social context, that love can be extended to the love for one's superior, or the love of a subject for the emperor. The same principle applies to a father's love for the son, which is in essence analogous to the emperor's love for his people. It is in this sense that love serves to bind together the members of a society and stabilize its sociopolitical order.

In *The Cantos* Pound either cites or refers to the term *yi* 義 eight times, four of which are related to the second concept in Mencius's theory of *si duan*, or four beginnings. In Mencius's theory, the virtue of *yi* is believed to grow out of an innate sense of shame that compels us to do what is right or just. Hence this term is often rendered as 'righteousness' or 'justice' in English. In Pound's poetic discourse, however, the Confucian-Mencian *yi* or justice is synonymous with 'equity,' signifying something in opposition to the unnatural desire for 'profit' (*li* 利). Pound derived the dichotomy of *yi* (equity) and *li* (profit) from *Da xue*, which ends with a statement to the effect that what can truly benefit a nation is not *li*, but *yi*. This statement, which Pound often invokes in his writing, is construed by him as: 'Equity is the treasure of states' (*Con*, 91). In his formulation, *yi*, as the antithesis of *li*, stands for human beings' inborn propensity to follow what is natural and right. Such an understanding illuminates the following lines from canto LXXIV:

> Not words whereto to be faithful
>   nor deeds that they be resolute
>   only that bird-hearted equity make timber
>   and lay hold of the earth. (446)

The four lines are Pound's poetic rewriting of a passage from *Lun yu* 4.10. The original passage suggests that a superior person does not set his mind against or for anything, but only follows the right path naturally. In his prose translation, Pound renders the notion of following only the right path as 'he will be just' (*Con*, 207). In his poetic rendering, the notion of being just (*yi*) becomes 'bird-hearted equity' standing on the tree rooted in the earth. Such a radical revision would be beyond the imagination of any expert reader who knows the original Chinese text. I agree with Carroll Terrell's analysis: 'Pound's intent is probably to evoke the intelligence of nature in process. Neither birds nor trees think: they express themselves naturally and the right follows.'[27] In other words, by using the images of bird and tree, Pound seeks to capture the essence of *yi* or equity in its natural process.

The tension between *yi* (equity) and *li* (unnatural desire) is highlighted by Pound in canto LXXXIX (615), in which the Chinese characters for *yi* and *li* appear on the same page, representing two forces that come into conflict in a poeticized social space. The Chinese phrase here containing the character *li* – *hebi yue li* 何必曰利 – means 'why must say profit.' Pound also puts the English version of the phrase in canto LXXXVII (595). The phrase comes from Mencius's famous dialogue with King Hui of Liang. According to the account in *Mengzi* 1.1.1, during Mencius's visit to King Hui of Liang, the King asked Mencius what he had brought to 'profit' the kingdom since he came such a long way. Mencius then asked the King why his Majesty 'must speak of profit,' and said that the things the King should be concerned with were only *ren* and *yi*. If all people in the kingdom followed the call of *ren* and *yi*, Mencius argued, the individual person would live a happy and peaceful life, the family would enjoy harmonious relationships, and the kingdom would be stable and prosperous. Pound was deeply impressed by the story. What particularly attracted him in the story was, in his own words, the 'sense of EQUITY.' In his diatribe against usury, he liked to cite the story as a better formulation of political economy than the Marxian theory about the same subject.[28]

In his *Cantos*, Pound gives the least attention to *li* 禮 or propriety, the third of the four beginnings. Though he mentions *li* twice, both times when he spells out the four beginnings in their entirety (LXXXV/564, XCIX/731), he does not use the Chinese character either time. His lack of interest in this concept perhaps has to do with the fact that the idea of 'observing rites' suggested by this concept did not appeal to him. As for *zhi* 智 or wisdom, the last of the four, Pound mentions it three times, but only once does he single it out: 'Who leaves the sun out of / chic 智 / Religion?' (LXXXVII/595). Pound is interpreting the character 智 in his typical etymographic manner. The character consists of two components: *zhi* 知 (knowledge) and *ri* 日 (sun). Pound's line underscores his consistent recognition that religion is a mode of enlightened knowledge, or rather, a cognizance of the divine light. In other words, the innate desire to understand the source of divine creation forms an important part of human nature.

In short, the doctrine of *si duan*, which substantiates the intrinsic goodness of humanity in concrete ethical terms, tremendously reinforced Pound's humanist view of human nature. No wonder his poetic celebration of humanity always seems to culminate in his interpretation of this doctrine:

> Let a man do a good job at his trade,
> whence is honesty;
> whence are good manners,
> good custom
> this is tuan (XCIX/720)

Such a complete confidence in the noble spirit of human beings, in their potential for self-perfection, was rare among writers of the so-called lost generation, who had witnessed too much human self-destruction to entertain an unreservedly optimistic vision about humankind. To some extent, this attitude also differentiates Pound from his contemporary humanist thinkers, such as Irving Babbitt.

It is useful here to make a brief comparison between Irving Babbitt and Pound, for Eliot in *After Strange Gods* describes Babbitt, along with Pound, as one of the 'rebellious' Protestants spellbound by Confucianism. Although both Babbitt and Pound were interested in the humanistic elements of Confucianism, each felt its appeal in a fundamentally different way. At first glance, the difference may have been only one of degree – Confucianism did not attract Babbitt as strongly as it did Pound. For one thing, it was Buddha (whom Pound despised), not Confucius, whom Babbitt saw as the embodiment of the ultimate achievement of Eastern wisdom. In Babbitt's view Confucius only served to supplement Aristotle in exemplifying the enlightenment of the law of measure, or the law of self-discipline. A more substantial difference between Pound and Babbitt can be found in their varying conceptions of human nature. Unlike Pound, who favoured the theory of the natural goodness of humanity and rejected the doctrine of Original Sin, Babbitt believed that the theory of the natural goodness of humanity was precisely what had disrupted Western thought since its popularization by Rousseau. The argument Babbitt makes in his major works, such as 'What I Believe: Rousseau and Religion' and *Rousseau and Romanticism*, is that Rousseau's theory misrepresents human nature, for it uses a false dualism of man versus society to replace an older and true dualism. This older dualism, according to Babbitt, emphasized a constant tension between a human being's natural impulses that often lead to vice and the vital force of human will that always strives to control human impulses. To counter Rousseau's theory, interestingly, Babbitt did not resort to the Christian doctrine of Original Sin, but to the Buddhist doctrine that human beings' natural laziness is the greatest vice of all, one that makes them intrinsically inclined to succumb to the impulse of temperament. For Babbitt, therefore, the redemption of humanity depends on disciplines empowered by a conscious and diligent exercise of the will.

In contrast, Pound's orientation to Confucian humanism resists any attempt to redeem humanity by suppressing the natural tendencies of human beings. The Christian notion of Salvation has no place in

Pound's spiritual belief system precisely because the notion denies the reality of earthly existence and deprives human beings of the chance for self-perfection, leaving them as powerless, sinful creatures at the mercy of a mysterious transcendental force. In Confucianism, the way towards redemption, if any, lies in education in the form of self-cultivation rather than in salvation by an external force. The relationship between human nature and education is persuasively elucidated in Pound's version of the first paragraph of *Zhong yong*:

> What heaven has disposed and sealed is called the inborn nature. The realization of this nature is called the process. The clarification of this process [the understanding or making intelligible of this process] is called education. (*Con*, 99)

Pound's 'inborn nature,' a proper rendering of the Chinese term *xing* 性 (intrinsic nature), designates the primordial nature of humanity originating from Heaven. Since Heaven in Confucianism is essentially benevolent, it is inconceivable that the inborn nature of humanity could contradict the *Dao* (Pound's 'process') of Heaven. The way to regain this heavenly origin is through cultivating human nature, bringing to light what human beings have been endowed with by Heaven, namely the four beginnings of benevolence, righteousness, propriety, and wisdom.

Such a pursuit constitutes the fundamental mission of what Pound ascertains in the Confucian notion of *jiao* 教 (education) in the above passage. The Chinese character *jiao* 教 has two meanings, education and religion, both of which inform Pound's intent in deploying this character three times in *The Cantos* (LXXXV/577, 579; LXXXVI/581). While *jiao* refers to the passing down of knowledge from one generation to the next, it also suggests that what is passed down must concentrate on human concerns. 'Knowledge,' as Pound insists in *Guide to Kulchur*, 'is to know man' (98). Actually, his definition of knowledge is derived from Confucius's answer to a disciple's question in *Lun yu* 12.22. In this context, Confucius seems to suggest (and Pound obviously concurs) that human beings can only come to know the world in which they live by first obtaining a firm grasp of the knowledge of themselves. On the other hand, Pound's understanding of *jiao* reaffirms his belief that human beings can achieve self-redemption by developing what is intrinsic to them and, in so doing, attain a connection with the divine light of

Heaven. Such a theological vision, reinforced by the concept of *jiao*, informs Pound's Confucian notion of internal transcendence, which I will discuss at length in the fourth section of this chapter.

3. 'Man and Earth: Two Halves of the Tally'

Pound's characterization of human nature in Confucian terms reasserts the humanistic view cherished by Western intellectuals since the Renaissance. This view, which culminated in the Enlightenment philosophy, champions human beings as the legitimate agent of history and human intelligence as the driving force of progress. But Pound's formulations about human nature would be much less interesting if he merely reiterated the assertion of humanity as the autonomous subject. His resort to Confucian doctrines of humanity was also a result of his search for a vigorous counterforce against the anthropocentric tendency that he found pervasive in Western humanist thought since the Renaissance. Keenly aware of the adverse effects of overstating the autonomy of humanity in the universe, Pound started to critique anthropocentrism as early as 1910 in *The Spirit of Romance*: 'After the Treconto we get Humanism, and as the art is carried northward we have Chaucer and Shakespeare, (Jacques-père). Man is concerned with man and forgets the whole and the flowing' (93). By 'the whole and the flowing' Pound means the 'vital universe' of things, the world of 'fluid force.' For Pound, forgetting this world, no less a sin than forgetting 'man' himself, is a clear sign of human beings' alienation from the natural world in which they live.

Pound's recognition that Confucianism represented a counterdiscourse to anthropocentrism is clearly evidenced in much of his work, including his poetry. In canto LXXXVIII, for instance, he alludes to a poem by e.e. cummings, in which cummings deplores the monstrous actions of 'manunkind' that have engendered the 'disease' of 'Progress.'[29] Pound notes that it is not 'un-man,' but 'all-men,' who should be held responsible for this disease, and then invokes the Confucian concept of *jing* 敬 (revere, respect) as the cure (LXXXVIII/601). In his etymographic reading of Confucius, Pound describes *jing* as: 'Respect for the kind of intelligence that enables grass seed to grow grass; the cherry-stone to make cherries' (*Con*, 193). Used specifically in relation to human follies committed against nature, the concept of *jing* comes to signify a kind of Confucian rationalism, pointing to a proper understanding of the relationship between humanity and nature.

Thus, Pound's use of Confucian ideas about humanity and nature should not be seen as a superficial attempt to decorate the humanistic position he inherited from the Western tradition. He sought instead to find a way to overcome the theoretical pitfall of separating humanity from nature, a pitfall that always haunted Western humanists who relished the supremacy of the 'rational self' and its works and privileged man as the master of the world. Pound believed, with Fenollosa, that European thinkers in general had an inherently flawed view about the relationship between humanity and nature, because European philosophy since Aristotle had not been able to equip them with an adequate attitude towards nature. With its aversion to mythological cosmology and its indulgence in abstract analysis, the Aristotelian tradition produced a philosophy that in Pound's opinion was 'an attack upon nature,' a negative influence in sharp contrast with the teachings about nature in the 'school of Kung,' which 'included intelligence without cutting it from its base' (*SP*, 86).

Yet Pound had a more urgent reason to be so intensely concerned with the issue of the relationship between humanity and nature. Among all alarming repercussions of this deteriorating relationship, he found it particularly menacing that usury, the sole beneficiary of the perversion of human thinking, could have a better chance to exploit human beings' misconception of nature to advance its evil cause. For this reason, he constantly instructs the readers of *The Cantos* to keep on guard against 'usura, sin against nature' (XLV/229). To some extent, Pound even believed that the increasing estrangement of human beings from nature, as evidenced by their growing ignorance of nature, was largely orchestrated by the manipulative usury, because its own survival depended on undermining human perception of the world of objects. As Pound saw it, 'Usury is contra naturam. It is not merely in opposition to nature's increase, it is antithetic to discrimination by the senses. Discrimination by the senses is dangerous to avarice. It is dangerous because any perception or any high development of the perceptive faculties may lead to knowledge. The money-changer only thrives on ignorance' (*GK*, 281). It is clear that for Pound the problem posed by usury was more than an economic one and called for solutions that would operate within a broader context. As a result, while he tried to fight usury in the field of economics by advocating an agenda that blended some contemporary economic theories (such as C.H. Douglas's doctrine of social credit), he also argued within the realms of philosophy and theology for a theory that would resist the corrupting force of usury by clarifying the relationship between the mind and the world of objects, that is, the relationship between humanity and nature.

It is within this context that Pound appropriated Confucian ideas in formulating a compelling theory of nature that addressed different but related aspects of his concerns. Pound's theory, which is totalitarian in its general world outlook and unorthodox in its theological implications, consists of three major premises. The first premise is that the appropriate relationship between human beings and nature is that of partners, not that of a ruler and his 'dominion.' The second premise maintains that the world of things is an organic whole, full of living spirits sustained by the same inviolable laws of dynamic creation. The third premise calls for an ample respect for nature because it can serve as the source of knowledge and guidance for moral conduct of human beings.

Pound's vision of a human partnership with nature derives its philosophical framework from his reading of Confucius. The notion of 'partner' appears in chapter 22 of *Zhong yong*. Pound's translation of it reads:

> Only the most absolute sincerity under heaven can bring the inborn talent to the full and empty the chalice of the nature.
> He who can totally sweep clean the chalice of himself can carry the inborn nature of others to its fulfillment; getting to the bottom of the natures of men, one can thence understand the nature of material things, and this understanding of the nature of things can aid the transforming and nutritive powers of earth and heaven [ameliorate the quality of the grain, for example] and *raise man up to be a sort of third partner with heaven and earth.* (*Con*, 173–5; emphasis mine)

These two paragraphs envision an idealized state of being that only the most 'sincere' individuals can achieve. Pound's rendering here shows a fairly adequate understanding of the Confucian ideal of human existence in its original context. In classical Confucian works such as *Zhong yong*, heaven and earth are not two separate things but rather two aspects – physical and metaphysical, or natural and supernatural – of one entity, and they combine to make the world of things that both is inhabited by us and exists beyond us. To be a 'partner' with heaven and earth is to exist in harmony with the world outside us and simultaneously to entertain an intimate knowledge of it.

Pound's interpretation of the Confucian passage conveys an important assumption on which rests his advocacy of the partnership between human beings and nature: that the 'nature of man' is identical, and thus continuous, with the 'nature of things.' Such an assumption must have been attractive to Pound because it was compatible with his previous conception of the same relationship; this conception, which he had received from the ancient pagan tradition, maintained that 'the little cosmos "corresponds" to the greater, that man has in him both the "sun" and "moon"' (*SR*, 94). In his early work on the *Spirit of Romance*, Pound already used 'kinship,' a term not very far from 'partnership' in meaning, to describe the relationship between humanity and nature: 'Let us consider the body as pure mechanism. Our kinship to the ox we have constantly thrust upon us; but beneath this is our kinship to the vital universe, to the tree and the living rock, and, because this is less obvious – and possibly more interesting – we forget it' (*SR*, 92). This passage contains several important points concerning Pound's early view of nature. First, the idea of 'kinship' is intended to highlight the physical mechanism of humanity, suggesting that the reality of human nature is informed by the materiality of human beings, similar to other things in the universe. 'Man is,' Pound observes in the same work, 'a mechanism rather like an electric appliance, switches, wires, etc. Chemically speaking, he is *ut credo*, a few buckets of water, tied up in a complicated sort of fig-leaf' (*SR*, 92). Second, the idea of such a kinship derives from the belief that nature must emanate from a mind like ours. That is why the human mind, working 'like soap-bubbles reflecting sundry patches of the macrocosmos' (*SR*, 92), can absorb the messages of nature and penetrate its secrets. Furthermore, this kinship demonstrates a shared principle of creativity. The human mind, structured to function in the same way as the mechanism of nature, is capable of creation by producing thoughts in human beings just as the tree begets its thought 'in the seed, or in the grass, or the grain, or the blossom' (*SR*, 92).

In addition to reaffirming Pound's early belief in a human 'kinship' with the world of things, the Confucian notion of a human partnership with heaven and earth also reinforced his radical formulations about the individual self. In this case, Pound was able to find ways to bring Confucian ideas to bear on his agenda and to apply them to his concerns systematically and consistently. In the preceding chapter I pointed out that the notion of introspection, or 'looking into oneself' (a notion Pound derived from his unique interpretation of the Confucian text), forms the essential part of Pound's assertion of the primacy of individuality. His postulation of a human partnership with nature, premised on the continuousness between the nature of humanity and the nature of things, takes that assertion one step further in his particular individualism. An individual person's introspection, as a result, is no longer seen as leading to isolation from the outside world, but rather to opening up a direct entrance into it, because the authentic discovery of the self is also the revelation of the secrets of the universe, thus setting the stage for further actions that are bound to have impact on the outside world. In other words, as made clear in Pound's etymographic interpretation of another passage in *Zhong yong*, the aim of self-examination is anything but egocentric: 'The inborn nature begets this activity naturally, this looking into oneself and thence acting. These two activities constitute the process which unites outer and inner, object and subject, and thence constitutes a harmony with the seasons of earth and heaven' (*Con*, 179). If human nature is at one with the nature of things, there is no way one's actions will conflict with the outside world as long as one acts in accordance with true self-knowledge. Thus, it seems that the division between 'outer and inner, object and subject,' the Cartesian division that has always troubled the Western mind, is resolved in Poundian Confucianism.

In the passage above, Pound's interpretation of the Confucian solution to the subject-object dichotomy also stresses the idea of 'acting.' His emphasis deserves attention because the idea of 'acting' conveys his awareness that living in 'harmony' with the outside world is not a guaranteed state of being for all humans, but rather a reward earned by an individual through persistent, strenuous spiritual pursuit and through actions undertaken in keeping with the nature of humanity and things. In other words, true partnership with nature is not merely a condition of human existence to be recognized, but rather an active engagement in the process of creation, a moral praxis that must be maintained in one's life at all times. Without such a commitment, a human life is incomplete, or lacking in 'full manhood,' to use a Poundian expression. In *The Cantos*, Pound envisions a rapturous moment when the pursuit of the ethical norm of *yi* (equity) and the principle of the *Dao* or process enables the human spirit to fill in the space between earth and heaven, a state of true companionship in which

    this breath wholly covers the mountains
        it shines and divides
    it nourishes by its rectitude

       does no injury
overstanding the earth it fills the nine fields
            to heaven
Boon companion to equity
    it joins with the process
            lacking it, there is inanition. (LXXXIII/551)

These lines are based on a passage from *Mengzi* 2.1.2, where Mencius speaks to a disciple about what he calls *haoran zhi qi* 浩然之氣 (grand air), something cultivated in the inner world of the individual through consistent commitment to righteousness. The *haoran zhi qi*, according to Mencius, is the source of moral strength and can bring about the union of the human heart/mind and the *Dao* 道 or Way (Pound's 'process'). Mencius appears to have difficulty identifying what this *qi* 氣 (air) actually is, for he admits that 'it is difficult to describe it.'[30] However, since Mencius in describing it uses terms that suggest its largeness (*da* 大) and hardness (*gang* 剛), the *haoran zhi qi* seems to be a material attribute of some kind. This is why, when properly nourished, that is, sustained by righteous deeds, it can grow and fill up the space between earth and heaven. Legge translates this concept into 'passion nature,' making it almost a pure spiritual entity.[31] In contrast, Pound, who always esteemed the human body and even viewed it as sacred, chooses the word 'breath' for this concept in his verse, with the obvious intention of emphasizing its physical dimension.

Pound's rendering of this Mencian passage in *The Cantos*, because of his eccentric treatment of Chinese characters, is problematic from a sinologist's point of view.[32] However, in this particular case, he deserves the benefit of poetic licence, because what we have here is not a literal translation of Mencius's words but a creative transformation. The interesting thing in Pound's translation is not the lack of correspondence between his lines and the original passage in *Mengzi*, but the way in which these lines correspond to his overall vision. By means of his etymographic reading strategy, Pound is able to create in these lines the central poetic image of 'boon companion.'[33] Such an image, restating the notion of partnership in a more figurative manner, confirms the attainable union of human beings with the world of things through the blessing of the 'process' of the *Dao*. In addition, through its associations with a merry, festive atmosphere, the image of the 'boon companion' celebrates the enjoyment of sensuous experience derived from human beings' pursuit of such a relationship, which in fact rests on the material reality of the universe. In short, with the idea of 'boon companion,' Pound further clarifies his vision of the ideal relationship between humanity and nature.

The celebration of human companionship with nature is heightened in *The Cantos* by the recurrence of the theme 'man, earth: two halves of the tally' (LXXXII/546). The 'tally' metaphor, also invoked in canto LXXVII (487–8), derives from Mencius's remarks about sagehood in *Mengzi* 4.2.1. The original passage makes the point that two sage-kings, even though separated by time and space, may achieve a spiritual union because they share the same ethical principles. In Pound's metaphorical revision, the two parties of humanity and earth replace the two sage-kings, yet he stresses a similar point that the two parties can enjoy a harmonious union in a cosmos sustained by the omniscient principles of divine creation. Pound envisages a number of historical moments at which such a harmonious relationship has supposedly been achieved. One instance is his imagined life of the Na-khi tribe in China, where human beings are able to live in a tranquil environment between heaven and earth (CX/798). According to Pound's vision, such a partnership is beneficial not only to human beings but also to things in nature. For instance, when the ancient Chinese kingdom of Hia (*Xia*) respected the 'great sensibility' of Heaven, 'Birds and terrapin lived under Hia, / beast and fish held their order, / Neither flood nor flame falling in excess' (LXXXV/565).

Pound's notion of a human partnership with nature also derives its cogency from the recognition that the world of things is an organic and patterned whole alive with spiritual beings. Like many of Pound's other ideas, much of this view can be traced to his early works, but it did not take on a consistently persuasive form until he fully integrated Confucian teachings with his thought. With an unorthodox theological position that incorporated polytheism and pantheism, Pound believed that the world of natural objects was abundant in spiritual beings and had its own dynamic life. It is important to note that although he viewed nature as a divine emanation, he did not conceive of the divine in terms of a single monopolizing God, but rather as the collective power characterizing the various invisible or supernatural forces that sustain the individual, dynamic existence of natural objects. The essence of things, from this perspective, is both spiritual and physical. Such an approach to the world of things had been the working basis for Pound's analysis of pagan mythology in his early prose work. In Confucianism, he found a comparable approach as a result of his forcible reading of Confucian works. Note, for instance, Pound's version of *Zhong yong* 16:

> Kung said: The spirits of the energies and of the rays have their operative *virtu*. The spirits of the energies and the rays are efficient in their *virtu*, expert, perfect as the grain of the sacrifice. We try to see them and do not see them; we listen and nothing comes in at the ear, but they are in the bones of all things and we can not expel them, they are inseparable, we can not die and leave them behind us. (*Con*, 131)

In this version Pound inserts his ideas into the original passage. The notion of 'spirits' comes from the Chinese term *gui shen* 鬼神, which both Legge and Chan translate as 'spiritual beings.'[34] Pound's rendering of the 'spirits of the energies and of the rays' not only allows these supernatural beings stronger connections with earthly existence (which smacks of his early mystical vision sustained by European paganism) but also recognizes the enlightening force of such beings from the perspective of a Neoplatonic light philosophy. In Pound's rendering of the passage that follows the quotation above, Confucius goes on to suggest that an adequate reverence for the 'spirits of the energies and the rays' would lead to 'cognizance of the gods.' Confucius's remarks, or rather, Pound's version of Confucius's remarks, reinforces the belief that these divine spirits inform the inexhaustible dynamism of nature, and that despite their invisibility, they cannot be separated from the existence of finite objects, including human life. The latter idea is articulated in the statement that these divine beings reside 'in the bones of all things.' That sentence is a creative translation Pound produces through his etymographic reading of the Chinese character *ti* 體 (body). In his rendering of the above passage, the divine spirits, by maintaining a powerful presence, appear to have a direct impact on our life and thus deserve our tribute.

Closely related to Pound's ideas about the spiritual dynamism of the world of things is his recognition of the totalitarian and organic nature of this world. He explicitly and repeatedly attributed a totalizing view of nature to the teachings of Confucianism. To a considerable extent, such a totalizing outlook should also be interpreted as a profound reflection of the collective psyche of Pound's generation, a desire to reinstate the vision of a unified and all-encompassing world that might resist the fragmentation of modern experience brought about by wars, economic depression, and cultural nihilism. This desire accounts for Pound's intense interest in Confucianism, which, in his view, shows appropriate respect for the 'oneness' of nature. In his discussion of Mencius, Pound observes: 'At no point does the Confucio-Mencian ethic or philosophy splinter or split away from organic nature. ... The nature of things is good. The *way* is the process of nature, *one*, in the sense that the chemist and biologist so find it. Any attempt to deal with it as split, is due to ignorance and a failure in the direction of the will' (*SP*, 87). When making this observation, Pound is pitting the 'totalitarian' Confucianism against the 'Greek splitting' of Western analytical philosophy derived from the Aristotelian tradition. According to Pound, this philosophy breaks the objects of its investigation into abstract fragments in order to force them into a preconceived structure of knowledge, rather than getting a good grip on them as organic parts of an inseparable whole. Such an argument for the wholeness of nature finds convincing expression in Pound's version of *Zhong yong*. In a passage of this work, which is intended to present a holistic picture of the visible universe (heaven and earth), Pound's diction again calls attention to the idea of 'unsplittability': whether 'great' or 'minute,' the universe remains 'something which nothing can contain' or 'something which nothing can split' (*Con,* 117). Not only is nature 'unsplittable,' but the moral lessons derived from nature resist 'splitting' as well. The 'five activities of high importance under heaven ... and the three efficient virtues,' that is, the basic moral principles that define the appropriate social relationships of human beings and regulate their social behaviour, 'are to be united in practice,' and we must 'not attempt to split them apart one from the other' (*Con,* 151–3). The unity of moral codes with practice then leads to the oneness of knowledge, that is, the unity between the knowing mind and the known object, for 'the scope of knowing is one, it does not matter how one knows, the cult of knowledge is one' (*Con,* 153).

As the antidote to 'Greek splitting,' the Confucian virtue of 'non-split' suggested in Pound's own work and his Confucian translations points to three ideal states of being: the oneness of nature, the oneness of humanity with nature, and the oneness of the individual with himself. The oneness of nature means the recognition that nature abides by its own consistent laws and resists the intention of human beings to superimpose their wills upon its existence. Pound liked to retell a well-known parable from *Mengzi* 2.1.2 as a means of ridiculing the human folly of attempting to interfere with nature's course and violate its dynamic

Confucianism and Pound's Spiritual Beliefs   167

integrity. The parable, as Pound told his readers, is about a man in ancient China 'who pulled up his corn because it didn't grow fast enough, and then told his family he had assisted the grain' (*SP*, 87). There is an explicit reference to the parable in *The Cantos*:

勿
助
長
as it stands in the Kung-Sun Chow. (LXXXIII/552)

'Kung-Sun Chow' is the title of the section in *Mengzi* where the parable is narrated. The three Chinese characters, which mean 'don't assist [the grain] grow,' pose the warning against similar human actions, which are both harmful to nature and self-destructive to all of humanity.

When human beings fracture the oneness of nature, according to Pound, an inevitable outcome is their splitting off from nature. This is precisely the aberration that he tried to remedy with his theory of the nature-humanity partnership. For Pound, any individual with a truly totalizing vision not only recognizes the unity of nature and honours the harmonious relationship between humanity and nature, but also makes an effort to maintain the oneness of his selfhood, for a human person, after all, is part of the material world and should obey its laws as well. Thus, 'the man of breed looks at his own status, seeing it in clear light without trimmings; he acts, and lusts not after things extraneous to it'; furthermore, 'the man of breed cannot be split in such a way as to be shut off and unable to rejoin himself' (*Con*, 125). In this case, the 'splitting' of the individual bespeaks his alienation from himself. Pound gives his readers concrete examples of such a 'man of breed' who successfully resists 'splitting.' For instance, in canto XCVIII (713):

>   and with the colour of Nature
> Iong Ching, Canto 61
>   of the light of 顯 hsien
>   明 ming,
> by the silk cords of the sunlight,
> Chords of the sunlight (*Pitagora*)
>   non si disuna

In Pound's portrayal, Emperor Yong Zheng (Iong Ching, 1723–1736), a Confucian hero, was able to honour the unbroken signatures of nature (the 'colour of Nature'), because he was enlightened by the same 'non-divisible' ('non si disuna') light that had informed Pythagoras's mind as well as Dante's poetry.

In addition to being dynamic and holistic, nature in Pound's vision also appears to be rationally organized. The objective world, Pound once explained by using what he called Dante's 'sense of gradations,' is made of 'things neither perfect nor utterly wrong, but arranged in a cosmos, an order, stratified, having relations one with another' (*SP,* 150). Besides, the presence of such a cosmic order assures the human mind of the chance to get closer to the essence of the universe. If Pound often entertained a point of view that tended to mystify nature, he was no less inclined to rationalize nature, turning it into something with which the human mind can come to grips, as if nature would become an anti-human force if it were unknowable or incomprehensible to human beings. Thus, in Pound's conception, nature, so symmetrically and rationally patterned as to suggest the working of a supreme intelligence, provides for human beings not just a world of material abundance, but also an inexhaustible source of knowledge, guidance for moral conduct, and a norm of wisdom and beauty that transcends the conflicts and accidents of history.

For too long, Pound felt, human beings had over-asserted their supremacy; it was time for them to acknowledge their ignorance and start learning from nature. 'Pull down thy vanity, it is not man / Made courage, or made order, or made grace,' he vehemently calls in his poetry, 'Learn of the green world what can be thy place / In scaled invention or true artistry' (LXXXI/541). According to Pound, what human beings need to learn from nature are first of all moral lessons. Based upon his discoveries in Confucian classics, Pound in his poetry is able to create a sort of eco-ethical discourse rare in his time:

> Manners are from earth and from water
> They arise out of hills and streams
> The spirit of air is of the country
>   Men's manners cannot be one
>   (same, identical)
> Kung said: are classic of heaven,
> They bind thru the earth
>   and flow
> With recurrence,
>   action, humanitas, equity (XCIX/718)

More importantly, human beings need to learn from nature the secrets of life and, on the basis of this awareness, obtain an intimate knowledge of the divine intelligence. Pound's commitment to this agenda is strengthened by his understanding of the 'great learning' of the Confucian *Da xue*. The 'great learning,' as envisioned in his translation, is an epistemological journey that begins with 'sorting things into organic categories' and ends 'in coming to rest, being at ease in perfect equity' (*Con*, 27–31). The knowledge of nature is thus the 'root' and leads to ultimate revelation, for 'things have ends (or scopes) and beginnings. To / know what precedes 先 and what follows 後 / will assist yr / comprehension of process' (LXXVII/485). These lines, paraphrasing a key passage from *Da xue*, assert that in addition to self-knowledge, an eventual understanding of the 'process,' namely, the *Dao* or the true Way of Heaven, must be grounded in the knowledge of nature.

4. *Dao*: The Tensile Light from Heaven

As with many Western writers in the nineteenth and twentieth centuries, and in particular his American predecessor Emerson, Pound's search for spiritual experience in the natural world was part of the search for a path to the ultimate source of life, conventionally explained in terms of God in the West. As noted earlier, Pound was not an atheist; he never doubted the existence of an almighty deity, the invisible supreme force of creation that unifies all finite beings in its absolute reality. Although he occasionally remarked that he would not mind calling this divine force 'God,' he often used other terms to refer to it, such as 'eternal state of mind,' '*theos*,' 'intimate essence,' 'supreme intelligence,' 'luminous principle of Reason,' or the Neoplatonic '*nous*.' These various terms for the same entity emerged from his attempt to redefine this transcendental category in non-conventional terms, and revealed his difficulty in capturing an unorthodox theological vision in one consistent description.

Although Pound's religious beliefs often appeared fragmented in the works written in his early years, his overall spiritual position at that time had already taken on a discernible shape through his exploration of European pagan mythologies. Whether called 'God' or 'eternal state of mind,' Pound's divinity comprehends the sum of reality or the totality of the creative powers of the cosmos; within the frame of this belief, 'God' and 'gods' are interchangeable terms. In spite of Pound's recognition of the mysterious nature of the divine force, he believed that divinity manifests itself through the rational ordering of nature, rather than through miracles, particularly of the sort found in the Old Testament. For Pound, the absolute being of divinity is in some ways identical with the world, which is deemed the emanation of the divine force and its logical self-expression. Pound's overriding concern was with the connection between the human and the divine, a concern reflecting a deep-seated longing for the presence of the kind of divinity the believer could confidently relate to and joyfully place his faith in. The questions Pound raised in his early writing focused on this concern, such as, 'When is a god manifest?' and more specifically, 'When does a man become a god?' The answer, according to Pound, was when the human being 'enters one of these states of mind,' that is, the eternal mind (*SP,* 47). The notion of man becoming god, in Pound's early theological observations, could also be expressed as god becoming human, for both ideas point to the same mysterious human experience of spiritual transformation and elevation. According to Pound, such an experience could be found in European paganism, in which 'the god has at least succeeded in becoming human' to fulfil the 'goal of the love and the invocation' (*SR,* 98). Pound's notion conveys the belief that divinity shares some essential dimensions with human beings, and so makes its presence known through the development of human intelligence.

With such a theological vision, what Pound needed from Confucianism was the complementary vocabulary and paradigms that would allow him to articulate his belief with a renewed persuasiveness and consistency. In addition, his search in Confucian works for theoretical provisions also enriched the theological implications of Confucianism and enlarged its spiritual perspectives. In fact, the Confucian tradition does not have a fully developed theology, especially with regard to the belief in an almighty transcendental being. Pound had to bring his received ideas from the Western tradition into his reinterpretation of the concepts in Confucian cosmology he deemed useful for his theological reconstruction. By adopting such a revisionary approach, he produced a synthesized theory about the relationship between the human world and the world above, a theory in which unorthodox Western ideas and Confucian ideas are mutually illuminating. The theory addresses Pound's spiritual concerns in three primary aspects. First, it confirms the legitimacy of a belief in the existence of a transcendental force, called *Tian* or Heaven in its Confucian sense. Second, the theory reassures the believer of the immanence of the divine force in the form of Light and through the operation of the *Dao* or Heavenly process. Third, it articulates a strong confidence in the human capability for internal transcendence empowered by self-cultivation of the innate predispositions of the heart/mind, a capability enabling human beings to embrace eternal truth and to attain sagehood.

The Chinese character *tian* 天, commonly translated as 'heaven,' can mean vastly different things because of its obscure etymology and loose applications in classical works. In a recent study on the historical evolution of the Chinese conception of the relationship between *Tian* and humanity, Feng Yu lists as many as fifteen 'major' meanings that have been attached to this term in the course of history, ranging from deity to human energy.[35] The ambiguity of the term, a subject of speculation among Western sinologists, has compounded the difficulty of elucidating Confucian cosmology.[36] Based on Legge's English translations alone, which Pound consulted while studying the Four Books during the 1930s, the Confucian concept of *Tian* can yield at least six different meanings in English: a personal deity (*Lun yu* 6.26; 9.5), the transcendental force of creation (*Zhong yong* 17.3), the absolute principles of ethical values (*Lun yu* 7.22; 8.19), fate (*Lun yu* 12.5), the cosmological whole (*Lun yu* 17.19), and the physical sky (*Lun yu* 19.25).[37] In other words, the Confucian *Tian* can be seen to inscribe dimensions that are at the same time divine and worldly, spiritual and material, eternal and provisional, creating and created. For Pound, who always longed for a theological paradigm that would overcome the separation between the divine and the human, *Tian* seemed to offer an attractive solution.

In Pound's own translations, the attributes of the Confucian *Tian* generally fall into three categories: the divine and intangible entity, the essential force of material reality, and something between the infinite and the finite. Pound uses three forms of the English word 'heaven' to distinguish these three possible aspects of this Confucian concept. When *Tian* designates the transcendental power, the ultimate source of creation, he capitalizes the English word, such as: 'From of old, Heaven, in creating things, of necessity concentrates their materials in them, with energy and in due proportions' (*Con,* 135). If *Tian* refers to the material dimensions of this entity, which nevertheless embody the universal moral principles of existence, he uses the plural form of the English word: 'In the heavens present to us, there shine separate sparks, many and many, scintillant' (*Con,* 183); or, 'wanting to know mankind he must perforce observe the order of nature and the heavens' (*Con,* 151). In only one particular case does he suggest that the emphasis of this concept should fall exclusively on the material aspect of heaven, that is, when Confucius famously asserts that *Tian* is no more than a non-personal force of nature (*Lun yu* 17.19). In this case, Pound uses 'sky' to render the master's word: 'Sky, how does that talk? The four seasons go on, everything gets born' (*Con*, 277). If Pound intends to retain the original ambiguity of the concept *Tian*, he mostly uses the singular 'heaven' without a capital letter. In such a case, 'heaven' may refer to the divine being, such as in, 'What heaven has disposed and sealed is called the inborn nature' (*Con*, 99), or it may stress its earthly affiliation, such as in 'Great as are heaven and earth men find something to say against them in criticism' (*Con*, 117). The flexibility of *Tian* permits Pound to avoid rigid dogmatism in theological formulation, dogmatism being what he strongly dislikes in Christianity. More importantly, the interchangeability of the semantic attributes of *Tian* enables him to reinstate the essence of finite being in a divine or heavenly origin, and to accord worldly reality and material grounding to the eternal and spiritual presence of the divine being. In the framework of such a perspective, what seems to separate the absolute from the provisional, the spiritual from the corporal, is also what brings them into unity.

The image of *Tian* or Heaven constitutes an important part of the spiritual vision in Pound's poetry. His first mention of *Tian* or Heaven appears in one of the 'China Cantos': 'the spirit Chang Ti, of heaven / moving the sun and stars' (LIII/263). 'Chang Ti' refers to the Chinese term 上帝 (*Shangdi*) meaning 'the Lord Above' or literally 'the Higher Emperor.' Here, Pound's associating heaven with this strongly anthropomorphic concept of a supreme deity bears the influence of his reading of the works by Christian missionaries to China, something that he would soon get rid of as he came to study Confucian works more closely. Pound's 'China Cantos' is based on *Histoire générale de la Chine* by the French Jesuit de Moyriac de Mailla, who went to China in the early eighteenth century. De Mailla's book is a translation of a condensed version of *Zizhi tongjian* 資治通鑒 (A Comprehensive Mirror for the Aid of Government) by the Chinese historian Sima Guang (1019–1086). Jesuit missionaries to China during the seventeenth century and the early eighteenth century for the most part followed the so-called accommodationist policy, which encouraged the priests to synthesize Chinese culture, and especially Confucianism, with Christian teachings in order to ensure the success of their mission. One major ideological synthesis these Jesuit fathers pursued was the equation of the Christian God with the Chinese *Shangdi* and *Tian*. De Mailla's French representation of Chinese history similarly treats Chang Ti (*Shangdi*) and *le Ciel* (Heaven) as the equivalent of God. Such an equivalence, as John Nolde has noted, was picked up by Pound.[38]

But the association of the Christian God with *Tian* is quickly negated in Pound's poetry as he comes to posit *Tian* as the alternative to the Christian God, especially the part of God that he regards as derived from 'Jewish elements.' That the Confucian *Tian* or Heaven is antithetical to this Christian God is purposely proclaimed by Pound in *The Pisan Cantos*:

> With justice,
> by the law, from the law or it is not in the contract
>   Yu has nothing pinned on Jehoveh
>   sent and named Shun who to the
> autumnal heavens *sha-o*
> with the sun under its melody
>   to the compassionate heavens (LXXIV/460)

These lines mainly allude to a passage in *Lun yu* 20.1, where the old sage-king Yao (Pound mistakes Yu for Yao),[39] at the moment of passing the throne to Shun, is advising the new king on following the mandate of Heaven. The phrase of 'compassionate heavens' derives from Legge's translation note on Mencius's idea of Heaven in *Mengzi* 5.1.1, and it is used here to assert the righteous and humane nature of Heaven's decrees. By contrasting the Confucian Heaven and Jehovah in these lines, Pound makes the clear point that the God of the Old Testament has no place in a world where people, and especially their leaders, are guided by the sound and light of the benevolent Heaven.

Recognized as the transcendental origin of beings, *Tian* or Heaven is depicted in Pound's poetry not as the stern and aloof Ruler of all things but rather as the Supreme Intelligence, which endows the universe with meaning and provides human life with moral guidance. As Pound maintains in canto LV while referring to Zhou Dunyi's neo-Confucian theory (Pound's Tcheou Tun-y, 1017–1073), 'Reason from heaven' constitutes 'the beginning of all things' (LV/298). In Confucianism, the enlightening will of Heaven is called *Tian ming* 天命, which in Pound's prose translation is either 'the luminous decree of heaven,' 'the orders of heaven,' or simply 'the destiny' (*Con*, 35–6, 198, 23). The Confucian concept of *Tian ming* has both political and existential implications. I will dwell on the second implication later in relation to the concept of internal transcendence. In its political sense, *Tian ming* is usually translated in

English as the 'mandate of heaven,' approximating the Western notion of the 'divine right.' However, it is important to note that the Confucian *Tian ming* does not mean an absolute privilege allowing a ruler to transcend his social obligations. The legitimacy of *Tian ming*, according to Confucius, and Mencius in particular, cannot be established unless the ruler proves his right to his mandate through actions that win the recognition and approval of his people. In a recent study on Pound, Leon Surette, having misconceived the notion of the Confucian *Tian ming*, voices a sweeping opinion that characterizes Pound's embrace of Confucian politics as an automatic endorsement of tyranny. Observing on Pound's resort to 'Confucius and Mencius,' Surette argues: 'Confucian political theory legitimates tyranny in that the just ruler reigns with "the mandate of heaven," not of the people.'[40] On the contrary, what Pound appreciates in the Confucian-Mencian concept of *Tian ming* is precisely its emphasis on the connection between the efficacy of *Tian ming* and the will of the people, even though there is no denying that he often interprets the will of the people from an elitist perspective. As he repeatedly insists in his poetic allusion to the concept of *Tian ming*: ' 命 extend to the people's subsidia, / that it was in some fine way tied up with the people' (LXXXV/578).

For Pound, the authority of *Tian ming* rests on its central quality of eternal benevolence, because Heavenly decrees are always just, compassionate, and beneficial to human beings. In his poetry, he also utilizes the character 靈 *ling* (spirit) to signify the benevolent *Tian ming*. He calls *ling* the 'great sensibility' and maintains that 'Ling 靈 / was basis of rule' (LXXXV/563, 572). If a ruler follows *ling*, that is, loving and caring for his people, as did King Wu in ancient China, then he can bring stability and prosperity to his country; otherwise, as demonstrated by the tyrannical King Zhou, the ruler will incur calamities upon himself and his people.

The belief that the primordial power of *Tian* or Heaven derives from its benevolent will permits Pound to view all nurturing forces in the cosmos as constitutive of the essence of Heaven, thus placing his conception of the divine within a polytheistic framework. More remarkably, he even allows feminine forces a place in such a spiritual construction of Heaven. In canto XCVII, we are presented with a marvellous picture: 'Out of ling 靈 / the benevolence / Kuanon, by the golden rail,' is sailing on the Heavenly river (the 'celestial Nile'), as 'the flames gleam in the air' (695). Kuanon (Guanyin), the compassionate bodhisattva, is a goddess figure from Chinese Buddhism, a religion Pound was usually biased against. In this dramatic mingling of Confucian and Buddhist elements, however, his reverence for the Heavenly principle of ecumenical benevolence enables him to overcome his ideological prejudice. In canto CX (798), where he is imagining a paradise between heaven and earth, Kuanon appears again, this time joined by the beautiful moon goddess Artemis. It seems that in Pound's vision, Heaven as the unity of divine forces is sustained, or to be more accurate, inhabited, by all benevolent *ling* or spirits, whether they are from the East or the West, androgynous or otherwise.

Pound's quest for a belief in the benevolent force of Heaven is also furthered by his integration of two concepts: *Dao* 道 (or *Tao*, usually rendered 'way') from Confucian metaphysics and Light from Neoplatonism. While the *Dao* in Pound's exploration mostly points to the metaphysical process of Heaven's operation, Light seems to configure that process in its luminous physical or spatial presence. For one thing, by exploring the two important concepts in a mutually illuminating context, Pound sought not only to reinstate the intelligibility of the Neoplatonic philosophy of light that he always favoured, but also to give his reconstruction of a modern Confucian belief a Western philosophical grounding. What's more important, he employed the two concepts to make a coherent and compelling case for the existence of a divine immanence, an assertion that was intended to console the Western mind in a post-Nietzschean world filled with doubt and fear after the 'death' of God.

Dao or way, an ambivalent term in classical Chinese works, can apply to multiple spheres of existence in Confucianism. For Pound, however, there is only one *Dao*, which originates in Heaven and completes itself in humanity. *Dao* in that sense mostly signifies the transcendental law of Heaven. It is noteworthy that Western commentators tend to construe this *Dao* in terms of a static form of permanent truth. For instance, Pauthier translates it as 'la règle de conduite morale' (the rule of moral conduct);[41] Waley defines the term as 'the infallible method of rule'; Lau calls it 'the sum total of truths about the universe and man,' and Fingarette reads it as a 'single, definite order.'[42] In contrast, Pound interprets *Dao* in terms of a 'process,' that is, the 'process' of realizing 'what heaven has disposed and sealed' in human nature and the ever-flowing movement that makes the divine law evident and comprehensible. Pound's interpretation of *Dao* as 'process' is based on his etymographic reading of the Chinese character for *Dao*. The character, 道, consists of two components: the lower part, the radical, denotes 'go' or 'walk' and the upper part means 'head.' Hence, Pound's gloss: 'The process. Footprints and the foot carrying the head; the head conducting the feet, an orderly movement under lead of the intelligence' (*Con*, 22). In Pound's translation of Confucian works, *Dao* 道 is consistently rendered as 'process,' contextualized with the image of light.

Pound's notion of light came from the medieval philosopher John Scotus Erigena, whose famous dictum, 'all things that are are lights,' is a recurrent theme in *The Cantos* (LIIIX/449). From Erigena's Neoplatonic perspective, the world is a theophany of divine radiation, in which God is light and his creations are lights; divine creation is thus God's act of manifesting himself in his creatures. Yet Pound seems to be more interested in the 'corporeal' dimension of the light metaphor. In his long essay on Guido Cavalcanti, who in Pound's view was also influenced by the light philosophy, Pound approvingly quotes from Etienne Gilson's 1925 book on medieval philosophy: 'Light is a very subtle corporeal substance and it is almost incorporeal. Its characteristic properties are to engender itself perpetually and to diffuse itself spherically and instantaneously about a point. ... This extremely tenuous substance is also the stuff of which all things are made; it is the primary corporal form and some people call it corporeality.'[43] In quoting this passage, Pound clearly points to his inclination to characterize light in terms of its materiality.

The affinity between the worldview of Confucianism and that of the Neoplatonic philosophy of light is Pound's discovery, and one which he repeatedly asserts. In an Italian article published in *Meridiano di Roma* in November 1941, he describes the universe presented by Confucianism as 'un mondo di luce' (a world of light) much like the world envisioned by Erigena and Cavalcanti.[44] Pound's 'discovery' largely relies on his reading of the Chinese character *ming* 明 (bright). In Confucian works, *ming* does not carry the heavy philosophical weight perceived in it by Pound, but the character is indeed often used in contexts where the transcendental supreme intelligence is the topic, such as in the mention of *Dao* in the opening paragraph of *Da xue* (*ming de* 明德, 'illustrious virtue'), or in the description of *Tian* in *Zhong yong* 26.5 (*gao ming* 高明 'high and bright'). Pound discovers the linkage between Confucianism and Neoplatonism, then, in this contextual significance of *ming*. Thus, he states: ' 明. The sun and moon, the total light process, the radiation, reception and reflection of light; hence, the intelligence. Bright, brightness, shining. Refer to Scotus Erigena, Grosseteste and the notes on light in my *Cavalcanti*' (*Con*, 20). Such a perception informs Pound's consistent strategy of superimposing the Neoplatonic vision of light on Confucian metaphysics in his translations. For example, Pound translates a key *Zhong yong* passage on the *Dao* of Heaven in the following way:

> From these hidden seeds it moves forth slowly but goes far and with slow but continuing motion it penetrates the solid, penetrating the solid it comes to shine forth on high. ... The celestial and earthly process pervades and is substantial; it is on high and gives light, it comprehends the light and is lucent, it extends without bounds, and endures. (*Con*, 181–3)

In this instance, *Dao* is not only construed as the vigorous 'process' of creation, but also 'substantiated' in the form of flowing light.

In *The Cantos*, by similarly reconfiguring the transcendental *Dao* of Confucianism in terms of a perpetual process of generating light, Pound through a poetic persona conveys to his readers a strong belief in the divine presence:

> Gentlemen from the West,
>   Heaven's process is quite coherent
> and its main points perfectly clear.
>   顯 hsien. (LXXXV/572)

The Chinese character 顯 *xian* (Pound's 'hsien,' meaning 'manifest' or 'manifestation'), often used by Pound to highlight the effects of *ming* or 'tensile light,' reinforces the idea that the divine manifests itself not only in the depths of its perfect creation, but also in the coherence and clarity of its creational plan. Moreover, Heaven's intent to communicate its 'points' is such an unstoppable force that, according to Pound in *The Cantos*, its 'definition can not be shut down under a box lid' (LXXVIII/499). The 'box lid' metaphor derives from Pound's rendering of a poetic passage in *Zhong yong*, where the 'bright silk of the sunlight / pours down in manifest splendor' and nothing can 'shut it down under a box-lid' (*Con*, 133). By merging the light image with the Confucian *Dao* or process, Pound makes the originally elusive concept of *Dao* a coherent expression for the heavenly process of creation and enlightenment. In addition, because the divine light is a familiar biblical image of the Genesis to Christians, by juxtaposing it with the Confucian *Dao*, Pound makes this abstract Chinese notion more intelligible and accessible to his Western readers.

The *xian,* or manifestation, of the divine light only attests to the presence of Heaven's benevolent will, however. The *Dao* as an ideal process should be a reciprocal communication between the godhead and the human mind. In other words, the enlightening process originating from Heaven cannot be completed until it is joined by the responding movement of the human mind. After all, the central concern of Pound's new humanist belief is not simply with the existence of the ultimate origin of permanent truth, but rather with the ability of human beings to transcend their limitations in order to partake of the grace of that permanent truth. Pound is deeply convinced that it is largely up to human beings to bring the *Dao* or process into completion. That is why, in his revisionary translation of one Confucian statement (*Lun yu* 15.28), he stresses: 'A man can put energy into the process, not the process into the man' (*Con,* 267). But the question is: how can a man put his 'energy' into the 'process' of the *Dao*? This brings us to the final, but not the least important, theme in Pound's belief system: how to establish a compelling way towards internal transcendence, namely, a connection with Heaven that the individual believer can obtain through his or her own efforts rather than by means of external assistance.

In his spiritual quest Pound explored two theories to that end. The first one is the theory of reason. Regardless of Pound's tendency to associate his notion of reason with the theory of the medieval Erigena (XXXVI/179), his understanding of reason is largely derived from two slightly earlier sources. One of these sources is Enlightenment philosophy. This philosophical tradition assumes that the universe is ordered by the same rational principle that also characterizes the working of the human mind and, therefore, that the human mind can discover and understand universal truths through the capacity of reason. The other source is the Romantic tradition, especially that of Emerson, in which reason indicates a willingness for total openness to the mystery of the supernatural, and thus a capacity of higher intuition enabling humanity to apprehend and partake of divinity. It is in the Emersonian sense that Pound sees poetry as the superior expression of reason. In *Guide to Kulchur,* he states: 'The worship of the supreme intelligence of the universe is neither an inhuman nor bigoted action. Art is, religiously, an emphasis, a segregation of some component of that intelligence for the sake of making it more perceptible' (189–90).

Both aspects of Pound's notion of reason, the rationalistic and the mystical, inform his early understanding of Confucian works. For instance, in his 1928 translation of *Da xue,* the human pursuit of perfect virtue is construed as an action of 'developing the luminous principle of reason which we receive from the sky, and of making it shine with full glory' (*TH*, 11). Also, in one of the 'China Cantos,' in his brief mention of the neo-Confucian philosopher Zhou Dunyi, Pound imposes the notion of reason on Zhou's theory: 'Reason from heaven, said Tcheou Tun-y / enlightens all things' (LV/298). It seems that the appeal of reason is what initially enabled Pound to perceive a linkage between Confucianism and the mystic philosophy of light, and he would go on to valorize reason as what could open up a path towards the Transcendental. Interestingly, however, after the 'China Cantos,' Pound is no longer seen to superimpose the notion of reason on Confucian doctrines. Nor does he explicitly apply this concept again to his rendering of Confucian ideas about Heaven and the *Dao* in his Confucian translations in the 1940s, although the implication of the *Dao* as the working of the supreme intelligence remains deeply entrenched in his interpretations. Such a subtle change may have been partly due to his growing desire to avoid using too openly Western a concept in his Confucian reconstruction, a concept for which he may have also begun to lose the kind of enthusiasm he once entertained. A more important cause for this change, however, might have been Pound's discovery of Mencius's formulation of *xin* or heart/mind, a concept to which he became increasingly attracted in the course of his intensive study of Mencius's works from the late 1930s to the late 1940s.

Mencius's theory of *xin* 心 (heart/mind) appealed to Pound not only because it offers an insightful explanation of the unity between humanity and Heaven but also because it places human development at the centre of its concerns. In my earlier analysis of the Mencian doctrine of *si duan*, or four beginnings, I discussed Mencius's view that the four ethical predispositions of the human heart/mind constitute the inborn good nature of human beings. For Mencius, the ethical inclination of the heart/mind is what defines humanity as such on three accounts. First, the four predispositions of the heart/mind distinguish human beings from animals; second, the development of these predispositions is entirely within human control and thus verifies the significance of the human will; and third, developing these predispositions takes priority over other pursuits like the satisfaction of sensory desires, making the human being essentially a moral being. Based on these insights, Mencius put forth his famous theory of *jin xin* 盡心 (to complete the heart/mind, or to exert the heart/mind to the utmost) to clarify the relationship between humanity and Heaven. According to this theory, cultivat-

180   Ezra Pound and Confucianism

ing the ethical predispositions not only preserves one's innate nature, but is also the way to serve Heaven. If one gives full development to one's heart/mind, one will be able to gain full knowledge of one's inborn nature. Having known one's inborn nature, one will be able to know Heaven. By giving full development to one's heart/mind and nourishing one's inborn nature, then, one is serving Heaven (*Mengzi* 7.1.1).

In *The Cantos* Pound makes direct references to Mencius's notion of the heat/mind at least four times, using transliterations in two instances and, in the other two instances, citing the Chinese character for heart. His most explicit mention of Mencius's theory of *jin xin* 盡心 occurs in canto LXXXVI (581):

> 即   kiue sin
> 心
>   leading to
> Mencius, chi (453, Mathews)

The two Chinese characters Pound uses here are not directly from Mencius's work, but from *Shu jing* or Book of History in Seraphin Couvreur's trilingual edition (French, Latin, and Chinese) of this Confucian classic. In *Shu jing* 5.14.15, Pound finds the phrase 既厭心 (*ji jue xin*, Pound's *chi kiue sin* based on Couvreur's transcription), which Couvreur renders as 'il vous suffira de lui donner toute votre application,'[45] and which Legge renders as 'exert your mind to the utmost.'[46] Pound's understanding of the first character 既 is also reinforced by his reference to the explanation of entry 453 in Mathews's Chinese-English Dictionary, in which 既 can mean 'to complete.' The second character Pound quotes, *xin* 心, is the same *xin* in Mencius's theory. In other words, for Pound *ji xin* 既心 coincides with *jin xin* 盡心, for both stand for the idea of 'completing or exerting the heart.' Hence Pound uses 既心 to 'lead' his readers to Mencius's doctrine.[47]

Pound in his poetic elaboration takes Mencius's doctrine of the heart/mind farther than many of its exegetes perhaps would permit. For Pound, the human heart is not a teleological vehicle, a transitional station on the spiritual journey to a higher level of existence. The purpose of exerting the human heart to its utmost degree does not mean to run beyond the bounds of the heart in the search for eternal truth, but rather to secure a firmer dwelling within the human heart because the heart is precisely the dwelling place of the divine. Pound proclaims that belief in another poetic reference to Mencius, where the emphasis falls on the theme of 'tien t'ang hsin li,' meaning 'Heaven's Temple [is] in the heart' (XCIX/722). Striking a parallel with the Protestant belief that God stays in the soul of the faithful and the Zen Buddhist belief that Buddha sits in the heart of the pious, Pound's claim that the human heart enshrines Heaven gives the most radical expression to the religious appeal of Confucianism. By asserting the human ability to build Heaven's temple in the heart, such a claim endows the human subjectivity with an active and important role in actualizing the 'oneness of Heaven and humanity' (*tian ren he yi* 天人合一), the perfect state of being that has been vehemently sought after by Confucian believers.

Finally, in Mencius's historical accounts, several sage-kings in ancient China, in particular Yao and Shun, exemplify the greatest achievements that humankind has ever made in developing the heart/mind. At the same time, Mencius insists that 'Yao and Shun are like everyone else' (*Mengzi* 4.2.32), that is, everyone else is endowed with the same ethical predispositions of the heart/mind as Yao and Shun. With proper and vigorous self-cultivation of this ethical inclination, then, everyone else should be able to obtain similar sagehood. Mencius's view of the spiritual equality among human beings has attracted a great deal of attention from modern Confucian defenders because for them it contains what can be regarded as the seeds of a Confucian formulation of democracy. Pound also shows interest in this view, echoing Mencius in *The Cantos*: 'The Sage Emperor's heart is our heart' (XCIX/715). The irony here is that although such a view acknowledges the universal human potential for achieving greatness and moral transformation, it represents universal humanity by limiting its meaning to the selected cases of the few cultural heroes. Here again, in Pound's subscription to Mencius's doctrine about the universal value of the sagely heart/mind, we see the contradiction between a liberal humanism and a cultural elitism. It is not surprising, then, that Pound's attempt to universalize the experience of human spirituality ends up in zealous portrayals of the privileged sage-kings. These superior individuals are believed to have embodied the perfect human personality after which we should all model ourselves, as their pursuits are purported to have opened up the path to authentic spiritual transcendence. In *The Cantos*, Pound's celebration of such Confucian heroes characteristically marks the height of his spiritual quest, a moment of joy and triumph when the poet witnesses the ascendance of the sage-kings in the glory of the divine light, testifying to the perfect union between humanity and Heaven:

>   in tensile 顯
> in the light of light is the *virtù*
>   'sunt lumina' said Erigena Scotus
>   as of Shun on Mt Taishan
> and in the hall of the forebears
>   as from the beginning of wonders
> the paraclete that was present in Yao, the precision
> in Shun the compassionate
> in Yu the guider of waters (LXXIV/449)

Conclusion
Poundian-Confucian Humanism at the Crossroads

At the end of *The Great Digest*, his retranslation of *Da xue* completed in the mid-1940s, Pound quotes his artist friend Tami Kume: 'We are at the crisis point of the world' (*Con*, 89). To many people, the labelling of a certain historical moment as a point of crisis may seem a cliché, an ideologue's self-serving strategy of crying wolf. After all, human beings have experienced many crises, big and small, and yet history never turns back or stops but rather keeps moving forward, much to the satisfaction of some and the dismay of others. In the case of Pound, however, who had lived through the devastating tumult of two world wars, an overwhelming sense of crisis was undoubtedly genuine. Such a sense did not necessarily entail a pessimistic view of history, as has been ascribed to the so-called lost generation to which Pound belonged; rather, that Pound acknowledged a sense of crisis indicated his belief in the necessity of historical changes and thus the possibility of a future invested with hope and choice, awakening to a new dawn. From this perspective, his notion of 'crisis' can be construed as a 'crisscross,' a historical crossroads that afforded an opportunity to search for a way out of the impasse that humankind had entered. One may even argue that the profundity of Pound's sense of historical crisis, together with his resultant recognition of unavoidable responsibilities, parallels that of Confucius two and half millennia ago. Both of these men, when confronted with what appeared to them a turning point in history, took upon themselves the task of guiding 'Kulchur,' and made every possible effort to reinstate what they considered universal and permanent values in the face of forces they believed threatened the continuity of human civilization.

Thus, Pound's emphasis on a historical crisis at the end of his version of *Da xue* is immensely meaningful in two ways. First, with an almost apocalyptic urgency he tells his readers that he is not presenting his Confucian reinterpretation as the leisurely mental exercise of a speculative philosopher, or the plaything of a curious writer seeking satisfaction in an exotic Oriental fantasy, but rather as a recharged force for human redemption, a renewed value system that gains its life and dynamism in resisting cataclysmic historical anomalies. Such an agenda accounts for Pound's repeated call, during the 1930s, for the 'immediate need of Confucius.' Second, by underwriting his Confucian translation with a realistic sense of crisis, Pound is trying to contextualize his modern project of reclaiming Confucianism, thus asserting his right to rehistoricize the value of Confucian teachings in the Western world. In other words, Pound's revised Confucianism declared its *modern* and *Western* relevance, serving as the philosophy, the political claims, and the aesthetics of an oppositional writer in his quixotic fight against what he perceived to be the enemy of humanity.

In this concluding chapter, by placing Pound's Confucianism in broader historical contexts, I am returning to my central argument that this particular form of Confucianism makes sense only as a special discourse, formulated at a specific historical moment to confront contradictory conditions of human existence generated by the social milieu of Pound's time. By so doing, I hope to illuminate the historical implications of Pound's Confucianism in its three manifestations of a counter-discourse: (1) as an alternative vision of human existence to Western capitalist modernity, (2) as a new humanist program in the Western tradition of humanism, (3) as a unique reconstruction of Confucianism in the transnational development of the Confucian tradition.

Pound's Confucianism, first of all, posits a counterweight against the discourses that in his view are responsible for the dehumanizing apparatus of the modern Western world. From the several major areas of his concerns that I have examined thus far, it is clear that Pound's critique of Western culture concentrates on the period from the Reformation to his time, the historical span during which capitalist sociopolitical formations, represented by Western Europe and North America, went through the process of rationalization and legitimation as the universal model of social development. Although Pound's criticism covers a wide array of targets ranging from arts and politics to religion, the main thrust of his critical charge is always directed at the core constitutive element of Western modernity – finance capitalism, especially its banking system, which he simply called 'usury.' Not only did Pound accuse modern 'usurocracy' of perpetuating an immoral system of the distribution of wealth, he also held it accountable for breeding the 'Cult of Lucre,' a mercantile culture in which 'man has been reduced not even to a digestive tube, but to a bag of money that gradually is losing its value' (*SP,* 161, 178).

For Pound, the ruthlessly pragmatic, profit-driven impulse of the capitalist mind has shaped the modern mode of material production in such a way that the human subject as well as his works are reduced to a sort of tool serving objectives irrelevant to the development of human nature. In the modern procedure of material production, according to Pound, the aim of labour is alienated from its essential human needs. Contrary to the Jeffersonian small producer who understands and controls his own work, a modern factory worker is hired to do a job without much knowledge of the meaning and purpose of his work, let alone a vision of how his work connects with the progress of humanity. Such a worker, Pound deplored, 'is little better than the mechanism he works with' (*SP,* 199). Pound also saw the invisible hand of usury behind the unrestrained, wasteful exploitation of natural resources, which has characterized the way of material production since the Industrial Revolution. It is Pound's belief that nature's abundance is not only the sole material blessing for human beings, but also the source of spiritual enlightenment from which issues human beings' confidence in the earthly life and optimism about the future. In his view, this precious source is being jeopardized because modern financiers have 'plotted against abundance' to serve their money-hungry agenda (*SP,* 176).

Parallel to this alienation of the nature of humanity from their activities in material production, according to Pound, is the same value deduction of human products in cultural spheres. In general Pound was not against the advancement of modern science, even though he thought that, since Leibniz, the ever-worsening scientific tendency towards abstraction was part of the cause for the overwhelmingly imprecise use of European languages. What he opposed in the production of knowledge is that modern institutions of learning have adopted an instrumentalist attitude, by which knowledge is no longer the means to the self-cultivation of the individual learner, a means of helping the individual to become 'a more complete man,' but rather serves as the rationalistic tool for controlling things extraneous to human self-fulfilment (*SP,* 191, 197). For Pound, the most disappointing aspect of modern culture is the degradation of arts. As Mauberley laments in Pound's autobiographical poem:

> The age demanded an image
> Of its accelerated grimace,
> Something for the modern stage,
> Not, at any rate, an Attic grace.[1]

The making of modern arts is seen to be dictated by the same, contemporaneous demand for fast and mass production of commodities. The aesthetic criteria fashioned by the self-reflexive logic of the mercantile age favour the kind of arts wrought for easy consumption and transitory pleasure, but not for the pursuit of intellectual insights and visions of eternal beauty. Such arts, in Pound's view, are the products of the machine, not genuine human creations as represented by Greek sculpture, the lyrics of Li Bai (Li Po, 701–762), or the epic of Dante, all of which embody universal human wisdom in a form as solid as marble and as precise as stone-cutting.

Pound inveighed against the dominant discourses of Western modernity from a humanistic position enforced by Confucianism. In sharp contrast to modern Western culture, 'where once we read "men," we read now "money,"'[2] what he found in Confucian works was 'man, man, man, humanity all over the page, land and trees' (*SP*, 94). Pound's humanist orientation has received neither due attention nor adequate appreciation in contemporary scholarship. For instance, in his study on the genealogy of Western humanism, Alan Bullock explicitly excludes Pound from the humanist tradition based on Pound's connection with mysticism.[3] In Pound studies, John Heath-Stubbs was the only commentator to ever categorize Pound as a 'humanist' writer. In the 1950 essay 'The Last Humanist,' which has attracted little attention from Pound scholars, Heath-Stubbs calls Pound 'the last and most tragic representative' of the humanist tradition established by Italian Renaissance writers. While he admires this great tradition for its commitment to preserving the universal human value of classical European works, Heath-Stubbs is critical of its 'too purely humanistic conception of Man,' one that has prevented practitioners like Pound from properly diagnosing the 'daemonic' force in human nature.[4] Heath-Stubbs's characterization, notwithstanding his insights, does not give us a full picture of Pound's humanist position. For one thing, Pound would object to being imprisoned in the Renaissance tradition of humanism because, as I noted in chapter 4, he was strongly opposed to its anthropocentrism and held it partly responsible for the separation between humanity and nature. More importantly, sustained by his extensive incorporation of Confucian tenets, Pound's humanist outlook cannot be explained only in terms of the Western canon of humanism.

To be sure, Pound inherited a number of premises from the humanist tradition of the West. These basic premises include a belief in the essential goodness of humanity, the recognition of the human capability of self-perfection and the human creative power to enrich human existence, and the ideal vision of happiness and fulfilment in the earthly life. But Pound also rejected many of the assumptions that have characterized Western humanism, including its central tenet, which endorses man as the measure of all things, its blind faith in human rationality, and its all-out negation of anything supernatural and transcendental. This fundamental disagreement set Pound apart from major contemporary humanist thinkers of the West, such as the advocates of the 1933 American 'Humanist Manifesto' (including John Dewey), the 'New Humanists' headed by Irving Babbitt, and the philosophical humanists represented by the British-born F.C.S. Schiller.[5] Furthermore, Pound believed that the Western tradition of humanism had been in irreversible decline since reaching its heyday in the Renaissance, and that under the existing circumstances in the West humanist thought could hardly find a nurturing base for further development. He once remarked that 'humanism [had] no choice in the occident, in life,' and therefore had 'taken refuge in the arts.'[6] However, the humanism hiding in the arts, from his point of view, already became a mockery of human creativity and, isolated from reality, could no longer serve as the constructive force for human life. Pound's resort to Confucianism, then, was obviously a consequence of his disillusionment with the Western tradition of humanism.

Although Pound was initially drawn to Confucianism by what appeared to him a Confucian individualism positing the primacy of self-development, the Confucian doctrines that increasingly attracted him and, in the end, irresistibly convinced him were those that stressed human interrelatedness over absolute individuality, and social harmony over competition, without at the same time denying the agency of the human subject in social formations. These doctrines define the human individual as a moral being whose personal fulfilment is informed by his recognition of, as well as contributions to, the social relations that give meaning to the existence of the individual and the community. Within the framework of these doctrines the creative powers of humanity are invested with huge social responsibilities that require the individual to work consciously to serve a common good in all spheres of life – language, arts, economy, politics, etc. Such doctrines also provided Pound with a totalizing cosmic vision in which human beings are supposed to find their appropriate position in relation to both natural and supernatural forces.

Here, I should note that by arguing for the humanist orientation of Pound's Confucian reconstruction I have no intention of exonerating him from the problematic implications that his ideology is often seen to contain. Instead, I am trying to highlight the uniqueness of his humanist discourse, its differences from and similarities to the formulations of his forerunners and contemporaries in the Western humanist tradition. More importantly, I seek to convey the often-ignored point that Confucian humanism lends Pound's articulation a coherent ideological basis in his battle against the undesirable process of Western modernization. Pound's readers often complain about the difficulty of his poetry, mostly because his works seem to lack the sustenance of a coherent ideological viewpoint. Pound himself, towards the end of *The Cantos*, also remarks, perhaps in an ironic manner: 'And I am not a demigod, / I cannot make it cohere' (CXVI/816). Despite such impressions, Pound's humanist concerns in light of Confucian doctrines may provide us with a revealing thematic line, a consistent perspective, a unifying structure, with which we can better understand his work.

As a humanist discourse against the hegemony of modernity, Pound's Confucianism occupies a significant place in the history of Western engagement with Confucianism. Before Pound embarked on his Confucian quest, Western treatments of Confucianism had undergone three stages, each marked by different attitudes towards this particular Chinese tradition. None of these attitudes, it is noteworthy, was sufficiently informed or convincingly grounded. The first was a stage of *accommodating* Confucianism with Christian teachings, represented by the practice of Matteo Ricci (1552–1610), the renowned Jesuit priest who headed the China Mission until his death. After staying in China for a while, Ricci realized that Confucianism held such an authoritative place in all aspects of Chinese life that, to convert the Chinese, the missionaries must accommodate basic Confucian doctrines by reinterpreting them in Christian terms. Three strategies were essential to Ricci's policy. First, he maintained that Confucianism was a moral philosophy, not a religion, and that Confucius was a mortal, the 'Prince of Chinese Philosophers,' not a 'deity.'[7] In other words, Confucius was not a competitor with Jesus Christ for believers. Second, Ricci rejected contemporary neo-Confucianism on the grounds that its naturalistic formulation of *Tian Li*

(Heavenly Principle) was a product of theological adulterations by the heretical doctrines of Buddhism and Daoism and contradicted the Christian notion of a personal God. Third, Ricci advocated returning to classical Confucianism for elements reconcilable with Christian belief. He claimed that, except in a few instances, Confucianism in its earliest manifestations was 'so far from being contrary to Christian principles, that such an institution could derive great benefit from Christianity and might be developed and perfected by it.'[8]

Even though Ricci's accommodationist policy concerning Confucianism met with objection by some priests, in particular Niccolo Longobardi (1565–1655), Ricci's successor as the mission superior, it was supported by the majority of missionaries to China during the sixteenth and seventeenth centuries. Their implementation of this policy produced, among other things, the first complete translation of the first three of *Si shu* or Four Books in a Western language (Latin). This translation, published in 1687 together with a biography of Confucius under the title of *Confucius Sinarum Philosophus* (Confucius: The Philosopher of China), had an enormous impact on the worldview of European intellectuals. In Europe, Ricci's accommodationist approach was adopted by Leibniz, although with significant modifications, in the latter's philosophical explications of Confucian thought. Interestingly, what appealed to Leibniz most in Confucianism was the neo-Confucian concept of *Li* or Principle, the very idea that Ricci had denounced as heresy. In his 1716 *Discourse on the Natural Theology of the Chinese*, Leibniz attempts to make the case that *Li* is a sophisticated formulation by which Confucian philosophers explain the supreme creative force of the universe. He thus identifies *Li* with Reason, 'the foundation of all nature, the most universal reason and substance.'[9] In this conception, the neo-Confucian principle of *Li* becomes identical with the Christian notion of God, for both refer to the transcendental cause of creation and perfection, the absolute law informing the material and spiritual existence of human beings. It is in such an enlightening unity of *Li* and God that Leibniz sees the possibility of creating a world theology, something that Mungello has insightfully characterized as 'an ecumenism that included not only the reunion of Catholic and Protestant Christendom but an ecumenism with which the religious and intellectual beliefs and practices of non-Westerners, such as the Chinese, could be reconciled.'[10]

The second stage of Western encounter with Confucianism, which I term the stage of *idealization*, is marked by the promotion of Confucian 'rationalism' as a weapon against the hegemony of Christian theology, and thus as an empowering force that could help Europe to move from an obscurant dark age into a modern world ruled by reason, science, and progressive ethical knowledge. This new attitude towards Confucianism coincided with the Enlightenment and its leading proponents were Voltaire and François Quesnay. For Voltaire, Confucius embodied all the virtues that reason could foster: 'Confucius has no interest in falsehood: he did not pretend to be a prophet; he claimed no inspiration: he taught no new religion; he used no delusions; flattered not the emperor under whom he lived.' On the contrary, said Voltaire, Confucius 'unveiled the light of reason to mankind.'[11] Confucianism, based on the sage's teachings, was thus seen as a rational religion effectively guiding human life by the authority of reason rather than by superstition and dogmatism. Moreover, according to Voltaire, Confucian ethics represented the crown of human knowledge that anchored the admirable Chinese civilization, and the Chinese polity supported by Confucian literati testified to the success of a government run by philosophers. While Voltaire envisioned in Confucian China an idealized sociopolitical order, Quesnay found in the same China an idealized economic structure. Quesnay believed that the moral and political rationalism manifested in Confucian teachings conformed to natural laws and had contributed to the continuity and prosperity of China's remarkable agricultural economy. He further maintained that a rational government should model itself after the Chinese empire, making the pursuit of wisdom derived from 'the natural laws' the 'principal administrative objective of the government' as well as the basis of civil society.[12]

In the third stage of Western response to Confucianism, a stage of *negation*, what had been previously seen in Confucianism as capable of strengthening history's progress towards modernity now became an undesirable element that would hinder, and thus must be excluded from, the process of modernization. Hegel's attitude most tellingly reflects this change. In his *Lectures on the History of Philosophy*, Hegel critiques Confucianism by placing it in the context of China's historical evolution. He contends that China has failed to reach the higher level of civilization that Western cultures have achieved. On the historical road to absolute freedom, Chinese society, which for Hegel is a patriarchal order and despotic hierarchy, has missed the freedom of the individual. Such historical conditions in the real China, according to Hegel, are largely generated by the institutionalized belief system of Confucianism. For Hegel, Confucianism is not a real philosophy, because he finds it to be incapable of abstract analysis of the relationships of the world and of speculative contemplations of the ideal. Nor does Confucianism posit any special appeal as an ethical tradition for, in Hegel's view, it has not presented any moral lessons that have not been 'as well expressed and better, in every place and amongst every people.'[13] Hegel deems Confucianism an underdeveloped religion with two negative features. First, as the state religion of China serving the interest of the emperor, Confucianism is not the religion of the ordinary individual believer and has not developed to the point where spirituality and individual consciousness are established. Second, Confucianism is the 'religion of magic,' according to Hegel in *Lectures on the Philosophy of Religion*.[14] Hegel's 'magic' refers to an immediate relationship between human beings and nature, in which human beings hold a 'direct' power over nature. In Hegel's view, the direct power of magic, which is bound to prevent human beings from an objective observation of nature, should be distinguished from the 'indirect' power over nature manifested in a higher culture. Such an indirect power is achieved by stepping back from an immediate relationship with nature and understanding the physical laws of the natural world in a scientific manner and through technical instruments.

The Hegelian dichotomy of Western/higher culture versus Chinese/lower culture underlies the sociological study of Confucianism by Max Weber, another important figure in the third stage of Western encounter with Confucianism. Weber's interest in Confucianism derived from his need to seek a cultural antithesis to Protestantism, an unfavorable alterity by which he could prove that the religious ethic of Protestantism was the sole driving force for modernity, that is, the capitalist mode of production, rationalized political structures, and modern sciences. In *The Religion of China*, Weber critiques Confucianism from a variety of angles. But his conviction that Confucianism could not bring China into a modern world derived primarily from examining three aspects of Confucianism: the degree of its rationalization, its ethical relationship with the world, and its way of cultivating individual personality. In the first respect, borrowing from Hegel's concept of 'magic,' Weber classifies Confucianism as a religion of primitive rationalism characterized by preserving the worship of magic. The power of magic, in this case, is maintained by the spirits of ancestors. Hence, 'from magic there followed the inviolability of tradition as the proven magical means and ultimately all bequeathed forms of life-conduct were unchangeable if the wrath of the spirits were to be avoided.'[15] In the second respect, without the belief in a transcendental God, thus lacking the 'consciousness of sin and need for salvation, conduct on earth and compensation in the beyond,' Confucianism 'reduced the tension with the world to an absolute minimum.'[16] Therefore, in contrast to Protestantism, which is bent on conquering the world in order to reshape it according to its ethical vision, Confucianism finds the world the best possible site of existence and thus makes efforts to adjust itself to the conditions of the world. With regard to this third aspect, for the same reason that it lacks a sense of sin and salvation, Confucianism assumes that human beings are capable of unlimited perfection and that the individual ideal of the self is 'a universal and harmoniously balanced personality.' The way to achieve that ideal is through education in classical works and by 'fulfilling traditional obligations.'[17] Weber's analysis points to one conclusion: Confucian ethics fosters radical traditionalism that prefers stagnation to change, hence intrinsically resisting modernization.

The delineation of Western engagement with Confucianism outlined above may help us to better understand the historical context for Pound's Confucian program. It is not coincidental that Western interest in Confucianism began almost simultaneously with Western economic and cultural expansion to the East, a process leading to the global domination of capitalist modernity. The attitudes underlying each stage of the West's engagement with Confucianism prior to Pound are parts of their respective ideologies that have all participated in enforcing that process, albeit in different ways. It is in its questioning of the values of capitalist modernity that Pound's reconstruction of Confucian humanism marks its fundamental departure from the three previous attitudes. Nevertheless, Pound's Confucianism was not invented suddenly or independently from the entire Western institution of Confucian studies; actually, this institution enabled the development of Pound's approach, including both its insights and misconceptions. In his study of *Orientalism*, Edward Said makes the point that the success of Western domination rests on two assumptions: the superiority of Christian civilization and the triumph of free trade; the two assumptions constitute the main content of modern Western life and the entire achievement of the capitalist economy. The assumed cultural superiority of the Christian tradition, among other things, is precisely what Pound intended to subvert. His relentless attack on the questionable role that Christian establishments have played in Western socio-economic life since the Reformation differentiates his Confucian project from that of the early Christian missionaries, whose dealings with Confucianism were driven by the mission of converting Confucian China into a territory of the Christian God's kingdom. This distinction renders Pound's Confucian discourse a rare alternative practice to Orientalism in general.

However, Pound was not totally exempt from these missionaries' misunderstanding of Confucianism and Chinese history. For one thing, he inherited their prejudice against Buddhism and Daoism. This prejudice, which inhibited Pound from adequately grasping the dynamic interactions of various Chinese cultural traditions as well as the evolution of Confucianism, was largely responsible for his serious misrepresentation of Chinese history, as evidenced in his 'China Cantos.' Pound's historiography is a dualistic narrative marked by its reduction of complex history to the conflict between good and evil, or light and darkness; he situates all historical events – political doctrines, cultural trends, and economic activities – in either one or the other of the two categories. The demonized Buddhism and Daoism conveniently fit the stereotype of the dark force in Pound's poetic representations, in which the entire Chinese history appears to be nothing more than an incessant struggle between the Confucian tradition and the anti-Confucian tradition represented by Buddhism and Daoism.

Such a misconception of Chinese history on Pound's part was reinforced by the Enlightenment writers' romanticized conception of Confucian China. In so far as his Confucian position is concerned, Pound made no secret of his affinity with this Enlightenment tradition. For instance, when speaking of some cryptic 'verses' in Confucian works, he quoted from Voltaire: 'One must take them in the perspective of Voltaire's: "I admire Confucius. He was the first man who did *not* receive a divine inspiration"' (*Con*, 191).[18] Pound shared with the Enlightenment writers the same incredibly uncritical acceptance of Confucian teachings. Neither the Enlightenment writers nor Pound seriously examined Confucianism by situating it in the historical realities of China – partly because of their reluctance to do so, partly because of the inadequate knowledge about Confucianism and Chinese history provided by the institution of Western Chinese studies. It seems to have sufficed for them that Confucianism could conveniently serve as a time-honoured, authoritative paradigm of the constellation of values and ideas to which they eagerly subscribed in their ideological struggles. In this idealized conception, Confucianism became the panacea for all social problems. Thus, in their romanticized historiography, when Confucianism went up, so did China; when Confucianism went down, China ran into trouble. Such an idealized configuration of the Confucian tradition is by and large what Pound and his Enlightenment predecessors transferred into the imaginative space for their Western readers. Notwithstanding this similarity, there exists a crucial difference between Pound and his Enlightenment forerunners. Whereas the Enlightenment writers used Confucianism to justify their subversion of sociopolitical conditions hostile to their vision of a rationalized modern world, Pound used Confucianism to undermine the rationality of that very world.

Pound completely reversed Hegel's and Weber's evaluations of Confucianism in almost all major aspects. While it is not clear if Pound ever read or knew of the two German thinkers' studies of Chinese history and Confucianism, it is certain that his refusal to accept Western capitalist modernity as the privileged model of human progress enabled him to form a totally different assessment of Confucianism. From this perspective, Pound's undertaking anticipated the trend in Confucian studies unfolding over the last several decades in China and the West, since most of those engaged with this trend have ultimately responded, in one way or another, to the challenge posed especially by the Weberian negation of Confucianism. In addition, what makes Pound's reconstruction of Confucian humanism refreshing is his effort to avoid a Eurocentric posture, an effort apparently sustained by his awareness that there exist outside of the Western tradition other compelling models of human existence. Yet Pound was not much interested in the differences between the Western tradition and the Confucian tradition; for him these differences were superficial, contingent, and only constitutive of temporary historical aberrations. Instead, he seemed more interested in the intrinsic, and often hidden, similarities between the two traditions. He saw such similarities as informed by the permanent human values that laid the common foundation of all cultures. And he was committed to uncovering these similarities in order to reestablish the common ground for the universal history of humanity, a history that might cogently connect to its past as well as lead to a promising future.

The overtly oppositional gesture of Pound's ideological praxis determines the dialogical and revisionist nature of his Confucian discourse, which generates meaning more through its immediate and antagonistic relationship with opposing ideologies than by harking back to the supposedly authentic voice in the original Confucian works. It is true that to engage in ideological dialogue is the defining feature of any discursive practice. But what informs the operation of Pound's Confucian program is that from its inception it functioned as an aggressive counterforce against social establishments that he held responsible for the corruption of Western civilization. More remarkably, Pound's Confucianism, empowered as it was by its combatant instinct for targeting various opposing discourses, constantly reframed its concerns, redefined its terms, and readjusted its positions – even at the risk of self-contradiction, such as the contradiction between its early individualist claims and its subsequent authoritarian stance. In a sense, all crosscultural interpretations are revisionist. Pound's Confucianism is just more so, not only because he was an iconoclastic reader, but because he had to 'update Confucius's formula' in order to reclaim Confucian ideas in a way demanded by his oppositional agenda.[19] Pound had a term for such a revisionist approach: 'Make It New.' He found this doctrine in Confucian works and made it better known through his own writings.[20] Life is in perpetual metamorphosis, he believed, and ideas ought to be continuously renewed to accommodate changes; hence, 'Seeking a word to make change / 變' (LVII/313). For Pound, the idea of *bian* 變 (change, metamorphosis), another expression for the doctrine of 'Make It New,' constitutes the dynamic spirit of the Confucian tradition. That is, the imperative of constant renewal should apply not only to other things but also to Confucianism itself. Otherwise, Pound told his Western readers, Confucianism would be diminished to 'a static and inactive doctrine, inactive enough to please even the bank of Basel and our western monopolists' (*SP*, 93). Yet the 'metamorphosis' to which he subjected Confucianism, as we know now, is unprecedentedly drastic and challenging.

Despite all its radical and often problematic revisions, Pound's reinterpretation of Confucianism under specific modern circumstances has made contributions worthy of serious attention as well as dialectical evaluation. His rethinking of the nature of language enabled by his revision of Confucian doctrines has turned out to be profoundly thought-provoking and shed light on an important aspect of the political motives behind the experimental practices of the modernist writers. By investing his experience of poetic language in the Confucian doctrines of *zheng ming* and *cheng yi*, Pound has enlarged the scope of Confucian perspectives by bringing the major modern issue of representation into the analytical focus of the Confucian mind, immensely enriching the aesthetic and epistemological dimensions of Confucian thought on poetry, language, and politics.

Another peculiar contribution by Pound lies in his exploration of the relationship between the individual and the state from a perspective sustained by integrating premises from Confucianism and Western liberalism. The question of how to position the individual in the modern state is an overriding concern for Confucian thinkers today, and Pound's exploration has left lessons that are valuable in both positive and negative senses. On the one hand, given the prevalent Western assumption that Confucianism is inimical to the interest of the individual, Pound's early formulation of the rights-based Confucian individual, a pioneer corrective to the Hegelian-Weberian prejudice, opens up a new horizon for the development of Confucianism. On the other hand, however, his formulation becomes highly problematic when, in an attempt to solve the conflict of diverse individual interests, he misinterprets the Confucian notion of a relational individual in terms of a collective individual whose universally virtuous personality incarnates the wills of all individual members of the state. Such a super-individual, in Pound's vision, is embodied by the cultural heroes whose achievements have sustained the continuity of human civilization. The controversial ideal of a collective individual magnifies the polemic inherent in Pound's cultural elitism, for the ideal situates the hope for a harmonious social order in the subjective will of the privileged cultural hero rather than in a social system designed to balance and protect diverse individual interests. It is tragic that Pound's conceptualization of an idealized perfect individual eventually turned into a valorization of autocracy.

Pound comes closest to Confucianism through his search in Confucian teachings for valid spiritual beliefs, a search that produced many insights. When those like T.S. Eliot, following Hegel, disparaged Confucianism as an 'inferior religion,' Pound was one of the very few Western writers in the first half of the twentieth century to praise Confucianism, openly and whole-heartedly, as an inspiring and compelling belief system. Obtaining from Confucianism a set of well-formulated concepts about human nature, Pound was able to provide the development of Western humanism with a strong ethical grounding as well as a powerful spiritual vision. His postulate of an ecocriticism based on Confucian values offers a more attractive, holistic explanation of the relationship between human beings and nature than the one supplied by Western discourses grown out of the Judeo-Christian tradition. Moreover, Pound's religious vision, anchored on a thoughtful and artful mixture of European pagan polytheism, Neoplatonic philosophy of light, and Confucian doctrines about the Heaven-humanity relation, has given us some of the most beautiful verse in American poetry. Apart from a basic spiritual orientation free of the narrow-mindedness of monotheism and the rigidity of organized religion, such a religious vision of hybrid origins reflects the recognition that different cultural traditions from the East and the West can conduct a fruitful dialogue, in a constructive manner and on an equal footing.

By all means, Pound's special form of Confucianism is far from a perfect reconstruction and, in fact, appears highly questionable to many of his expert readers. His formulation may not even have offered truly satisfactory solutions to the problems that he thought were plaguing the Western world in which he found himself. Such shortcomings, however, cannot erase the valuable service that Pound did for Confucianism through his pioneer work, which displays unusual vision and courage in reclaiming Confucian values for the purpose of coping with the contradictions of modern conditions. The significance of such a service can be gauged only from the perspective of the crosscultural development of Confucianism. Over the last several decades, especially since the emergence of the East Asian model of socio-economic development, there has been a strong revival of interest in Confucianism in North America, China, and Chinese-speaking areas in East Asia. This intellectual trend, which is showing no sign of abating,[21] reflects the view that the Western tradition may have reached an impasse in trying to solve the problems generated by the modern conditions it created. Thus, efforts should be made to recuperate wisdom and insights from other traditions, such as Confucianism, in order to address the issues confronted now not only by the West but also by the rest of the world. Such a late-modern revival of Confucianism is seen by Confucian devotees as signifying the advent of a promising age full of opportunities, in which the Confucian tradition can reevaluate its ideological focus, redefine its theoretical structures, and regain its social relevance and credibility. Tu Wei-ming calls this phenomenon the 'third-epoch development of Confucianism.'[22]

In a 1985 interview, while speaking of his hope for the 'modern transformation of Confucianism,' Tu Wei-ming envisioned the next journey that Confucianism must make in order to fulfil its promise: 'Whether or not Confucianism can regain vitality in the twentieth century primarily depends on whether or not it can travel through New York, Paris, and Tokyo before returning to China. In other words, when looking forward to the twenty-first century from the perspective of the late twentieth century, Confucianism will find many goals to accomplish. I think it must first face the challenge of American culture, European cultures, East Asian cultures (the industrialized East Asia), planting its roots deeply in these cultures and growing up there. Only after that can it return to China in triumph.'[23]

Tu's remarks convey two important themes with which most students of Confucianism now agree. First, Confucianism must respond effectively to the challenges posed by the modern conditions of the West in order to justify itself as a dynamic tradition. Second, Confucianism should engage in crosscultural dialogues in order to draw new sustenance from other cultures as well as work with other cultures to find an answer to the problems they have in common in the modern world. These two themes, as we have seen, also animated Pound's great effort to reinstate Confucianism in the West. On Tu's visionary map, it is not hard for us to locate a position for Pound's endeavour, which, by any measure, constitutes an important step in such a transnational and crosscultural journey of Confucianism. It is in this sense that the lessons Pound left us from his undertaking as a professed Western Confucian – both his contributions and mishandlings – will no doubt prove over time to be of increasing historical significance.

Notes

Abbreviations of the Works by Ezra Pound

ABCR	*ABC of Reading*
CEP	*Collected Early Poems*
Con	*Confucius: The Great Digest, the Unwobbling Pivot, the Analects*
GB	*Gaudier-Brzeska: A Memoir*
GK	*Guide to Kulchur*
J/M	*Jefferson and/or Mussolini*
L	*Letters of Ezra Pound: 1907–1941*
LE	*Literary Essays of Ezra Pound*
PD	*Pavannes and Divagations*
PE	*Polite Essays*
PM	*Patria Mia*
SP	*Selected Prose, 1909–1965*
SR	*Spirit of Romance*
TH	*Ta Hio: The Great Learning*

Introduction

1 Stock, *The Life of Ezra Pound*, 176.
2 See Carpenter, *A Serious Character*, 218.
3 Pound, *Ezra Pound and Dorothy Shakespear*, 264.
4 According to Zhaoming Qian in his new book, much of Pound's interest in Confucianism may have been 'sparked' by the powerfully visualized Confucian 'ideals' in some Chinese paintings that he saw in the British Museum during his early years in London. Qian makes the stimulating argument that,

aside from Chinese poetry, Pound's enthusiasm for Confucian philosophy cannot be separated from his enthusiasm for Chinese art. See Zhaoming Qian, *The Modernist Response to Chinese Art*, especially the section on 'Pound and Pictures of Confucian Ideals,' 47–63.
5 Pound, 'The Words of Ming Mao "Least among the Disciples of Kung-Fu-Tse,"' *Ezra Pound's Poetry and Prose*, 1: 320. Researchers on Pound's relationship with Confucianism have never mentioned this article, perhaps because of its confusing authorship. Although signed by a certain 'M.M.' when published, the article actually was contributed by Pound. Donald Gallup guesses that 'M.M.' might be Pound's pseudonym (see his *Ezra Pound: Bibliography*, 505). In my opinion, 'M.M.' refers to 'Ming Mao' in the title. 'Ming Mao,' the transliteration of two Chinese characters – 明 (*ming*, 'bright') and 毛 (*mao*, 'hair') – was the Chinese nickname Pound used for his first article on Confucius. The two Chinese terms (*mao* in particular) were often used as affectionate salutations by Pound and his wife Dorothy in their letters to each other, a playful practice they had started before their marriage. For instance, in a letter dated 20 November 1913, Dorothy called Pound 'Beloved "Mao,"' even placing the Chinese character 毛 (*mao*) above the salutation. In several other letters, Dorothy again called Pound 'Dearest Mao' or simply 'Mao' (see Pound, *Ezra Pound and Dorothy Shakespear*, 275, 284, 329). In their letters during his post–Second World War captivity, Pound frequently called Dorothy 'Mao,' while Dorothy called him 'Ming.' See Pound, *Ezra and Dorothy Pound*, 91, 95, 99, 155.
6 In the 1930 article 'Credo,' in reply to T.S. Eliot's question about his religious belief, Pound asked his 'enquirer to read Confucius and Ovid' (*SP*, 53). Then in 'Date Line,' published in 1934, Pound made an even clearer statement: 'As to what I believe: I believe the *Ta Hio*' (*LE*, 86).
7 This is the title of Pound's essay 'Confucius' Formula Up-to-date,' published in *British-Italian Bulletin* 2.3 (18 January 1936): 4. The essay advocates a 'Confucian' doctrine that came to dominate Pound's political vision, namely 'to promote the peace of the world by the good internal government of one's country.' See Pound, *Ezra Pound's Poetry and Prose*, 7:19. Pound elaborates on the 'immediate need of Confucius' in the 1938 essay bearing that title (*SP*, 75–80).
8 A number of works on Pound's translation of *Shi jing* (Pound's *The Classic Anthology Defined by Confucius*) have been produced, such as L.S. Dembo's *The Confucian Odes of Ezra Pound* and Eugene Eoyang's 'The Confucian Odes.' Because *Shi jing* is a collection of ancient poems that do not necessarily convey Confucian ideas, these works should not be equated with studies of Pound's Confucian ideology; rather, they are largely concerned with his

translation of Chinese poetry. Mention should also be made of John Nolde's *Blossoms from the East*. Although Nolde's work contains a brief discussion of 'Pound and Confucius' (13–23), it focuses on clarifying the sources of Pound's 'China Cantos' from de Moyriac de Mailla's *Histoire genérérale de la Chine*, a French translation of the condensed version of *Zizhi tongjian* (A Comprehensive Mirror for the Aid of Government) by the eleventh-century Chinese historian Sima Guang.
9 Cheadle, *Ezra Pound's Confucian Translations*, 4.
10 Hegel, *Lectures on the Philosophy of Religion*, 2:548.
11 Kuberski, *A Calculus of Ezra Pound*, 13.
12 Ostriker, 'The Poet as Heroine,' 35.
13 Wilhelm, *Ezra Pound: The Tragic Years*, 24, 27.
14 Surette, *Pound in Purgatory*, 74.
15 Cheadle, 'Ezra Pound's Confucian Translations,' 65–6. To make the case that 'Pound is not the only one to see seeds of fascism in Confucianism,' Cheadle in her study tries to invoke observations by others that associate Confucianism with Fascism. However, she is unable to pinpoint a single piece of evidence from the original Confucian works that reflects the 'seeds of fascism,' thus placing her claim on very questionable grounds. The inadequacy of such a view becomes even more evident when it rests simply on suspicion, or ad hoc logical fallacy. Donald Davie, for instance, did not find a 'necessary connection' between Confucianism and Fascism. But Davie still believed that there must be something 'in the Confucian texts that can lend itself to such perilous applications as Pound was to make,' for it was after Pound's encounter with Confucius that he showed 'for the first time ... the strain of thought and feeling that ultimately brought the poet to face the charge of treason.' Davie, *Studies in Ezra Pound*, 158, 157.
16 Peter Nicholls: 'His [Pound's] fascism was, in short, a curious hybrid, and the metaphysics of the state which came to occupy a central place in his work was as much a product of his enthusiasm for Cavalcanti and Confucius as it was of the actual ideology of fascism.' *Ezra Pound: Politics, Economics and Writing*, 3.
17 Chan, review, 371.
18 Tu Wei-ming, *Centrality and Commonality*, 132.
19 Pound often used 'totalitarian' to describe Confucianism. Upon comparing Confucianism and Greek philosophy, he claimed that 'the Confucian is totalitarian' (*SP*, 85) and that Confucius 'is superior to Aristotle by totalitarian instinct' (*GK*, 279). Pound also believed that Fascism started with Confucianism. As Romano Bilenchi, an Italian writer and friend of his, recalled: 'One day he [Pound] explained to me that Fascist doctrine has its origin in Con-

fucius, passed by way of Cavalcanti, Flaubert, the German ethnologist Leo Frobenius and Enrico Pea directly to Mussolini, Hitler and Oswald Mosley.' Bilenchi, 435.

20 For example, I noticed on the check-out record of the 'Date Due' slip in the Florida State University Library copy of Pound's *Confucius* that twelve patrons had used this book from 1980 to 2001; similarly, according to the 'Date Due' slip of Pound's *Ta Hio* that belongs to the Library of University of Southwestern Louisiana, fifteen patrons used this book from 1983 to 2001.

21 On Amazon.com, customer reviews give consistently high rankings to Pound's translation of the three Confucian prose works: an average of four stars in comparison with James Legge's three stars. One reader said: 'My own copy of Pound's "Confucius" was purchased many years ago. It's very well-thumbed and heavily annotated, and I often return to it. I've also studied Arthur Waley's more exact translation carefully, and a few others. But the Confucian lines that stick in my mind always seem to be those of Pound's.' Tepi, 'Those who know aren't up to those who love,' Customer Reviews, 24 May 2001 (http://www.amazon.com).

22 Levenson, *Confucian China and Its Modern Fate*, 1:120–3.

23 I use 'New Confucians' to refer to the modern Confucians who share largely similar concerns regarding the further development of Confucianism in modern times. These Confucian thinkers, now collectively known in Chinese as *xiandai xin rujia* 現代新儒家 (modern New Confucians), are represented successively by Xiong Shili (1885–1968), Mou Zongsan (1909–1995), and Tu Wei-ming. Thus the term 'New Confucianism' is distinct from the term 'neo-Confucianism,' which I use to refer to the Song-Ming Confucianism.

Chapter 1: Five Types of 'Misreading' in Pound's Confucian Translations

1 Pound says of himself in *Guide to Kulchur*: 'To read and be conscious of the act of reading is for some men (the writer among them) to suffer. I loathe the operation. My eyes are geared for the horizon. Nevertheless I do read for days on end when I have caught the scent of a trail. And I, like any other tired business man, read also when I am "sunk", when I am too exhausted to use my mind to any good purpose or derive any exhilaration or pleasure from using it' (55).

2 Hugh Kenner called Pound's *Confucius* 'one of Pound's most important poems.' Kenner, *The Poetry of Ezra Pound*, 312. When Marianne Moore praised the same work as the 'high thing' that can 'supplant life,' what impressed her was its poetic quality, a quality that 'makes most bards look very shabby.' See David Gordon, 'And Moore,' 149. Similarly, it is in view of

'the literary context' that Kathleen Raine placed Pound's *Confucius* on the same rank as 'Chapman's Homer or Dryden's Virgil.' Raine, 'There Is No Trifling,' 17. These opinions suggest the extent of difficulty that critics have encountered in categorizing Pound's 'prose' translation.

3 Cited in Gordon, 'And Moore,' 149.
4 Fang, 'Metaphysics and Money-Making,' 92.
5 Chan comments on Pound's Confucian translation: 'One can expect beautiful English and poetic insight from Ezra Pound, and one gets them here in abundance. Unfortunately, he was not willing to confine himself to these, but ventured off to a translation on the basis of Chinese ideographs. This is not a field in which he is expert.' Review, 372.
6 Chang Yao-xin, 'Pound's Chinese Translations,' 131.
7 Chan, review, 372.
8 John Dryden: 'The Qualification of a translator worth reading must be a Master of Language he Translates out of, and that he Translates into. ... If he be but Master enough of the Tongue of his Authors, as to be Master of his Sense, it is possible for him to express that Sense.' Dryden, *The Works of John Dryden*, 20:226.
9 For Arnold, 'the translator of Homer ought steadily to keep in mind where lies the real test of his success of his translation. ... He is to try to satisfy *scholars*, because scholars alone have the means of really judging him. A scholar may be a pedant ... and then his judgment will be worthless, but a scholar may also have poetic feeling, and then he can judge him truly.' Arnold, *Matthew Arnold on the Classical Tradition*, 117.
10 'During August and the first half of September 1937,' recalled Pound, 'I isolated myself with the Chinese text of the three books of Confucius, Ta Hio, Analects and the Unwavering Middle, and that of Mencius, together with an enormously learned crib but no dictionary' (*SP,* 82). Pound was referring to the pirated edition by the Commercial Press of Shanghai, and at that time he did not know the 'crib' was by James Legge, the 'anonymous' translator (*GK,* 20).
11 See Cheadle, *Ezra Pound's Confucian Translations,* 44.
12 For a brief discussion of the difference between the Stone Classic text and Zhu Xi's text, see Achilles Fang's 'A Note on the Stone Classic' in Pound's *Confucius,* 11–15.
13 'I observed Pound's Chinese studies,' James Laughlin remembered. 'Most days after lunch he would go up to his bedroom to take off into China. ... Lying on the bed, in Rapallo, his big black hat shading his eyes, he would prop a huge Chinese dictionary on a pillow on his stomach. He had been drawn to Chinese in 1913 by the notebooks of Ernest Fenollosa, an extraor-

dinary linguist but one who apparently had not cottoned to the fact that not all of the Chinese characters are ideoglyphic. There, then, was Ezra lying on his bed, looking for the pictures of things or people or signs that he thought should be in the characters. Often they weren't, and he couldn't reconcile what he saw in the characters with the dictionary meanings. As a result he invented meanings of his own. Sinologists deplore these inventions. But for most of us his language and his lines are so beautiful that the inaccuracies hardly matter.' Laughlin, *Pound as Wuz*, 8.

14 Kenner, *The Pound Era*, 447. But Kenner does not believe that Pound could digest the Chinese texts, stating elsewhere: 'Pound never worked directly from the ideograms; he worked to improve an existing version, Fenollosa's, or Pauthier's, or Legge's or Karlgren's.' Kenner, 'Ezra Pound and Chinese,' 40.
15 Cheadle, *Ezra Pound's Confucian Translations*, 38.
16 See William McNaughton, 'A Report on the 14th Biennial International Conference on Ezra Pound,' 111.
17 The poem Fang cites is entitled "蝴蝶": "兩個黃蝴蝶，／ 雙雙飛上天，／ 不知爲什麽，／ 一個忽飛還。／ 剩下那一個，／ 孤單怪可憐。／ 也無心上天，／ 天上太孤單。" Fang to Pound, 26 August 1952. Ezra Pound Papers (Mss 43). Yale Collection of American Literature, Beinecke Rare Book and Manuscript Library, New Haven, Connecticut.
18 Cheadle, *Ezra Pound's Confucian Translations*, especially 35–45.
19 The original Chinese text is from Zhu Xi's *Si shu jizhu*. Throughout my work, I follow James Legge in designating the textual division of the Four Books, which was also adopted by Pound. In the case of *Lun yu*, the first Arabic numeral refers to the book, the second the chapter, and the third the paragraph.
20 Waley, *The Analects of Confucius*, 131.
21 Ibid., 103.
22 Pauthier, *Confucius et Mencius*, 161.
23 The several English versions of *ming ming de* which I consider to be thoughtful include Legge's 'to illustrate illustrious virtue,' in *The Chinese Classics*, 1:356; Derk Dodde's 'to exemplify illustrious virtue,' in Yu-lan Fung (Feng Youlan), *A History of Chinese Philosophy*, 1:362; Wing-tsit Chan's 'manifesting clear character,' in *A Source Book in Chinese Philosophy*, 86; and Daniel K. Gardner's 'keeping one's inborn luminous Virtue unobscured,' in *Chu Hsi and the Ta-hsueh*, 88–9.
24 Pauthier, *Confucius et Mencius*, 45.
25 Ibid., 5–6.
26 Mungello, *Curious Land*, 258. I am indebted to Mungello's study on the Jesuits' translation of Confucius as well as the origins of sinology.

27 Pauthier displays his knowledge of previous translations by the early Christian missionaries in the Introduction to his own translation of Confucius. Mungello also notes that Pauthier was very much interested in Couplet's writings on Chinese subjects. See Mungello, *Curious Land*, 256.
28 This is Mungello's English translation; see his *Curious Land*, 278. The Latin version reads: 'Magnum adeoque virorum Principum, sciendi institutm consistit in expoliendo, seu excolendo rationalem naturam a coelo inditam; ut scilicet haec, ceu limpidissimum speculum, abstersis pravorum appetituum maculis, ad pristinam claritatem suam redire possit.' Couplet, *Confucius Sinarum Philosophus*, 1.
29 Voltaire, *Ancient and Modern History*, in *The Works of Voltaire*, vol. 15, part 2, 172.
30 Cited in Gallup, *Ezra Pound: A Bibliography*, 167.
31 Legge, *The Chinese Classics*, 1:171.
32 Zengzi's definition of *junzi* appears in *Lun yu* 8.6: '*Keyi tuo liu chi zhi gu, keyi ji bai li zhi ming, lin da jie er bu ke duo ye. Junzi ren yu? Junzi ren ye!* 可以托六尺之孤，可以寄百里之命，臨大節而不可奪也，君子人與，君子人也．' Legge renders this passage as: 'Suppose that there is an individual who can be trusted with the charge of a young orphan *prince*, and can be commissioned with the authority over a State of a hundred *li*, and whom no emergency however great can drive from his principles; – is such a man a superior man?' *The Chinese Classics*, 1:210.

Pound's rendering reads: 'Fit to be guardian of a six cubits orphan (a prince under 15) in governing a state of an hundred *li* who cannot be grabbed by the approach of great-tallies [ta chieh 795 (e) 6433.30 *must mean something more than L's 'any emergency,' i.e., must indicate not getting rattled either at nearing the annual report to the overlord, or by the coming near it, i.e., to the chance of appropriating to himself the symbol of power*] a proper man? aye, a man of right bread' (*Con*, 225). Pound does at least two things to make his case here. On the one hand, he tries to discredit Legge by singling out Legge's alleged liability in light of Mathews's dictionary, entries 795 (e) and 6433.30. On the other hand, in an attempt to remedy what he sees as his mentor's inadequacy, Pound reorganizes this passage to ensure a different reading, altering the grammatical features and syntactical order of the original passage, in addition to changing its main tropes.
33 Pound explains that he displays Pauthier's versions in his own translations 'sometimes as alternative interpretation, sometimes for their own sake even when I do not think he is nearer the original meaning' (*Con*, 194).
34 Apart from the relevant sections in Kenner's *The Pound Era*, especially 150–62, one may find three works particularly informative: Laszlo Gefin,

Ideogram: History of a Poetic Method; Akiko Miyake, 'Contemplation East and West'; and Hwa Yol Jung, 'Misreading the Ideogram.'
35 Fenollosa, *The Chinese Written Character*, 8.
36 Ibid., 22.
37 Ibid., 25.
38 Ibid., 23.
39 Ibid., 23.
40 Pound, 'L'Ebreo, patologia incarnate,' *Ezra Pound's Poetry and Prose*, 8:144. Pound's original text in Italian reads: 'L'ideogramma è baluardo contro coloro che distruggono il linguaggio. L'ideogramma ... è divenuto tesoro di sapienza stabile, arsenale del pensiero vivo.'
41 Pound, 'Ta Hio,' *Ezra Pound's Poetry and Prose*, 8:149. Pound's article is in Italian. The original text reads: 'L'ideogramma rappresenta più d'una parola; cioè per tradurlo bisogna qualche volta adoperare tutta una frase. E in questa frase bisogna indicare la fonte, ed il fondo dell'idea "graffiata." ... Per esempio una idea sorge da un concetto: acqua, da un concetto: albero, grano, bambou. Una idea sorge da un concetto: fuoco o luce; da un concetto d'uomo che corre, o che guarda con attenzione. Queste radici delle idee devono conservarsi nella traduzione se vogliamo capire la natura e la portata dell'originale.'
42 A typical example of Pound's early practice of etymographic interpretation is his elaboration, in the 1928 *Ta Hio*, on the several characters that generate his favourite aphorism of 'make it new': 'The pictures ... are: sun renew sun sun renew (like a tree shoot) again sun renew. That is to say a daily organic vegetable and orderly renewal; no hang-over. The "orderly" I should derive from the upper left-hand bit of the ideograph' (12).
43 Legge's version reads: 'The Master said, "How majestic was the manner in which Shun and Yu held possession of the empire, as if it were nothing to them."' *The Chinese Classics*, 1:213.
44 Benjamin, 'The Task of the Translator,' 80.
45 See note 2 of this chapter.
46 Fenollosa, *The Chinese Written Character*, 23.
47 John Irwin, *American Hieroglyphics*. See especially part 1 and the first chapter on Poe.
48 See Jung, 'Misreading the Ideogram,' 212–18.
49 Cited in Mungello, *Curious Land*, 199.
50 Bacon, *The Advancement of Learning and The New Atlantis*, Book 2, XVI. 2, 131.
51 For Mungello's detailed account, see the chapter on 'Proto-Sinology and the Seventeenth-Century European Search for a Universal Language,' *Curious Land*, 174–207.

52 Fenollosa, *The Chinese Written Character*, 6.
53 There are six categories of Chinese characters formed under different structural principles. These categories are: 'pictographic' characters, 'self-explanatory' characters, 'associative' characters, 'picto-phonetic' characters, 'mutually explanatory' or 'synonymous' characters, and 'phonetic loan' characters.
54 Wilder and Ingram, Introduction, *Analysis of Chinese Characters*.
55 Ibid.
56 Fenollosa, *The Chinese Written Character*, 25.
57 The passage actually records a dark moment in Confucius's career, as his ambition to rebuild civilization had suffered one defeat after another. In this instance, lamenting the long absence of the portents – the arrival of the phoenix and the revelation of the magic river chart – which would herald the advent of the enlightened era, an anguished, seventy-one-year-old Confucius uttered these words. Such words, according to commentator Yang Bojun, 'articulate Confucius's despair over the impasse of the *Dao*.' *Lun yu yizhu*, 96. Legge's translation also offers a configuration of Confucius different from Pound's: 'It is all over with me.' *The Chinese Classics*, 1:219. Waley, whose version is identical with Legge's, suggests in a note that at this moment Confucius felt that 'Heaven does not intend to let me play a Sage's part.' *The Analects of Confucius*, 140. Roger Ames's rendering is even more straightforward: 'All is lost with me!' *The Analects of Confucius: A Philosophical Translation*, 128.
58 Legge, *The Chinese Classics*, 1:223. For major Chinese commentators' readings, see Yang Bojun, *Lun yu yizhu*, 100; Qian Mu, *Lun yu yaolue*, 130; Mao Zishui, *Lun yu jinzhu jinyi*, in Wang Yunwu et al., eds., *Si shu jinzhu jinyi*, 137.
59 Zhu Xi, *Lun yu*, in *Si shu jizhu*, 60.
60 Waley, *The Analects of Confucius*, 143. For similar versions of this passage, see Lau, *The Analects*, 99; Ames, *The Analects of Confucius*, 131.
61 Legge's version of this phrase is: 'To rest in the highest excellence.' *The Chinese Classics*, 1:356.
62 Achilles Fang highly praised Pound's interpretation of *zhi*, claiming that such an interpretation 'seems to solve a number of knotty problems in Kung's book.' Even though Fang's praise only concerns Pound's translation in *Da xue*, it still appears to be overzealous for the reason I have stated. See Fang's letter to Pound, 12 January 1951. Ezra Pound Papers (Mss 43). Yale Collection of American Literature, Beinecke Rare Book and Manuscript Library, New Haven, Connecticut.
63 'Latin is sacred, grain is sacred,' Pound once observed, believing that the sacred nature of this language reflects the strength of the culture before the

Reformation, and that the culture was disrupted as absolute 'faith' was replaced by 'argumentation' and the 'mystery of fecundity' by the 'cult of sterility.' Pound, *Impact*, 55.

64 Part of the reason I bring up this issue is that Pound's position has been misunderstood as leaning towards recognition of untranslatability. As Kathryne Lindberg puts it when explaining Pound's radical reading strategies, 'Pound finds in translation the greatest potential for creative and wayward interpretation, for disrupting cognition and mocking the very notion of translatability that rests on perfect cognates.' Lindberg, *Reading Pound Reading*, 243.

65 The central argument of George Steiner's monumental study, *After Babel: Aspects of Language and Translation*, is based on the notion of untranslatability. Steiner's theory is influenced by Heidegger, whose view is representative of the modern philosophical rethinking of translation. Heidegger's view on translation is summarized in these remarks: 'Sometime ago I called language, clumsily enough, the house of Being. If man by virtue of his language dwells within the claim and call of Being, then we Europeans presumably dwell in an entirely different house than Easternasian man. ... And so, a dialogue from house to house remains nearly impossible.' Heidegger, *On the Way to Language*, 5.

66 Pound first published his Italian version in several parts as Confucius's aphoristic sayings. 'Saggezze,' *Il Popolo di Alessandria* (23 April 1944): 1; 'Confucio parla [I],' *Il Popolo di Alessandria* (23 December 1944): 4; 'Confucio parla [II],' *Il Popolo di Alessandria* (2 Janaury 1945): 4; 'Poundiana,' *Il Popolo di Alessandria* (23 Janaury 1945): 2. He then collected these pieces in one pamphlet, *Chiung Iung. L'asse che non vacilla* (Venice: Casa Editrice delle Edizioni Popolari, February, 1945).

67 Cheadle, *Ezra Pound's Confucian Translations*, 106.

68 Tu Wei-ming, *Centrality and Commonality*, 132.

Chapter 2: Confucianism and Pound's Rethinking of Language

1 Pound offers this definition in *Guide to Kulchur*, in which he attempts to clarify his vision of the 'new civilization' by combining Frobenius's concept of Paideuma, 'the tangle or complex of the inrooted ideas of any period' (57), with the Confucian *zheng ming*, the attainment of 'clear terminology whereof no part can be mistaken for any other' (59).

2 Sima Qian, *Shi ji*, 1513.

3 Zhu Xi, *Lun yu*, in *Si shu jizhu*, 86.

4 Han Ying, *Han shih wai chuan*, 190. The story reads: 'Confucius was sitting by [one of the] Chi-sun [family]. The Chi-sun's minister T'ung said, "If the

prince should send someone to borrow a horse, should it be given him?" Confucius said, "I have heard that when a prince takes [a thing] from his subject, it is termed 'taking'; one does not speak of 'borrowing.'" The Chi-sun understood and said to the minister T'ung, "From now on when your prince takes a thing, call it taking. Do not speak of borrowing." Confucius rectified the expression "borrowing a horse," and as a result the proper relation between prince and subject was established.'
5 Wang Yunwu, *Lun yu*, in *Si shu jinzhu jinyi*, 198.
6 Ibid.
7 Feng Youlan, *Zhongguo zhexue shi xinbian*, 1:99. Yang Bojun also insists: 'What Confucius wanted to correct was only the phenomenon of improper use of words concerning ancient rites and social status, not the phenomenon of ordinary misuse of words. Improper use of words in ordinary situations is an issue in the categories of grammar and rhetoric, while the improper use of words concerning rites and social status is an ethical and political issue.' Yang Bojun, *Lun yu yizhu*, 142.
8 Cheng Zhongying, *Zhongguo zhexue yu Zhongguo wenhua*, 75.
9 From Legge's nineteenth-century version to Roger Ames's recent 'philosophical' rendering, the Confucian *ming* has always been translated as 'names.' See, Legge, *The Chinese Classics*, 1:263; Lau, *The Analects*, 118; Hinton, *The Analects*, 139; Leys, *The Analects of Confucius*, 60; Ames, *The Analects of Confucius*, 162. Waley was the only translator who rendered *ming* as 'language.' At the same time, however, Waley argued that the concept of *zheng ming* was not articulated by Confucius himself but rather invented in later ages, on the grounds that no historical evidence was found to support the conjecture that Confucius was troubled by a 'language crisis.' In other words, Waley fell into the trap of his own fundamentalist paradox. Thus, according to him, *ming* for Confucius would not mean 'language'; and if *ming* must be construed as 'language' in general, it should not be taken as an authentic Confucian concept. See Waley, *The Analects of Confucius*, 22, 171.
10 Pauthier, *Confucius et Mencius*, 53.
11 Legge, *The Chinese Classics*, 1:358. Chan, *A Source Book in Chinese Philosophy*, 86.
12 *Zhou yi*, in Wu Shuping et al., *Shisan jing*, 2. Cary Baynes's version of the complete statement reads: 'The Master said: "The superior man improves his character and labors at his task. It is through loyalty and faith that he fosters his character. By working on his words, so that they rest firmly on truth, he makes his work enduring."' Baynes, *The I Ching or Book of Changes*, 13.
13 Zhang Dainian, *Key Concepts in Chinese Philosophy*, 140.
14 Hall and Ames, *Thinking through Confucius*, 58.
15 It is useful to make a brief distinction between Pound's pursuit of precise

language and the advocacy of precision in artistic representations maintained by some of his contemporaries. The term 'precision' seems to have had a special appeal to poets and artists in the early twentieth century. Marianne Moore, for instance, in the poem 'Bowl,' explicitly identifies herself as a 'precisionist': 'I learn that we are precisionists, / not citizens of Pompeii arrested in action / as a cross-section of one's correspondence would seem to imply.' *The Complete Poems of Marianne Moore*, 59. However, the term 'precisionism' is mainly associated with a group of American artists in the 1920s, also known as the New Classicists and the Immaculates. The leader of this group was Charles Demuth and its practitioners included Georgia O'Keeffe and Charles Sheoler. These artists shared a similar interest in painting cityscape and in attempting to capture the spirit of modernity by a sort of cubist realism. Pound was not connected with this group, nor did he share their interests.

16 Eliot, *Collected Poems*, 16.
17 There is no doubt that the crisis of language, as noted by Richard Sheppard in an article on this subject, is 'an aspect of a much wider socio-cultural problem' and in essence reflects the crisis of established social values (324–5). For a detailed analysis of this crisis, see Sheppard's 'The Crisis of Language.'
18 Herbert Schneidau has specifically linked Pound to the mysticism of G.R.S. Meed and Allen Upward: 'The tinge of mysticism in Pound's conception seemed to have something to do with certain people he met in London, notably, G.R.S. Mead and Allen Upward.' In his discussion, Schneidau makes a convincing case for Mead's and Upward's influence on Pound. See Schneidau, *Ezra Pound: The Image of the Real*, 118–27.
19 *The Poetry and Prose of William Blake*, ed. Geoffry Keynes (London and New York, 1939) 637. Cited in M.H. Abrams, *The Mirror and the Lamp*, 313.
20 T.E. Hulme, *Speculations* (London, 1936) 138. Cited in Abrams, *The Mirror and the Lamp*, 320. For a brilliant exploration of this topic, see Abrams's discussion of 'Poetic Truth and Sincerity' in *The Mirror and the Lamp*, 312–20. I am indebted to Abrams's study of representative theories of sincerity in the nineteenth century.
21 Pound, 'Pastiche. The Regional. VIII,' *Ezra Pound's Poetry and Prose*, 3:323.
22 Fenollosa, *The Chinese Written Character*, 12.
23 In his thorough study of Gourmont's influence on Pound, Richard Sieburth asserts that Pound had read Gourmont's *Le problème du style* in 1912, and that all the problems of language with which Pound came to be concerned were raised in Gourmont's work. See his *Instigations: Ezra Pound and Remy de Gourmont*, 95, 102.
24 Gourmont, *Remy de Gourmont: Selected Writings*, 16.

25 Pound presented *ABC of Reading* as a showcase of 'great literature' or 'good writers.' For him, while 'great literature is simply language charged with meaning to the utmost possible degree' (28), 'good writers are those who keep the language efficient. That is to say, keep it accurate, keep it clear' (32).
26 I certainly do not mean that Confucianism was the sole driving force behind this shift of emphasis in Pound's orientation. His reading of political and economic works by other writers, classical and modern, also contributed to this change. But to discuss their relevance is beyond the scope of my discussion. Regardless, in so far as Pound's theory of language is concerned, Confucian doctrines were doubtless the dominant influence at this time in his career.
27 Eliot, *On Poetry and Poets*, 20.
28 Brooks, 'Irony as a Principle of Structure,' 738. The idea of the poet as a language keeper does not just remain a theoretical speculation. Brooks's argument in this essay, which is among the major documents of the New Criticism, is an example of how this theory can be employed to evaluate poetry and shape the direction of its development.
29 To further illustrate the impact of Pound's theory, I would like to mention Allen Tate's defence of his decision to vote in favour of awarding Pound the Bolligen Prize in 1949. Tate's argument basically echoed Pound's assumptions about the modern poet's social duty: 'The specific task of the man of letters is to attend the health of society *not at large* but through literature – that is, he must be constantly aware of the condition of language in his age. As a result of observing Pound's use of language in the past thirty years I have become convinced that he had done more than any men to regenerate the language, if not the imaginative form, of English verse.' Consequently, Tate believed, whatever political prejudice Pound had expressed in his poetry, he still 'had performed an indispensable duty to society.' Tate, *The Man of Letters in the Modern World*, 266, 267.
30 Pound, *Selected Poems*, 98.
31 According to Chen Chun (1159–1223), it was the neo-Confucian masters, in particular Cheng Yi (1033–1107) and Zhu Xi, who rescued the concept from the moralistic interpretations of previous exegetes. See Chen Chun, *Neo-Confucian Terms Explained*, 97.
32 Ibid.
33 Chan, *A Source Book in Chinese Philosophy*, 96.
34 Tu Wei-ming, *Centrality and Commonality*, 73.
35 Terrell, *A Companion to the Cantos of Ezra Pound*, 2:365.
36 In classical Chinese philosophy, there is not a concept corresponding to the

notion of 'nature' that is so frequently used in modern Western philosophy. Chinese philosophers in the twentieth century tend to consider the concept of nature identical with the concept of heaven (*tian* 天) in classical Chinese philosophy. For instance, Tang Yijie, a major contemporary Confucian scholar in China, asserts that 'the dichotomy of "man" and "nature" is actually the dichotomy of "man" and "heaven" in ancient Chinese philosophy.' Tang Yijie, 'Cong Zhongguo chuantong zhexue de jiben mingti kan Zhongguo chuantong zhexue de tedian,' in *Lun Zhongguo chuantong wenhua*, ed. Li Zhonghua et al., 45.

37 Kenner has an illuminating discussion of the Emerson-Fenollosa-Pound relationship in regard to their notions of nature and language. See Kenner, *The Pound Era*, 157–62.

38 Legge's version reads: 'Mencius said, "All who speak about the natures of *things*, have in fact only their phenomena to *reason* from, and the value of a phenomenon is in its being natural."' *The Chinese Classics*, 2:331. Legge's dualistic view becomes clear in contrast to Wing-tsit Chan's rendering, which reads: 'Mencius said, "All who talk about the nature of things need only [reason from] facts [and principles will be clear]. The fundamental principle [of reasoning] from facts is to follow [their natural tendencies]." Chan, *A Source Book in Chinese Philosophy*, 76.

39 Robert Duncan, 'Beginnings: Chapter One of the H.D. Book,' 19.

40 Pound, 'Mr. Eliot's Mare's Nest,' *Ezra Pound's Poetry and Prose*, 6:141.

41 It was Michel Foucault who called attention to the connection between such an economics and classical linguistics. For his brilliant discussion of this subject, see *The Order of Things*, 166–214. Foucault's analysis focuses on the eighteenth-century physiocratic notions of economic values, which bear much resemblance to Pound's econo-linguistic orientation.

42 Speaking of this frightening situation, Eliot articulated a representative view: 'Among the varieties of chaos in which we find ourselves today, one is the chaos of language, in which there are no discoverable standards of writing.' Eliot, *On Poetry and Poets*, 192. Eliot's radical conservatism had much to do with a fear of the same 'chaos of language.'

43 Pound's long essay on Cavalcanti, from which I quote this passage, was published in 1934. It includes nine sections written over a long period of time dating back from 1931 to 1910. Judging from the fact that this passage is from the eighth section and emphasizes the notion of 'terminology,' I think the argument reflects Pound's concerns between the late 1920s and early 1930s.

44 In a recent study, Peter Makin divides Pound's preoccupation with the problem of language into two stages. The first stage witnessed Pound's practice of

Fenollosan 'ideogrammic writing,' a stage that unfortunately, according to Makin, discontinued before the mid-1930s. The second stage, which started in the mid-1930s, saw Pound's pursuit of an authoritarian theory of precise language resulting from his fascination with the Confucian *zheng ming*, or 'right naming' as Makin calls it. Although Makin thinks that Pound misread Confucius, he obviously still attributes Pound's pursuit in the second stage to a Confucian influence, for in his view Pound's formulations from that stage are 'un-Poundian, an aberration.' Makin, 'Ideogram, "Right Naming," and the Authoritarian Streak,' in Zhaoming Qian, *Ezra Pound and China*, 120.

45 For instance, Robert Duncan, who often championed Pound as a pioneer, expressed his disappointment with Pound's loss of the 'romantic spirit' to an authoritarian poetics. Duncan thought that such a change in Pound occurred in the 1930s when 'the ideogram which presented in configuration the inner response of the man became the ideogram of a proper sovereignty. Ideas in action became *idées fixes* acting upon a recalcitrant world.' Duncan, 'From the H.D. Book, Part II, Chapter 5,' 44.

46 Kenner, *The Pound Era*, 13. Kenner's report might not be accurate. It is the second character *da* 達 (reach), instead of the first one, that contains the ideographic components out of which Pound derived the three ideas of 'sheep,' 'go,' and 'earth.'

47 Nicholls, *Ezra Pound: Politics, Economics and Writing*, 95–7.

48 See Terrell, *A Companion to the Cantos of Ezra Pound*, 2:485.

Chapter 3: Confucianism and Pound's Political Polemic

1 Bernstein, *The Tale of the Tribe*, 56.
2 Hall, 'Interview with Ezra Pound,' 53, 54, 57.
3 Legge, *The Chinese Classics*, 1:250.
4 'Avoir un empire absolu sur soi-même, retourner aux rites [ou aux lois primitives de la raison céleste manifestée dans les sages coutumes], c'est pratiquer la vertu de l'humanité. Qu'un seul jour un homme dompte ses penchants et ses desirs déréglés, et qu'il retourne à la pratique des lois primitives, tout l'empire s'accordera à dire qu'il a la vertu de l'humanité. Mais la vertu de l'humanité depend-elle de soi-même, ou bien depend-elle des autres hommes?' Pauthier, *Confucius et Mencius*, 178.
5 'Virtue is the denial of self and response to what is right and proper. Deny yourself for one day and respond to the right and proper, and everybody will accord you virtuous. For has virtue its source in oneself, or is it forsooth derived from others?' Soothill, *The Analects or the Conversations of Confucius*, 115.

6 '"He who can himself submit to ritual is Good." If (a ruler) could for one day "himself submit to ritual," everyone under Heaven would respond to his Goodness. For Goodness is something that must have its source in the ruler himself; it cannot be got from others.' Waley, *The Analects of Confucius*, 162.
7 Chan, *A Source Book in Chinese Philosophy*, 38. According to Chan's note to his rendering on the same page, he uses the word 'master' in Zhu Xi's sense of conquering the self as 'an embodiment of self desires.'
8 'To return to the observance of the rites through overcoming the self constitutes benevolence. If for a single day a man could return to the observance of the rites through overcoming himself, then the whole Empire would consider benevolence to be his. However, the practice of benevolence depends on oneself alone and not on others.' Lau, *The Analects*, 112.
9 'Through self-discipline and observing ritual propriety (*li* 禮) one becomes authoritative in one's conduct. If for the space of a day one were able to accomplish this, the whole empire would defer to his authoritative model. Becoming authoritative in one's conduct is self-originating – how could it originate with others.' Ames, *The Analects of Confucius*, 152.
10 See Feng Youlan, *Zhongguo zhexue shi xinbian*, 1:139.
11 In Liu Baonan, *Lun yu zhengyi*, 483.
12 In Feng Youlan, *Zhongguo zhexue shi xinbian*, 1:139.
13 Zhu Xi, *Zhong yong*, in *Si shu jizhu*, 77.
14 De Bary, *Learning for One's Self*, 203. In this work de Bary argues that there existed a Chinese tradition of liberalism, which was sustained primarily by the Wang Yangming school of neo-Confucian philosophy and flourished during the Ming dynasty.
15 Li Zhi, *Fen shu xu fen shu*, 16.
16 Ibid., 101.
17 Ibid., 258.
18 Fang Yizhi, *Yiguan wen da*. Cited in Xu Sumin et al., *Ming Qing qimeng xueshu liubian*, 169.
19 It is interesting to note that although Confucian scholars in modern China have sought to revitalize Confucianism by reinterpreting its basic doctrines, they still follow Zhu Xi's interpretation of the *ke ji fu li* doctrine. The only major twentieth-century New Confucian scholar to give this doctrine a different reading is Qian Mu. According to Qian Mu's explanation, 'in [the phrase of] *ke ji*, *ke* means "competent" and "make competent." *Ke ji* thus means to empower the self, that is, to enable the self to do its own job.' Qian Mu, *Lun yu yaolue*, 80.
20 Tu Wei-ming, *Humanity and Self-Cultivation*, 6.
21 Tu Wei-ming, 'Rujia zhexue yu xiandaihua,' 101.

22 De Bary, *Learning for One's Self*, 23.
23 Tu Wei-ming, *Humanity and Self-Cultivation*, 6.
24 Wolfe, *The Limits of American Literary Ideology*. For Levenson's analysis, see especially the chapter on 'Egoists and Imagists,' *A Genealogy of Modernism*, 64–79.
25 Pound received such an opinion from the Swiss historian Jacob Burckhardt. He was familiar with Burckhardt's monumental work *The Civilization of the Renaissance in Italy* (1860) and made several references to Burckhardt (*SP*, 22, 201).
26 Pound, 'The Words of Ming Mao "Least among the Disciples of Kung-Fu-Tse,"' *Ezra Pound's Poetry and Prose*, 1:320.
27 During the first half of the twentieth century, when Confucianism was seriously discredited in China, it was hardly conceivable to defend it from a liberal perspective. Even for such a die-hard Confucian believer as Liang Shuming, the 'last Confucian' in China according to Guy Alitto, Confucianism was fatally flawed because of its neglect of the individual. Liang made this point consistently in his works from the 1920s to the 1940s. For instance, in *Zhongguo wenhua yaoyi*, he deplores: 'Western society which is based on the individual is alive to the concept of rights. In contrast, in China, which is dominated by the sense of responsibility, the individual has almost no place at all. ... The greatest deficiency of Chinese culture is the perpetual absence of the individual.' *Liang Shuming ji*, 342.
28 In his rendering of the Confucian passage in this 'Imaginary Letter,' Pound put the speakers in a wrong order. According to his version, the first one to answer the master's question is Zi Lu, the second is Zeng Xi, Ran Qiu comes next, and the last speaker is Gongxi Hua. He corrected the mistake in canto XIII and in his later translation of this passage as well (*Con*, 242).
29 Carroll Terrell has identified Pound's source in Pauthier's translation of *Lun yu* 1.1; this term in Pauthier's rendering is 'la déférence fraternelle.' See Terrell, *A Companion to the Cantos of Ezra Pound*, 1:63. However, in my view, Pound's term of 'fraternal deference' must have been informed by more than a single passage, since *ti*, a major Confucian concept, is elaborated frequently in all Confucian works.
30 Legge, *The Chinese Classics*, 1:139.
31 Gourmont, 'A French View of Nietzsche,' *New Age* 13, 2 (10 July 1913): 301. Cited in Levenson, *A Genealogy of Modernism*, 67.
32 Cited in Lukes, *Individualism*, 68.
33 For instance, Pound attacks Galsworthy in *Patria Mia*: 'The essence of Fabianism, Webbianism and all the patent brands of sociology now on the infant market would seem to be that every man, and especially John Galsworthy,

should look after everybody else's affairs' (41). Also: 'Shaw, being notably of his period, with his assertion of man's inferiority to an idea, [is] all part of one masochistic curse' (*SP,* 210).

34 Pound, 'Pastiche. The Regional. XV,' *Ezra Pound's Poetry and Prose,* 3:345.
35 Pound, 'The New Sculpture,' *Ezra Pound's Poetry and Prose,* 1:222.
36 Let me cite Waley's compelling translation of the original passage to illustrate my point. After the four disciples have presented their ideas: 'The Master heaved a deep sigh and said, I am with Tien [Dian]. When the three others went away, Tsêng Hsi [Zeng Xi] remained behind and said, What about the sayings of those three people? The Master said, After all, it was agreed that each should tell his wish; and that is just what they did. Tsêng said, Why did you smile at Yu [Zi Lu]? The Master said, "Because it is upon observance of ritual that the governance of a State depends; and his words were lacking in the virtue of cession. That is why I smiled at him."' Waley, *The Analects of Confucius,* 160–1.
37 Confucius's remarks on Nan Rong appear in *Lun yu* 5.2. What Confucius means is that Nan Rong is such a capable man that he will be given the opportunity to use his talents when order prevails and will not suffer punishment when chaos disrupts society.
38 Pound is alluding to a passage in *Lun yu* 13.18, in which Confucius remarks that in his hometown straightforward people tend to cover up for their family members, such as a father covering up for his son. The idea of a murderous son is Pound's own creation.
39 There is no doubt that any discussion of Pound's political position during the 1930s and early 1940s would hardly be valid without answering why Pound endorsed the Fascist regime in Italy. However, it should be recognized that Pound's support of Fascism is an enormously complicated topic, requiring an investigation that is beyond the scope of my discussion and would lead to unnecessary digression from my central concern. There have been a number of thoughtful studies on this topic and their conclusions may help us understand Pound's controversial position at that time. Generally, there are three kinds of explanation of Pound's attraction to Fascism. The first and also the dominant explanation is that Pound believed that the social and economic program of Fascist Italy was compatible with his economic vision and could solve the economic ills of the world (see Torrey, *The Roots of Treason,*137–8; Chace, *The Political Identities of Ezra Pound and T.S. Eliot,* 62–3; Wilhelm, *Ezra Pound: The Tragic Years,* 69–83; Surette, *A Light from Eleusis,* 177; Harrison, *The Reactionaries,*127). The second explanation is that Pound was fascinated by Mussolini's individual personality and his world outlook. This view is also adopted by most of those who hold the first explanation, but

there are some who specifically subscribe to this explanation, arguing that Pound perceived in the Duce the mixture of the ideal leader, true artist, and visionary prophet (Redman, *Ezra Pound and Italian Fascism*, 102), or that for Pound Mussolini embodied 'the apotheosis of the sign' signifying the clear 'origin' (Kuberski, *A Calculus of Ezra Pound*, 16). The last explanation, offered primarily by Casillo, insists that Pound's anti-Semitism played the decisive role in his pro-Fascist position (*The Genealogy of Demons*, 16).

40 Among many historical instances, perhaps the most familiar and compelling illustration of this ideological contradiction is the historical irony displayed in the American Revolution. When the founding fathers of America, most of them being the disciples of the Enlightenment philosophy of universal human rights, declared the birth of a nation in which it is decreed that all men are equal, this new nation had a large part of its population living under slavery, and its defenders were living in luxuries enabled by slave labour.

41 In a sense such a contradiction is captured by Adorno in his definition of the 'authoritarian personality.' According to this definition, an 'authoritarian type of man' is a combination of discrepancies: 'He is at the same time enlightened and superstitious, proud to be an individualist and in constant fear of not being like all the others, jealous of his independence and inclined to submit blindly to power and authority.' See T.W. Adorno et al., Preface, *The Authoritarian Personality*, ix.

42 The coexistence of conflicting positions in Pound has been noted by Pound scholars. For example, Casillo has observed: 'How can Pound simultaneously espouse the American (and indirectly the French) Revolution and Italian Fascism? These two movements seem categorically opposed in their liberalism and anti-liberalism, but Pound did not view them in this way. For Pound their affinity lies in their common populist forms of participatory democracy in combination with such authoritarian leaders as John Adams and especially Napoleon, whom Pound came increasingly to admire.' See *The Genealogy of Demons*, 135.

43 Pound's notion of 'totalitarian' has been a controversial subject. For a detailed analysis of his use of the term, see Matthew Little, 'Pound's Use of the Word *Totalitarian*.' While Little makes the argument that the primary meaning of Pound's term is philosophical rather than political, I use this term in its political sense.

44 The original is from *Lun yu* 6.28: '夫仁者，己欲立而立人，己欲达而达人.' Legge's translation reads: 'Now the man of perfect virtue, wishing to be established himself, seeks also to establish others; wishing to be enlarged himself, he seeks also to enlarge others.' *The Chinese Classics*, 1:194. Lau's translation is: 'Now, on the other hand, a benevolent man helps others to

218 Notes to pages 119-35

take their stand in so far as he himself wishes to take his stand, and gets others there in so far as he himself wishes to get there.' Lau, *The Analects*, 85.
45 As with the other three of the Four Books, in my reference to the original *Mengzi* (The Works of Mencius), I follow James Legge's textual division. The first arabic numeral refers to the book, the second the part, the third the chapter, and fourth the paragraph.
46 Legge, *The Chinese Classics*, 1:301. For an insightful discussion of the concept of 'reciprocity,' see Tu Wei-ming, *Centrality and Commonality*, 102–6.
47 For a representative expression of this argument, see Tu Wei-ming, 'Rujia chuantong de xiandai mingyun,' *Rujia chuantong de xiandai zhuanhua*, 234–77.
48 Tang Junyi, Mou Zongsan, Xu Fuguan and Zhang Junmai, 'Zhongguo wenhua yu shijie,' *Mingzhu pinglun*, January (1958), Hong Kong. Reprinted in Tang Junyi, *Wenhua yishi yuzhou de tansuo*, 360. This view is central to the major argument of this famous article, which has been generally seen as the manifesto of contemporary New Confucianism.
49 For Mou Zongsan's elaboration on this theory, see especially his 'Daode de lixiang zhuyi chuban xu,' *Mou Zongsan ji*, 84–8.
50 Mou Zongsan, *Lishi zhexue*, 192.
51 Mou Zongsan, *Daode lixiang zhuyi de chong jian*, 9.
52 Tu Wei-ming, *Centrality and Commonality*, 36.
53 Ibid., 35, 31.
54 Pound quotes directly from Legge's translation: 'Mencius said, "In the 'Spring and Autumn' there are no righteous wars."' Legge, *The Chinese Classics*, 2:478.
55 Angela Palandri, 'Homage to a Confucian Poet,' 305.
56 Legge, *The Chinese Classics*, 1:296.
57 Legge, *The Chinese Classics*, 2:453.
58 'The man who would be benevolent is like the archer. The archer adjusts himself and then shoots. If he misses, he does not murmur against those who surpass himself. He simply turns around and seeks *the cause of his failure* in himself.' Legge, *The Chinese Classics*, 2:205.
59 Peter Nicholls has made a thought-provoking analysis of the nature of Pound's self-examination in his *Ezra Pound: Politics, Economics and Writing*. See especially the section of 'The Power of Memory,' 170–81.
60 Legge, *The Chinese Classics*, 2:299.

Chapter 4: Confucianism and Pound's Spiritual Beliefs

1 Eliot, 'Isolated Superiority,' 6–7.
2 Ibid., 7.

3 Although Eliot began his lectures with the assertion that he sought to address the 're-establishment of a native culture' of America, his primary concerns throughout these lectures clearly focused on how to revitalize the Euro-American tradition as a whole. Eliot, *After Strange Gods*, 16.
4 Ibid., 41.
5 Ibid., 41.
6 Ibid., 42–3.
7 Pound's immediate counterattack appeared in his seven reviews of Eliot's book, published in the *New English Weekly* in 1934: 'Mr. Eliot's Mare's Nest,' 4.21 (8 March): 5; 'Mr. Eliot's Quandaries.' 4.24 (29 March): 558–9; the second 'Mr. Eliot's Quandaries,' 5.2 (26 April): 48; 'Mr. Eliot's Looseness,' 5.4 (10 May): 95–6; 'Ecclesiastical History,' 5.12 (5 July): 272–3; 'Mr. Eliot's Solid Merit,' 5.13 (12 July): 297–9; 'A Problem of (Specifically) Style,' 6.6 (22 November): 127–8. Kathryne Lindberg in her work has given a detailed, well-documented analysis of Pound's responses in these 'disorganized reviews.' See Lindberg, *Reading Pound Reading*, 100–25. Apart from these essays, Pound later revived this debate again and again, implicitly or explicitly, in his letters, prose (such as *Guide to Kulchur*), and poetry (such as *The Pisan Cantos*).
8 'Belief,' Pound stated in a discussion of religious conviction, 'is a cramp, a paralysis, an atrophy of the mind in certain positions' (*SP*, 49).
9 Pound, 'A Problem of (Specifically) Style,' *Ezra Pound's Poetry and Prose*, 6:215.
10 Pound, 'Mr. Eliot's Mare's Nest,' *Ezra Pound's Poetry and Prose*, 6:140.
11 Pound, 'Ecclesiastical History,' *Ezra Pound's Poetry and Prose*, 6:186.
12 Eliot, *After Strange Gods*, 42.
13 Pound, 'Letters on Rude Assignment,' 164.
14 For instance, Herbert Schneidau states: 'Polytheism, entailing respect for many forms of truth, became one of Pound's strongest commitments, and consequently he hated monotheistic religions for their coercive tendencies.' See his 'Ezra Pound: The Archaeology of the Immanent,' 220. William Cookson, editor of Pound's *Selected Prose*, also perceives the 'passion for liberty' in Pound's polytheism: 'His dislike of monotheistic religion is part of the same struggle against intolerance, monopoly and uniformity' (Introduction, *SP*, 9). Accusing Cookson of 'taking Pound's statements at face value,' Casillo asserts a totally different view. For Casillo, it is monotheism that embraces democracy by asserting the same absolute truth to all and thus eliminating inequality; therefore, Pound's polytheism is anti-democratic and harbours an 'intolerance of potentially universal religions.' *The Genealogy of Demons*, 129.

15 Pound saw the hierarchy in the 'grades and graduations' of the Dantesque or Catholic world undermined by the Protestants: 'The puritan is a pervert, the whole of his sense of mental corruption is squirted down a single groove of sex. The scale and proportion of evil, as delimited in Dante's hell (or the catholic hell) was obliterated by the Calvinist and Lutheran churches. I don't mean to say that these heretics cut off their ideas of damnation all at once, suddenly or consciously, I mean that the effect of Protestantism has been semiticly to obliterate values, to efface grades and graduations' (*GK,* 185). In 'The Jefferson-Adams Letters,' Pound again brings up this 'system of graduations, an hierarchy of values,' emphasizing its importance based on his regard for this system as one from which a sense of 'order' derives and wherein the 'Mediterranean state of mind, state of intelligence' resides (*SP,* 150).
16 Cited in Stock, *The Life of Ezra Pound,* 397.
17 Of course, we should not let Pound's accusation conceal the fact that in actuality Eliot was also prejudiced against the Jews. Even in the book for which Pound accused Eliot of being 'contaminated' by 'Jewish poison,' when addressing the issue of constructing a national culture of America Eliot emphatically upheld the notion of cultural and racial purity: 'The population should be homogeneous; where two or more cultures exist in the same place they are likely either to be fiercely self-conscious or both to become adulterate. What is still more important is unity of religious background; and reasons of race and religion combine to make any large number of free-thinking Jews undesirable.' Eliot, *After Strange Gods,* 28.
18 Pound's view of the 'true' origin of Christianity has long attracted critical attention. Clark Emery, for example, not only noticed Pound's assertion of paganism as the origin of Christianity but also pointed out the influence of Thaddeus Zielinski on Pound in this regard. He noted that Zielinski's work on Catholicism, *La Sibylle,* which Pound 'favored,' tries to prove that Catholicism 'derives, not from Judaism but from paganism, not from the waste of Asia Minor but from the Mediterranean basin. ... That is to say, the true Old Testament was pagan teaching rather than Mosaic. The implication of this position is that when Christian theologians turned from pagan teaching to Judaic, from Ovid and Hesoid to Moses and David, they falsified their true faith. It was Zielinski's hope to open his readers' eyes to that falsification. It is equally Pound's.' Emery, *Ideas into Action,* 9. For a more detailed analysis of Zielinski's impact on Pound, also see Casillo, *The Genealogy of Demons,* 70–5.
19 Tu Wei-ming, *Rujia chuantong de xiandai zhuanhua,* 4.
20 Pound, 'A Problem of (Specifically) Style,' *Ezra Pound's Poetry and Prose,* 6:215.

21 Kenner, *The Pound Era*, 231.
22 Zhu Xi, *Zhong yong*, in *Si shu jizhu*, 1.
23 Legge, *The Chinese Classics*, 2:395–6.
24 Besides Pound's transliteration, the Chinese character of *duan* appears in cantos LXXXV (565), LXXXVI (581), LXXXIX (621), and CIX (792).
25 Legge, *The Chinese Classics*, 2:476.
26 Ibid., 294.
27 Terrell, *A Companion to the Cantos of Ezra Pound*, 2:365. Terrell also cites Achilles Fang's frustration in the same note. Fang claimed that Pound's visual deciphering of the original passage 'cannot be reconciled with the Chinese language.'
28 See Pound, *Ezra Pound Speaking*, 109.
29 See Terrell, *A Companion to the Cantos of Ezra Pound*, 2:505.
30 Legge, *The Chinese Classics*, 2:189.
31 Legge's version provides a better clue to the original: 'This is the passion nature: – It is exceedingly great, and exceedingly strong. Being nourished by rectitude, and sustaining no injury, it fills up all between heaven and earth. This is the passion nature: – It is the mate and assistant of righteousness and reason. Without it, *man* is in a state of starvation.' *The Chinese Classics*, 2:190.
32 Achilles Fang, for instance, challenges the credibility of Pound's poetic version of this passage in his careful inspection of Pound's misreading of Chinese characters. He ends his analysis with this remark: 'All this is fantastic.' Fang, 'Materials for the Studies of Pound's "Cantos."' 4:121.
33 This idea derives form Pound's etymographic reading of the Chinese character 配 (*pei*, 'mate'). According to Achilles Fang, in Pound's rendering, 'the left part of the *pei* ideogram is identified with 酒 *chiu* ['wine' or 'liquor,'] hence Pound's "boon," but 酉 *you* is only a sound-giving element in *chiu*; the whole *pei* ideogram is then translated as "companion," so we have "boon companion."' See Fang, 'Materials for the Studies of Pound's "Cantos,"' 4:121.
34 Legge, *The Chinese Classics*, 1:397; Chan, *A Source Book in Chinese Philosophy*,102.
35 Feng Yu, *Tian yu ren – Zhongguo lishi shang de tian ren guanxi*, 25–6.
36 For an informative discussion of the interpretive history of *tian* by Western sinologists, see Hall and Ames, *Thinking through Confucius*, 201–8; also see Eno, *The Confucian Creation of Heaven*,181–9.
37 The following translations of *Tian* or heaven by Legge, from *The Chinese Classics*, vol. 1, can give us a vivid sense of the multifacetedness of this term: 'Wherein I have done improperly, may Heaven reject me! May Heaven reject me!' (193); 'Heaven produced the virtue that is in me' (202). 'Great indeed

was Yao as a sovereign! How majestic was he! It is only Heaven that is grand, and only Yao corresponded to it' (214). 'If Heaven had wished to let this cause of truth perish, then I, a future mortal, should not have got such a relation to that cause' (218). 'Does Heaven speak? The four seasons pursue their courses, and all things are *continually* being produced, *but* does Heaven say anything?' (326). 'Our Master cannot be attained to, just in the same way as the heavens cannot be gone up to by the steps of a stair' (348). 'Thus it is that Heaven, in the production of things, is bountiful to them, according to their qualities' (399).

38 For a detailed analysis of de Mailla's influence on Pound in this regard, see Nolde, *Blossoms from the East*, 36–45.
39 Yao preceded Shun on the throne while Yu succeeded Shun. Pound's mistake in confusing Yu with Yao in this allusion has been noted by Achilles Fang. See 'Materials for the Studies of Pound's "Cantos,"' 1:93.
40 Surette, *Pound in Purgatory*, 74.
41 Pauthier, *Confucius et Mencius*, 69.
42 See Hall and Ames, *Thinking through Confucius*, 232–7.
43 This is my translation. The original quotation is in French: 'La lumière est une substance corporelle très subtile et qui se rapproche de l'incorporel. Ses propriétés caractéristiques sont de s'engendrer ellemême perpetuellement et de se diffuser sphériquement autour d'un point d'une manière instantanée. ... Cette substance extremement ténue est aussie l'étoffe dont toutes choses sont faites; elle est la première forme corporelle et ce que certains nomment la corporété' (*LE*, 160).
44 Pound, 'Ta Hio,' *Ezra Pound's Poetry and Prose*, 8:149.
45 See Thomas Grieve, 'Annotations to the Chinese in *Section: Rock-Drill*,' 464.
46 Legge, *The Chinese Classics*, 3:577.
47 Thomas Grieve, in his well-researched study of Pound's Chinese sources of this canto, nonetheless fails to see what Pound found, that is, the meaning of 'completing' shared by *ji* 既 and *jin* 盡, which allowed Pound to connect *ji xin* 既心 with *jin xin* 盡心 . Thus Grieve notes: 'I have not been able to discover any special import attached to this character, chi 既, in the writings of Mencius (Mang-tsze), the ethical philosopher of the 4th century B.C.' Grieve, 'Annotations to the Chinese in *Section: Rock-Drill*,' 466n1.

Conclusion

1 Pound, *Selected Poems*, 98.
2 Pound, 'Patria Mia VI,' *Ezra Pound's Poetry and Prose*, 1:101.
3 Bullock places Pound in the tradition of an ancient mysticism represented by

Yeats in modern times: 'Great poet though he was, W.B. Yeats (1865–1939), for example, looked to a quite different, mystical-archaic-heroic, tradition which distrusted reason and felt the same aversion to a modern world born out of the Enlightenment as T.S. Eliot, Ezra Pound and Paul Claudel.' Bullock, *The Humanist Tradition in the West*, 153.
4 Heath-Stubbs, 'The Last Humanist,' in Russell, *An Examination of Ezra Pound*, 254.
5 For a succinct and well-documented introduction to these modern offshoots of Western humanism, see Vito R. Giustiniani, 'Homo, Humanus, and the Meanings of "Humanism."'
6 Pound, 'The New Sculpture,' *Ezra Pound's Poetry and Prose*, 1:221.
7 Ricci, *China in the Sixteenth Century*, 33, 335.
8 Ibid., 98.
9 Leibniz, *Writings on China*, 79.
10 Mungello, *Leibniz and Confucianism*, x.
11 Voltaire, *A Philosophical Dictionary*, in *The Works of Voltaire*, 4:81, 82.
12 Quesnay, *Oeuvres économiques et philosophiques*, 646.
13 Hegel, *Lectures on the History of Philosophy*, 1:121.
14 Hegel, *Lectures on the Philosophy of Religion*, 2:547.
15 Weber, *The Religion of China*, 240.
16 Ibid., 227.
17 Ibid., 228.
18 Pound is referring to the remarks Voltaire makes in *Ancient and Modern History*: 'He [Confucius] does not pretend to inspiration, or the gift of prophecy. He places all his merit in a constant endeavor to gain the mastery over his passions, and he writes only as a philosopher: accordingly, the Chinese consider him only as a philosopher.' *The Works of Voltaire*, vol. 15, part 2, 173.
19 Pound, 'Confucius' Formula Up-to-Date,' *Ezra Pound's Poetry and Prose*, 7:18.
20 Pound received the notion that ideas need to be constantly renewed from *Da xue*. He first translated this notion as 'renovate' (*TH*, 12), then as 'As the sun makes it new / Day by day make it new / Yet again make it new' (*Con*, 36). Besides entitling his 1934 collection of essays *Make It New*, Pound frequently utilized this notion in his prose, such as *Jefferson and/or Mussolini* (112–13) and *Guide to Kulchur* (278), as well as *The Cantos* (LIII/265, XCIII/649, XCIV/662).
21 The most recent example of this trend in North America is a group of academicians who call themselves 'Boston Confucians.' Their shared endeavour to shape their 'personal and social lives by Confucian standards' (xxv) is articulated by Robert Cummings Neville in his new book *Boston Confucianism: Portable Tradition in the Late-Modern World*. In mainland China, the continued

interest in reevaluating Confucianism recently culminated in a heated debate on Confucianism as a religion and its historical functions, caused by the publication in 1999 and 2000 of Li Shen's two-volume study of this subject, *Zhongguo rujiao shi* (The History of the Confucian Religion in China). Conducted both on the traditional platform of journal publications and on the Internet, the debate has involved many Chinese philosophers and historians.

22 Since its introduction by Tu Wei-ming, this term has become familiar to students of Confucianism and Chinese intellectual history. For a summary of Tu's vision, see especially the two essays: 'Towards a Third Epoch of Confucian Humanism,' in his *Way, Learning, and Politics*, 141–59; 'Ruxue di san qi fazhan de qianjing wenti,' in his *Rujia chuantong de xiandai zhuanhua*, 234–77.

23 Tu Wei-ming, *Rujia chuantong de xiandai zhuanhua*, 65.

Bibliography

Abrams, M.H. *The Mirror and the Lamp.* New York: Oxford University Press, 1953.
Adorno, T.W., et al. *The Authoritarian Personality.* New York: Harper and Row, 1950.
Alitto, Guy. *The Last Confucian: Liang Shu-ming and the Chinese Dilemma of Modernity.* Berkeley: University of California Press, 1979.
Ames, Roger T., and Henry Rosemont, Jr, trans. *The Analects of Confucius: A Philosophical Translation.* New York: Ballantine Books, 1998.
Arendt, Hannah. *The Origins of Totalitarianism.* New York: Harcourt, Brace and World, 1966.
Arnold, Matthew. *Matthew Arnold on the Classical Tradition.* Edited by R.H. Super. Ann Arbor: University of Michigan Press, 1960.
Babbitt, Irving. *Rousseau and Romanticism.* New York: Meridian Books, 1955.
Bacon, Francis. *The Advancement of Learning and the New Atlantis.* Edited by Arthur Johnson. Book 2, XVI. 2. Oxford: Clarendon Press, 1974.
Baynes, Cary F, trans. *The I Ching or Book of Changes.* New York: Pantheon Books, 1950.
Benjamin, Walter. 'The Task of the Translator.' *Illuminations.* Edited by Hannah Arendt. New York: Schocken Books, 1969. 69–82.
Bernstein, Michael Andre. *The Tale of the Tribe: Ezra Pound and the Modern Verse Epic.* Princeton: Princeton University Press, 1980.
Bilenchi, Romano. 'Rapallo 1941.' *Paideuma* 8.3 (1979): 431–42.
Bloom, Harold. *The Anxiety of Influence: A Theory of Poetry.* 2nd ed. New York: Oxford University Press, 1997.
Brooks, Cleanth. 'Irony as a Principle of Structure.' *Literary Opinion in America.* Edited by Morton Dauwen Zabel. New York: Harper Torchbooks, 1962. 728–41.
Bullock, Alan. *The Humanist Tradition in the West.* London: Thames and Hudson, 1985.

Bush, Ronald. *The Genesis of Ezra Pound's Cantos*. Princeton: Princeton University Press, 1976.
Carpenter, Humphrey. *A Serious Character: The Life of Ezra Pound*. London: Faber and Faber, 1988.
Casillo, Robert. *The Genealogy of Demons: Anti-Semitism, Fascism, and the Myths of Ezra Pound*. Evanston: Northwestern University Press, 1988.
Chace, William. *The Political Identities of Ezra Pound and T.S. Eliot*. Stanford: Stanford University Press, 1973.
Chan, Wing-tsit. Review of *The Great Digest, The Unwobbling Pivot*, by Ezra Pound. *Philosophy East and West* 3.4 (1954): 371–3.
– *A Source Book in Chinese Philosophy*. Princeton: Princeton University Press, 1963.
Chang, Yao-xin [Yao-hsin]. 'Pound's Cantos and Confucianism.' *Ezra Pound: The Legacy of Kulchur*. Edited by Marcel Smith and William A. Ulmer. Tuscaloosa and London: University of Alabama Press, 1988. 86–112.
– 'Pound's Chinese Translations.' *Paideuma* 17.1 (1988): 113–32.
Cheadle, Mary Paterson. 'Ezra Pound's Confucian Translations.' Ph.D. dissertation, University of California, Berkeley, 1987.
– *Ezra Pound's Confucian Translations*. Ann Arbor: University of Michigan Press, 1997.
Chen Chun 陳淳. *Neo-Confucian Terms Explained*. Translated by Wing-tsit Chan. New York: Columbia University Press, 1986.
Cheng Zhongying [Cheng Chung-ying] 成中英. *Zhongguo zhexue yu Zhongguo wenhua* 中國哲學與中國文化. Taipei: Sanmin shuju, 1974.
Ching, Julia. *Confucianism and Christianity*. Tokyo, New York, and San Francisco: Kodansha International, 1977.
Couplet, Philippe, et al., trans. *Confucius Sinarum Philosophus, Sive Scientia Sinensis*. Paris: Horthemels, 1687.
Dasenbrock, Reed Way. *The Literary Vorticism of Ezra Pound and Wyndham Lewis*. Baltimore: Johns Hopkins University Press, 1985.
Davie, Donald. *Ezra Pound*. New York: Viking, 1975.
– *Studies in Ezra Pound*. Manchester: Carcanet Press, 1991.
de Bary, Wm. Theodore. *Learning for One's Self*. New York: Columbia University Press, 1991.
– *The Liberal Tradition in China*. New York: Columbia University Press, 1983.
Dembo, L.S. *The Confucian Odes of Ezra Pound*. Berkeley and Los Angeles: University of California Press, 1963.
Dryden, John. *The Works of John Dryden*. Edited by Alan Roper. Vol. 20. Berkeley and Los Angeles: University of California Press, 1989.
Duncan, Robert. 'Beginnings: Chapter One of the H.D. Book.' *Coyote's Journal* 5/6 (1966): 8–31.

- 'From the H.D. Book, Part II, Chapter 5.' *Sagetrieb* 4.2–3 (1985): 39–86.
Eliot, T.S. *After Strange Gods: A Primer of Modern Heresy.* London: Faber and Faber, 1934.
- *Collected Poems.* London: Faber and Faber, 1980.
- 'Isolated Superiority.' *Dial* 84 (January 1928): 4–7.
- *On Poetry and Poets.* London: Faber and Faber, 1957.
- *Selected Essays.* London: Faber and Faber, 1932.
Emery, Clark. *Ideas into Action: A Study of Pound's Cantos.* Coral Gables, Florida: University of Miami Press, 1969.
Eno, Robert. *The Confucian Creation of Heaven.* Albany: State University of New York Press, 1990.
Eoyang, Eugene. 'The Confucian Odes.' *Paideuma* 3.1 (1974): 33–42.
Fang, Achilles. 'Fenollosa and Pound.' *Harvard Journal of Asiatic Studies* 20.1 and 2 (1957): 213–38.
- 'Materials for the Studies of Pound's "Cantos."' Ph.D. dissertation, Harvard University, 1958.
- 'Metaphysics and Money-Making.' *New Mexico Quarterly* 23.1 (1953): 91–4.
Fang Tianli 方天立, and Xue Jundu 薛君度. *Ruxue yu Zhongguo wenhua xiandaihua* 儒學與中國文化現代化. Beijing: Zhongguo renmin daxue chubanshe, 1998.
Feng Youlan [Fung Yu-lan] 馮友蘭. *Zhongguo zhexue shi xinbian* 中國哲學史新編. Vol. 1. Beijing: Renmin chubanshe, 1964.
- *A History of Chinese Philosophy.* 2 vols. Princeton: Princeton University Press, 1952–3.
Feng Yu 馮禹. *Tian yu ren – Zhongguo lishi shang de tian ren guanxi* 天與人 - 中國歷史上的天人關係. Chongqing: Chongqing chubanshe, 1990.
Fenollosa, Ernest. *The Chinese Written Character as a Medium for Poetry.* Edited by Ezra Pound. 1936. San Francisco: City Lights Books, 1969.
Fingarette, Herbert. *Confucius – the Secular as Sacred.* New York: Harper Torchbooks, 1972.
Flory, Wendy Stallard. *The American Ezra Pound.* New Haven: Yale University Press, 1989.
Foucault, Michel. *The Order of Things: An Archaeology of the Human Sciences.* New York: Vantage, 1970.
Freind, Bill. 'Why Do You Want to Put Your Ideas in Order?' *Journal of Modern Literature* 23.3–4 (2000): 545–63.
Gallup, Donald. *Ezra Pound: A Bibliography.* Charlottesville: University Press of Virginia, 1983.
Gardner, Daniel K. *Chu Hsi and the Ta-hsueh.* Cambridge and London: Harvard University Press, 1986.

Gefin, Laszlo. *Ideogram, History of a Poetic Method.* Austin: University of Texas Press, 1982.
Giustiniani, Vito R. 'Homo, Humanus, and the Meanings of "Humanism."' *Journal of the History of Ideas* 46.2 (1985): 167–95.
Gordon, David. 'And Moore: Marianne on Ezra's Confucius.' *Paideuma* 18.3 (1989): 149–50.
– '"Confucius, Philosophe": An Introduction to the *Chinese Cantos 52–61*.' *Paideuma* 5.3 (1976): 387–403.
Gourmont, Remy de. *Remy de Gourmont: Selected Writings.* Translated by Glenn S. Burne. Ann Arbor: University of Michigan Press, 1966.
Grieve, Thomas. 'Annotations to the Chinese in *Section: Rock-Drill.*' *Paideuma* 4.2 and 3 (1975): 361–508.
Habermas, Jürgen. *The Philosophical Discourse of Modernity.* Translated by Frederick Lawrence. Cambridge: MIT Press, 1987.
Hall, David, and Roger Ames. *Thinking through Confucius.* Albany: State University of New York Press, 1987.
Hall, Donald. 'Interview with Ezra Pound.' *Writers at Work: The Paris Review Interview (Second Series).* Edited by Van Wyck Brooks. New York: Viking Press, 1963. 35–59.
Han Ying. *Han shih wai chuan: Han Ying's Illustrations of the Didactic Application of the Classic of Songs.* Translated by James R. Hightower. Cambridge: Harvard University Press, 1952.
Hare, William Loftus. 'Chinese Egoism.' *Egoist* 1.23 (1 December 1914): 439–42.
Harrison, John R. *The Reactionaries.* New York: Schocken Books, 1967.
Heath-Stubbs, John. 'The Last Humanist.' *An Examination of Ezra Pound: A Collection of Essays.* Edited by Peter Russell. 1950. New York: Gordian Press, 1973. 249–56.
Hegel, Georg Wilhelm Friedrich. *Lectures on the History of Philosophy.* 3 vols. 1955. London: Routledge and Kegan Paul, 1974.
– *Lectures on the Philosophy of Religion.* Edited by Peter C. Hodgson. 3 vols. Berkeley: University of California Press, 1987.
Heidegger, Martin. *On the Way to Language.* Translated by Peter Hertz. New York: Harper and Row, 1971.
Hesse, Eva, ed. *New Approaches to Ezra Pound.* Berkeley and Los Angeles: University of California Press, 1969.
Hinton, David, trans. *Mencius.* Washington, DC: Counterpoint, 1998.
— *The Analects.* Washington, DC: Counterpoint, 1998.
Irwin, John. *American Hieroglyphics.* New Haven: Yale University Press, 1980.
Jackson, Thomas H. *The Early Poetry of Ezra Pound.* Cambridge: Harvard University Press, 1968.

James, William. *The Will to Believe.* New York: Dover, 1956.
Jensen, Lionel M. *Manufacturing Confucianism: Chinese Traditions and Universal Civilization.* Durham and London: Duke University Press, 1997.
Jin, Songping. 'Observation of Natural Scenes: *Ta Hsueh* and Pound's Later Cantos.' *Paideuma* 23.2–3 (1994): 7–44.
Jung, Hwa Yol. 'Misreading the Ideogram: From Fenollosa to Derrida and McLuhan.' *Paideuma* 13.2 (1984): 211–27.
Kelly, Alan Lawrence. 'Confucianism and the Meaning of *The Cantos* of Ezra Pound.' Ph.D. dissertation, Indiana University, Bloomington, 1986.
Kenner, Hugh. 'Ezra Pound and Chinese.' *Agenda* 4.2 (1965): 38–41.
– *The Poetry of Ezra Pound.* London: Faber and Faber, 1951.
– *The Pound Era.* Berkeley: University of California Press, 1971.
Kern, Robert. *Orientalism, Modernism, and the American Poem.* Cambridge: Cambridge University Press, 1996.
Kuang Yaming 匡亞明. *Kongzi pingzhuan* 孔子評傳. Jinan: Qilu shushe, 1985.
Kuberski, Philip. *A Calculus of Ezra Pound: Vocations of the American Sign.* Gainesville: University Press of Florida, 1992.
Lau, D.C., trans. *The Analects.* New York: Penguin Books, 1979.
Laughlin, James. *Pound as Wuz: Essays and Lectures on Ezra Pound.* St Paul: Graywolf Press, 1987.
Legge, James, trans. *The Chinese Classics.* Vol. 1, *Confucian Analects, the Great Learning, the Doctrine of Mean.* Hong Kong: Hong Kong University Press, 1960.
– *The Chinese Classics.* Vol. 2, *The Works of Mencius.* Hong Kong: Hong Kong University Press, 1960.
– *The Chinese Classics.* Vol. 3, *The Shoo King, or the Book of Historical Documents.* Hong Kong: Hong Kong University Press, 1960.
Leibniz, Gottfried Wilhelm. *Writings on China.* Translated by Daniel J. Cook and Henry Rosemont, Jr. Chicago and La Salle: Open Court, 1994.
Levenson, Joseph. *Confucian China and Its Modern Fate.* 3 vols. Berkeley and Los Angeles: University of California Press, 1968.
Levenson, Michael. *A Genealogy of Modernism.* Cambridge: Cambridge University Press, 1984.
Leys, Simons, trans. *The Analects of Confucius.* New York: W.W. Norton, 1997.
Li Zhengang 李振綱, and Jia Runguo 加潤國. *Zhongguo rujiao shihua* 中國儒教史話. Baoding: Hebei daxue chubanshe, 1999.
Li Shen 李申. *Zhongguo rujiao shi* 中國儒教史. 2 vols. Shanghai: Shanghai renmin chubanshe, 1999, 2000.
Li Zhi 李贄. *Fen shu xu fen shu* 焚書續焚書. Beijing: Zhonghua shuju, 1975.
Liang Shuming 梁漱溟. *Liang Shuming ji* 梁漱溟集. Beijing: Qunyan chubanshe, 1993.

Lindberg, Kathryne. *Reading Pound Reading: Modernism after Nietzsche.* Oxford: Oxford University Press, 1987.
Little, Matthew. "Pound's Use of the Word *Totalitarian.*" *Paideuma* 11.1 (1982): 147–56.
Liu Baonan 劉寶楠, ed. *Lun yu zhengyi* 論語正義. Beijing: Zhonghua shuju, 1990.
Liu Shuxian [Liu Shu-hsien] 劉述先. *Rujia sixiang yu xiandaihua* 儒家思想与現代化. Beijing: Zhongguo guangbo dianshi chubanshe, 1992.
– *Understanding Confucian Philosophy.* Westport, Connecticut: Greenwood Press, 1998.
Lukes, Steven. *Individualism.* New York: Harper Torchbooks, 1973.
Makeham, John. *Name and Actuality in Early Chinese Thought.* Albany: State University of New York Press, 1994.
Makin, Peter. 'Ezra Pound and Scotus Erigena.' *Comparative Literature Studies* 10.1 (1973): 60–83.
Marsh, Alec. *Money and Modernity: Pound, Williams, and the Spirit of Jefferson.* Tuscaloosa and London: University of Alabama Press, 1998.
Mathews, R.H. *Mathews' Chinese-English Dictionary.* Shanghai: China Inland Mission, 1931. Cambridge: Harvard University Press, 1950.
McNaughton, William. 'A Report on the 14th Biennial International Conference on Ezra Pound.' *Paideuma* 20.3 (1991): 89–118.
Metzger, Thomas A. *Escape from Predicament: Neo-Confucianism and China's Evolving Political Culture.* New York: Columbia University Press, 1977.
Michaels, Walter Benn. *Our America: Nativism, Modernism, and Pluralism.* Durham: Duke University Press, 1995.
Miyake, Akiko. 'Contemplation East and West: A Defense of Fenollosa's Synthetic Language and Its Influence on Ezra Pound.' *Paideuma* 10.3 (1981): 533–70.
Moore, Marianne. *The Complete Poems of Marianne Moore.* New York: Penguin Books, 1982.
Mou Zongsan 牟宗三. *Daode lixiang zhuyi de chong jian* 道德理想主義的重建. Beijing: Zhongguo guangbo dianshi chubanshe, 1992.
– *Lishi zhexue* 歷史哲學. Taipei: Taiwan xuesheng shuju, 1984.
– *Mou Zongsan ji* 牟宗三集. Edited by Huang Kejian 黃克劍. Beijing: Qunyan chubanshe, 1993.
Mungello, David E. *Curious Land: Jesuit Accommodation and the Origins of Sinology.* Honolulu: University of Hawaii Press, 1985.
– *Leibniz and Confucianism: The Search for Accord.* Honolulu: University of Hawaii Press, 1977.
– 'The Seventeenth-Century Jesuit Translation Project of the Confucian Four Books.' *East Meets West: The Jesuits in China, 1582–1773.* Edited by Charles

E. Ronan and Bonnie B.C. Oh. Chicago: Loyola University Press, 1988. 253–72.

Neville, Robert Cummings. *Boston Confucianism: Portable Tradition in the Late-Modern World*. Albany: State University of New York Press, 2000.

Nicholls, Peter. *Ezra Pound: Politics, Economics and Writing*. Atlantic Highlands, NJ: Humanities Press, 1984.

Nolde, John. *Blossoms from the East: The Chinese Cantos of Ezra Pound*. Orono: National Poetry Foundation, University of Maine, 1983.

– 'Ezra Pound and Ta Hio: The Making of a Confucian.' *Paideuma* 15.2 and 3 (1985): 73–91.

Ostriker, Alicia. 'The Poet as Heroine: Learning to Read H.D.' *American Poetry Review* 12.2 (1983): 29–38.

Palandri, Angela. 'Homage to a Confucian Poet.' *Paideuma* 3.3 (1974): 301–11.

Pauthier, Guillaume. *Confucius et Mencius: Les quatre livres de philosophie morale et politique de la Chine*. Paris: Charpentier, Libraire-Editeur, 1846.

Porteus, Hugh Gordon. 'Ezra Pound and His Chinese Characters: A Radical Examination.' *An Examination of Ezra Pound: A Collection of Essays*. Edited by Peter Russell. 1950. New York: Gordian Press, 1973. 203–17.

Pound, Ezra. *ABC of Reading*. London: Faber and Faber, 1951.

– *The Cantos of Ezra Pound*. 15th printing. New York: New Directions, 1996.

– *Collected Early Poems of Ezra Pound*. Edited by Michael John King. New York: New Directions, 1976.

– *Ezra and Dorothy Pound: Letters in Captivity, 1945–1946*. Edited by Omar Pound and Robert Spoo. New York: Oxford University Press, 1999.

– *Ezra Pound and Dorothy Shakespear. Their Letters: 1909–1914*. Edited by Omar Pound and Walton Litz. New York: New Directions, 1984.

– Ezra Pound Papers (YCAL Mss 43). Beinecke Rare Book and Manuscript Library, Yale Collection of American Literature. New Haven, Connecticut.

– *Ezra Pound Speaking: Radio Speeches of World War II*. Edited by Leonard W. Doob. Westport, Connecticut: Greenwood Press, 1978.

– *Ezra Pound's Poetry and Prose: Contributions to Periodicals*. 11 vols. New York: Garland Publishing, 1991.

– *Gaudier-Brzeska: A Memoir*. London: Faber and Faber, 1970.

– *Guide to Kulchur*. London: Faber and Faber, 1938.

– *Impact: Essays on Ignorance and Decline of American Civilization*. Edited by Noel Stock. Chicago: Henry Regnery, 1960.

– *Instigations*. New York: Boni and Liveright, 1920.

– *Jefferson and/or Mussolini*. London: Stanley Nott, 1935.

– *The Letters of Ezra Pound: 1907–1941*. Edited by D.D. Paige. New York: Harcourt, Brace, 1950.

- 'Letters on Rude Assignment.' *Blast 3*. Edited by Seamus Cooney. Santa Barbara, California: Black Sparrow Press, 1984.
- *Literary Essays of Ezra Pound*. Edited by T.S. Eliot. London: Faber and Faber, 1954.
- *Patria Mia*. Chicago: R.F. Seymour, 1950.
- *Pavannes and Divagations*. Norfolk, Connecticut: New Directions, 1958.
- *Polite Essays*. London: Faber and Faber, 1937.
- *Pound/Joyce: The Letters of Ezra Pound to James Joyce*. Edited by Forrest Read. New York: New Directions, 1967.
- *Selected Poems*. London: Faber and Faber, 1975.
- *Selected Prose, 1909–1965*. Edited by William Cookson. New York: New Directions, 1973.
- *The Spirit of Romance*. New York: New Directions, 1968.
- *The Translations of Ezra Pound*. Edited by Hugh Kenner. New York: New Directions, 1963.

Pound, Ezra, trans. *Confucius: The Great Digest, the Unwobbling Pivot, the Analects*. New York: New Directions, 1969.
- *Ta Hio: The Great Learning*. Seattle: University of Washington Book Store, 1928.

Qian Mu 錢穆. *Lun yu yaolue* 論語要略. Taipei: Taiwan shangwu yinshuguan, 1968.
- *Si shu shiyi* 四書釋意. Taipei: Taiwan xuesheng shuju, 1978.

Qian, Zhaoming. *Orientalism and Modernism*. Durham and London: Duke University Press, 1995.
- *The Modernist Response to Chinese Art*. Charlottesville and London: University of Virginia Press, 2003.

Qian, Zhaoming, ed. *Ezra Pound and China*. Ann Arbor: University of Michigan Press, 2003.

Quesnay, François. *Oeuvres économiques et philosophiques*. Darmstadt: Scientia Verlag Aalen, 1965.

Redman, Tim. *Ezra Pound and Italian Fascism*. Cambridge: Cambridge University Press, 1991.

Raine, Kathleen. 'There Is No Trifling.' *New Republic*, 24 March 1952, 17, 22.

Ricci, Matteo, and Nicola Trigault. *China in the Sixteenth Century: The Journals of Matthew Ricci: 1583–1610*. Translated by Louis J. Gallagher, SJ. New York: Random House, 1953.

Rule, Paul. *K'ung-Tzu or Confucius?: The Jesuit Interpretation of Confucianism*. Sydney and Boston: Allen and Unwin, 1986.

Russell, Peter, ed. *An Examination of Ezra Pound: A Collection of Essays*. 1950. Reprint, New York: Gordian Press, 1973.

Said, Edward. *Orientalism*. New York: Pantheon Books, 1978.

Schneidau, Herbert N. 'Ezra Pound: The Archaeology of the Immanent.' *Wak-

ing Giants: The Presence of the Past in Modernism. Oxford: Oxford University Press, 1991. 202–71
- *Ezra Pound: The Image of the Real.* Baton Rouge: Louisiana State University Press, 1969.
Sheppard, Richard. 'The Crisis of Language.' *Modernism: 1890–1930.* Edited by Malcolm Bradbury and James McFarlane. Hassocks, Sussex: Harvester Press, 1978. 323–36.
Sherry, Vincent. *Ezra Pound, Wyndham Lewis, and Radical Modernism.* Oxford: Oxford University Press, 1993.
Shun, Kwong-loi. *Mencius and Early Chinese Thought.* Stanford: Stanford University Press, 1997.
Sieburth, Richard. *Instigations: Ezra Pound and Remy de Gourmont.* Cambridge: Harvard University Press, 1978.
Sima Qian 司馬遷. *Shi ji* 史記. Shanghai: Shanghai guji chubanshe, 1997.
Soothill, William Edward, trans. *The Analects or the Conversations of Confucius.* 1910. London: Oxford University Press, 1962.
Steiner, George. *After Babel: Aspects of Language and Translation.* New York: Oxford University Press, 1975.
Stock, Noel. *The Life of Ezra Pound.* New York: Pantheon Books, 1970.
Surette, Leon. *A Light from Eleusis: A Study of Ezra Pound's Cantos.* Oxford and New York: Oxford University Press, 1979.
- *Pound in Purgatory: From Economic Radicalism to Anti-Semitism.* Urbana and Chicago: University of Illinois Press, 1999.
Tang Yijie 湯一介. "Cong Zhongguo chuantong zhexue de jiben mingti kan Zhongguo chuantong zhexue de tedian" 從中國傳統哲學的基本命題看中國傳統哲學的特點. *Lun Zhongguo chuantong wenhua* 論中國傳統文化. Edited by Li Zhonghua 李中華 et al. Beijing: Sanlian chubanshe, 1988. 44–69.
Tang Junyi 唐君毅, et al. 'Zhongguo wenhua yu shijie" 中國文化與世界. *Wenhua yishi yuzhou de tansuo* 文化意識宇宙的探索. Beijing: Zhongguo guangbo dianshi chubanshe, 1992. 323–80.
Tate, Allen. *The Man of Letters in the Modern World.* London: Meridian Books, 1957.
Tay, William. 'Between Kung and Eleusis.' *Paideuma* 4.1 (1975): 37–54.
- 'The Sun on the Silk: Ezra Pound and Confucianism.' Ph.D. dissertation, University of California, San Diego, 1977.
Terrell, Carroll. *A Companion to the Cantos of Ezra Pound.* 2 vols. Berkeley: University of California Press, 1980, 1984.
Torrey, E. Fuller. *The Roots of Treason.* New York: McGraw-Hill Book Company, 1984.
Tu, Wei-ming 杜維明. *Centrality and Commonality: An Essay on Confucian Religiousness.* Albany: State University of New York Press, 1989.

- *Confucian Thought: Selfhood as Creative Transformation.* Albany: State University of New York Press, 1985.
- *Humanity and Self-Cultivation: Essays in Confucian Thought.* Berkeley, California: Asian Humanities Press, 1979.
- *Rujia chuantong de xiandai zhuanhua* 儒家傳統的現代轉化. Beijing: Zhongguo dianshi guangbo chubanshe, 1992.
- 'Rujia zhexue yu xiandaihua" 儒家哲學與現代化. *Lun Zhongguo chuantong wenhua* 論中國傳統文化. Edited by Li Zhonghua 李中華 et al. Beijing: Sanlian chubanshe, 1988. 97–133
- *Way, Learning, and Politics: Essays on the Confucian Intellectual.* Albany: State University of New York Press, 1993.

Voltaire. *The Works of Voltaire.* Translated by William F. Fleming. Vols. 4 and 15. New York: St Hubert Guild, 1901.

Wakeham, John. *Name and Actuality in Early Chinese Thought.* Albany: State University of New York Press, 1994.

Waley, Arthur, trans. *The Analects of Confucius.* London: George Allen and Unwin, 1956.

Wang Yunwu 王雲五, et al., eds and trans. *Si shu jinzhu jinyi* 四書今注今譯. Taipei: Shangwu yinshuguan, 1989.

Weber, Max. *The Religion of China: Confucianism and Taoism.* New York: Macmillan, 1964.

Wilder, G.D., and J.H. Ingram. *Analysis of Chinese Characters.* Peking: North China Union Languages School, 1922. New York: Dover Publications, 1974

Wilhelm, James. *Dante and Pound: The Epic of Judgment.* Orono: University of Maine Press, 1974.

- *Ezra Pound: The Tragic Years.* University Park: Pennsylvania State University Press, 1994.

Wolfe, Cary. *The Limits of American Literary Ideology in Pound and Emerson.* Cambridge: Cambridge University Press, 1993.

Wu Shuping 吳樹平, et al., eds. *Shisan jing* 十三經. Beijing: Yanshan chubanshe, 1991.

Xie, Ming. *Ezra Pound and the Appropriation of Chinese Poetry.* New York and London: Garland Publishing, 1999.

Xu Sumin 許蘇民, et al. *Ming Qing qimeng xueshu liubian* 明清啓蒙學術流變. Shenyang: Liaoning jiaoyu chubanshe, 1995.

Yang Bojun 楊伯峻. *Lun yu yizhu* 論語譯注. Beijing: Zhonghua shuju, 1965.

Yang Hong 楊洪, and Wang Gang 王剛. *Zhong yong* 中庸. Lanzhou: Gansu renmin chubnashe, 1997.

Yu Yingshi 余英时. *Zhongguo sixiang chuantong de xiandai quanshi* 中國思想傳統的現代詮釋. Nanjing: Jiangsu renmin chubanshe, 1989.

Zhang Dainian 張岱年. *Key Concepts in Chinese Philosophy*. Translated by Edmund Ryden. New Haven and London: Yale University Press, 2002.

Zhang Litian 張立天, and Li Suping 李甦平. *Zhongwai ruxue bijiao yanjiu* 中外儒学比较研究. Beijing: Dongfang chubanshe, 1998.

Zheng Xuan 鄭玄, Kong Yingda 孔穎達, et al. *Li ji zhengyi* 禮記正義. Shanghai: Shanghai guji chubanshe, 1990.

Zhu Xi [Chu Hsi] 朱熹. *Si shu jizhu* 四書集注. Hong Kong: Taiping shuju, 1968.

Index

Abrams, M.H., 210n20
Adams, John, 82, 217n42
Adorno, T.W., on authoritarian personality, 217n41
Alitto, Guy, 215n27
Ames, Roger, 55, 86, 207n57, 221n36
anti-Semitism, 141–4
Aristotle, 146, 156, 159, 201n19
Arnold, Matthew, 18, 59

Babbitt, Irving, 135, 156, 187
Bacon, Francis, 35
Baynes, Cary, 209n12
belief, crisis of, 136–7
Benjamin, Walter, 34
Bernstein, Michael, 6, 84
Bilenchi, Romano, 201–2n19
Blake, William, 57
Bolligen Prize, 211n29. *See also* Tate, Allen
Brooks, Cleanth, 69
Buddhism, 156, 174–5, 181, 189, 193
Bullock, Alan, 186
Burckhardt, Jacob, 215n25

Calvin, John, 143
Cantos (canto numbers in Roman numerals): XIII, 3, 96, 106–9, 123, 129; XIV, 81; XXXIV, 65; XXXVI, 95; XLV, 159; LI, 65; LII, 147; LV, 173, 179; LVII, 195; LIX, 81; LX, 82; LXIII, 82; LXVI, 82, 128; LXVII, 82; LXVIII, 82; LXXIV, 72, 81, 128, 133, 134, 154, 173, 182; LXXV, 45; LXXVI, 132, 133; LXXVII, 131, 133, 164, 169; LXXVIII, 129, 132, 177; LXXIX, 80; LXXX, 81; LXXXI, 168; LXXXII, 164; LXXXIII, 163, 167; LXXXIV, 133; LXXXV, 151, 157, 164, 174, 177; LXXXVI, 82, 128, 146, 157, 180; LXXXVII, 73, 74, 154, 155; LXXXVIII, 158; LXXXIX, 154; XCIII, 148, 152–3; XCVII, 153, 174; XCVIII, 167; XCIX, 65, 122–3, 150, 151, 155, 168, 181; CX, 164, 175; CXVI, 188; as exemplification of verbal precision, 82–3; captivity narrative, 129–30, 131; 'China Cantos,' 5, 84, 172, 179, 193, 201n8; dualistic narrative of history, 193
Casillo, Robert, 217n39, 217n42; on Pound's polytheism, 219n14

Catholic Church, 143, 144, 145; and economic activities, 139; code worship, 140
Cavalcanti, Guido, 16, 40, 176, 202n19; as example of linguistic precision, 58
Chace, William, 216n39
Chan, Wing-tsit, 9, 15, 165, 212n38; on *cheng*, 71; translation of *ke ji fu li*, 86, 214n7
Chang, Carson. *See* Zhang Junmai
Chang Ti (*Shangdi*, God). *See* God
Chang Yao-xin (Yao-hsin), 15
Cheadle, Mary Paterson, 7, 19, 20, 42, 201n15
Chen Chun, 211n31
cheng (sincerity): as epistemological endeavour, 73–5; as ontological condition, 71–2; as 'perfect Word,' 45, 72; as self-actualization, 72–3; Chan on, 71; in *Yi jing* (Books of Changes), 54; Hall and Ames on, 55; Pound's interpretation of, 54, 70–1; Tu Wei-ming on, 71; Zhang Dainian on, 55; Zhu Xi on, 71. See also *cheng yi*; sincerity
Cheng Ming. See *zheng ming*
cheng yi (to make thought sincere), doctrine of, 11, 45, 195; Chan's translation of, 53; Dante's relevance to, 52; Legge's translation of, 53; Pauthier's translation of, 52; Pound's translation of, 53, 55, 75. See also *cheng*; sincerity
Cheng Yi, 211n31
Cheng Zhongying (Cheng Chungying), 49–50
Chinese characters: as 'primitive' and 'universal' language, 35; Bacon on, 35; Fenollosa on, 29–30; Leibniz on, 35; Pound's conception of, 30–2, 35–6; structural principles of, 207n53; Western study of, 36
Ch'ing Ming. See *zheng ming*
Christianity: and Judaism, 142–4; as 'coercive evil,' 95; as revealed religion of God, 25; doctrine of Salvation, 156–7; Pound's attack on, 12, 139–41; 'true' origin of, 144, 220n18
Chu Hsi. *See* Zhu Xi
Confucianism: against or for individual self-assertion, 84–5; and Judaism, 141, 142; appeal to Pound as humanist discourse, 148, 186; as counterdiscourse to anthropocentrism, 158; as humanist philosophy, 124; as moral idealism, 124; as natural religion, 25; as 'state religion,' 7; Christian missionary accommodation of, 188–9; Confucian works as Pound's 'bible,' 129; Enlightenment idealization of, 189–90; first Western translation of Confucian works, 25; Hegelian-Weberian negation of, 190–1; humanist orientation of religiosity, 147; late-modern revival of, 197; Pound's dedication to, 3; *Si-Meng xuepai* (school of Zisi and Mencius), 149; Western receptions of, 13. *See also* neo-Confucianism; New Confucianism
Confucius, 3, 37; and freedom of speech, 95–6; as guide in religion, 147; as guide of Kulchur, 183; as political failure, 129; in *Cantos*, 45, 81, 106, 107–8, 129; not as competitor with Jesus, 188; on heroic individuals, 130, 133; on human

nature, 149; on name and substance, 48, 49; on love, 152, 153; on self and rites, 85; political agenda of, 48
Cookson, William, on Pound's polytheism, 219n14
counterdiscourse, 11, 184, 194–5
Couplet, Philippe, 25–6
Couvreur, Seraphin, 180
cummings, e.e., 158

Da xue (Great Learning), 8, 41, 44, 52, 88, 99, 117, 124, 169, 178–9; *Confucio, Ta S'eu. Dai Gaku. Studio integrale*, 19; *Great Digest*, 6, 19, 183; *Ta Hio*, 4, 5, 18, 116
Daniel, Arnaut, 56, 60
Dante, 14, 52, 60, 146, 168, 186; as example of linguistic precision, 57; and Mencius on human will, 120; versus Calvin, 143
Dao (*Tao*, Way), 24, 130, 150, 157, 162, 163, 170; and reason, 179; and transcendence, 178; as 'process' in Pound's version, 175, 176; as 'tensile light,' 169, 177; bearing on humanity, 120–1; in *Zhong yong*, 42–3; Western interpretations of, 175
Daoism (Taoism), 189, 193
Davie, Donald, 6, 201n15
de (virtue), 117–18. See also *virtù*; *ming ming de*
de Bary, Wm. Theodore, 87; on Confucian selfhood, 89, 90
de Mailla, de Moyriac, 172–3, 201n8
Dembo, L.S., 200n8
Demuth, Charles, 210n15
Dewey, John, 187

divinity: immanence of, 137, 175; manifestation of, 169–70, 177. See also God; *Tian*
Dodde, Derk, 204n23
Douglas, C.H., 102, 125
Duncan, Robert, 77, 213n45

education. See *jiao*
egoism, 4, 92, 99
Eliot, T.S.: and Catholicism, 143, 145; as advocate of Original Sin, 140, 143; debate with Pound on religion, 135–8, 219n7; on Confucianism as 'inferior religion,' 135, 196; on language, 69; racial prejudice, 220n17; sense of linguistic crisis, 56, 212n42
elitism, cultural, 103–5, 127
Emerson, Ralph Waldo, 34, 73, 92, 169, 178; on poet as 'Seer,' 103
Emery, Clark, 220n18
Enlightenment, 10, 12, 13, 41, 112, 158, 193–4, 217n40, 222–3n3; influence of Confucianism on, 25–6, 189–90; postulate of reason, 94, 147, 178
Eno, Robert, 221n36
Eoyang, Eugene, 200n8
Erigena, John Scotus, 40, 145, 176

Fang, Achilles, 15, 19–20, 203n12, 207n62, 221nn27, 32, 33
Fang Yizhi, 88
Fascism, 8, 82, 141, 201nn15, 16, 201–2n19; and Pound, 216n39, 217n42
Feng Youlan (Fung Yu-lan), 49, 204n23
Feng Yu, 171
Fenollosa, Ernest, 4, 19, 34, 35, 36, 73, 203–4n13; on language, 62

Fingarette, Herbert, 175
Flaubert, Gustave, 61, 70, 202n29
Ford, Ford Madox, 92
Foucault, Michel, 212n41
French Revolution, 98, 112, 217n42
Frobenius, Leo, 144–5, 202n19; concept of Paideuma, 208n1

Galsworthy, John, 102
Gardner, Daniel K., 204n23
Gefin, Laszlo, 205n34
Giles, Herbert, 20
Gilson, Etienne, 176
Giustiniani, Vito R., 223n5
God, 25, 143; as 'spirit of heaven,' 172; Pound's terms for, 137, 169. *See also* divinity; *Tian*
Gordon, David, 202n2
Gourmont, Remy de, 92, 93, 98; on language, 63–4
Grieve, Thomas, 222n47
Grosseteste, Robert, 40, 176

Hall, David, 55, 221n36
Hall, Donald, 84
Hare, William Loftus, 4
Harrison, John R., 216n39
Hawley, W.M., 19
Heath-Stubbs, John, 186
Heaven. See *Tian*
Hegel, G.W.F., 7, 190–1, 194, 196
Heidegger, Martin, 41
Hitler, Adolf, 202n19
Homer, 14; Homeric world, 115
Hu Shi, 19–20
Huang Kan, 87
Hulme, T.E., 58, 59, 92
humanism: anthropocentric tendency in, 158; definition of, 10; 'Humanist Manifesto,' 187; humanist religion, 148; in Europe, 148; Italian tradition of, 92–3, 100, 186; New Humanists, 187; Pound's contributions to, 10–11, 184, 186–8, 196 (*see also under* Pound)

ideogram. See Chinese characters
Imagism, 61. *See also* linguistic precision
individualism: aesthetic, 92, 103–4; and social order, 105–6, 108–9; as self-contradictory ideology, 110–11, 217n40; autonomy, 94; *de facto* rights, 113; fraternity and equality, 97–8; freedom of speech, 94; 'man's divine right,' 91; Pound's commitment to, 84–5; rights-based Confucian individual, 196; *Rights of Man*, 111, 112; security of privacy, 96–8; self-actualization as redemption, 157; self-development, 98–101; super-individual, 196. *See also* self
Irwin, John, 34

James, Henry, 59, 97
James, William, 'will to believe,' 137
Jefferson, Thomas, 114
Jehovah, 143, 173. *See also under* Old Testament
Jesuits: missionaries to China, 172, 192–3; translation of Confucian works, 25–6, 189
ji (self). See *ke ji fu li*
jiao (education), as self-redemption, 157–8
Johnson, Lionel, 60
Judaism, 141, 142, 144
Jung, Hwa Yol, 206n34

Kang Xi (K'ang Hsi), 81–2
ke ji fu li, doctrine of: Confucius on, 85; major classical Chinese exegeses of, 87–8; major Western translations of, 86, 213–14nn4, 5, 214nn6, 7, 8, 9; New Confucians on, 89–90, 214n19; Pound's translation of, 85; textual ambiguity of, 86–7. *See also* self
Kenner, Hugh, 6, 19, 73, 80, 202n2, 205n34
Kuanon (Guanyin), 174–5
Kuberski, Philip, 7, 217n39
Kume, Tami, 183
Kung. *See* Confucius
K'ung fu Tsze. *See* Confucius

Lau, D.C., 86, 175, 217–18n44
Laughlin, James, 15, 19, 203–4n13
Lawrence, D.H., 110
Legge, James, 18, 21, 23, 28–9, 38, 70, 74, 120, 165, 205n32; as 'anonymous' translator, 203n10; as Pound's guide, 20; textual division of Confucian works, 204n19, 218n45; translation of *ji xin*, 180; translation of *ke ji fu li*, 86; translation of *Tian*, 171, 221–2n37
Leibniz, Gottfried W., 35, 185, 189
Levenson, Joseph, 10
Levenson, Michael, 92, 103
Lewis, Wyndham, 92, 140
li (rite, propriety), 155. See also *si duan*
Li Bai (Li Po), 186
Li Shen, 224n21
Li Zhi, on *ke ji fu li*, 87, 88
Liang Shuming, 215n27
Liberalism, 99, 110–11, 195; in opposition to Confucianism, 93–4; Pound's critique of, 110–13, 119. *See also* individualism
light: as divine manifestation, 177; Neoplatonic philosophy of, 145–6, 165, 175–6, 196
Lindberg, Kathryne, 208n64
ling (spirit), as 'great sensibility,' 174–5
linguistic precision: and economic value, 77–8; and social function of poetry, 68–70; as double correspondence of representation, 57, 58; as Imagist principles, 60–2; as response to crisis of language, 56; authority of, 78–9; in Troubadours, 56–7; precisionism in arts, 209–10n15. See also *zheng ming*
Little, Matthew, 217n43
Liu Xuan, 87
Longobardi, Niccolo, 189
Lun yu (Analects), 5, 6, 14, 41, 85, 115; *Confucius. Digest of the Analects*, 18–19; *Analects*, 19
Luther, Martin, 143

Ma Rong, 48–9, 87
Makin, Peter, on *zheng ming*, 212–13n44
Malatesta, Sigismundo, 81, 127
Mathews, R.H., 20
Meed, G.R.S., 210n18
Melville, Herman, 34
Men Tsze. *See* Mencius
Mencius, 7, 72, 141, 179; analogy of archery, 131; influence on Pound, 149; on 'grand air,' 163; on love, 152; on human nature, 150; on illustrious individuals, 130; on *li* (profit), 154–5; on nature, 73–4, 212n38; on noble will, 120; on war,

128–9; relationship with Confucius, 149–50
Mengzi (Works of Mencius), 6, 18, 41, 149
Mentzel, Johann Christian, 36
ming mind de (illustrate illustrious virtue), 24–7, 117, 204n23, 205n28
Miyake, Akiko, 206n34
modernity, 146, 190, 191, 192; as privileged model of progress, 194; Pound's critique of, 184–6
monotheism, 140, 196. *See also* polytheism
Monroe, Harriet, 61, 147
Moore, Marianne, 202n2; as 'precisionist,' 210n15
Morrison, Robert, 20
Mou Zongsan, 123–4, 126, 202n23, 218n48
Müller, Andreas, 36
Mungello, David, 25, 35, 189
Mussolini, Benito, 42, 82, 125, 128, 202n19
myth: in European pagan tradition, 145–7; of Wagadu, 134; Pound's notion of, 144

name. See *zheng ming*
nature: modern alienation from, 158; Aristotelian 'splitting' of, 166; as 'boon companion,' 163; as organic whole, 164; as source of knowledge, 168–9; full of divine spirits, 165; human partnership with, 160–4; identical with human nature, 161; in Cartesian division, 162; Pound's theory of, 160; Western attitude towards, 159
neo-Confucianism, 71, 87, 179, 188–9, 211n31, 214n14; distinction from New Confucianism, 202n23
Neoplatonism, 12. *See also under* light
Neville, Robert Cummings, 223n21
New Confucianism (modern), 10; and demand of democracy, 124; critique of volitional determinism, 126; differences from Pound's formulation, 125–7, manifesto of, 218n48; reclaims humanist values of Confucian tradition, 123–4; representatives of, 123, 202n23; theory of 'internal sagehood and external kinghood,' 124
Nicholls, Peter, 82, 132, 201n16
Nietzsche, Friedrich, 119–20
Nolde, John, 201n8

O'Keeffe, Georgia, 210n15
Old Testament, 142, 143, 144, 170, 220n18; God of, 173 (*see also* Jehovah)
Original Sin, doctrine of, 140, 144, 148, 156
Ostriker, Alicia, 8
Ovid, 147

paganism (European), 12, 144–5, 196
Palandri, Angela, 129
Pauthier, Guillaume, 4, 18, 21, 23, 205n33; as Pound's guide, 20; relationship with Enlightenment tradition, 25; translation of *Dao*, 175; translation of *ke ji fu li*, 86, 213n4; translation of *ming ming de*, 24–7
Plato, 115
Poe, Edgar Allan, 34, 206n47
polytheism, 140–1, 196, 219n14. *See also* monotheism
Pound, Dorothy Shakespear, 4, 200n5

Pound, Ezra: as 'rebellious Protestant,' 135; as translator of Confucius and Mencius, 4, 5, 6; attitude towards Catholicism, 143–4 (*see also* Catholic Church); debate with Eliot on religion, 136–8; early exposure to Confucian works, 3–4; encounter with Confucius in Chinese, 18–19; first article on Confucius, 4, 200n5; formulation of ecocriticism, 167–8, 196; humanist orientation, 10–11, 13, 84, 99, 120, 155, 178 186–8 (*see under* humanism); knowledge of Chinese language, 19–21; religious belief, 137–9, 169–71; self-criticism, 132; shift towards authoritarianism, 84; theory of language, 46, 70–1
precisionism. *See* linguistic precision
Propertius, Sextus, 14
Protestantism, 141, 143, 220n15; as antithesis to Confucianism, 191–2
Pythagoras, 168

Quesnay, François, 190
Qian Mu, 207n58; on *ke ji fu li*, 214n19
Qian, Zhaoming, 199–200n4

Raine, Kathleen, 203n2
reciprocity (*shu*), doctrine of, 120–1; in *Cantos*, 122
Redman, Tim, 217n39
Reformation, 142–3, 192, 207–8n63
ren (humanity, benevolence): and self, 85–6, 88–9; as love, 152–3; as utmost human virtue, 22; English translations of, 86; Pound's interpretation of, 88. See also *si duan*

Renaissance, 41, 92–3, 148, 158, 186, 187
Ricci, Matteo, 188–9
Richards, I.A., 135
Rousseau, Jean-Jacques, 156; on human nature, 148

sage-kings: King Wen (Wan), 40, 43, 133; King Wu, 42, 174; Shun, 33, 40, 42, 133, 173, 181, 182; Yao, 173, 181, 182; Yu, 33, 173, 182
Said, Edward, 192
Schiller, F.C.S., 187
Schlegel, Friedrich, 99
Schneidau, Herbert, 210n18; on Pound's polytheism, 219n14
self: actualization of, 116; and sagehood, 126; dualism of, 89; empowerment of, 130–2; New Confucian postulate of, 89–90; transformation in person-making, 118–19; self-knowledge as truth, 117–18; subjugation of, 86, 87; support of, 85. *See also* individualism; *ke ji fu li*
Shaw, George Bernard, 102
Sheoler, Charles, 210n15
Sheppard, Richard, 210n17
Shi jing (Book of Songs), 6, 200–1n8
Shu jing (Book of History), 180
si duan (four beginnings of human nature), doctrine of, 7, 151; as theme in *Cantos*, 151–2
Sieburth, Richard, 210n23
Sima Guang, 172
Sima Qian, 47, 149
sincerity, 54, 70; as verbal precision, 71 (*see also* linguistic precision); as Logos, 72; as ontological condition, 71–2; 'fidelity to given word,'

65; in Romantic writers, 59; technique as test of, 58–9. See also *cheng*; *cheng yi*
Soothill, William Edward, 86
state (political): as autocracy, 110, 123, 127–8, 196; as manipulative instrument, 101; as representation of collective interests, 113; as 'will system,' 125; Pound's idealized form of, 128; rights of, 113; totalitarian features of, 114–15
Stendhal, 61, 62
Sterne, Laurence, 60
Stirner, Max, 92, 98
Stock, Noel, 3–4
Surette, Leon, 8, 174, 216n39

Ta Hio. See *Da xue*
Tang Junyi, 218n48
Tang Yijie, on nature, 212n36
Tate, Allen, defence of Pound, 211n29
Thoreau, Henry David, 34
Tian (Heaven), 157, 170; as alternative to God, 173; as equivalent of God, 172; as Supreme Intelligence, 173; human union with, 181; Legge's translations of, 171, 221–2n37; mandate of Heaven, 173–4; multiple meanings in classical Chinese, 171; Pound's translations of, 171–2; Western interpretations of, 221n36
Torrey, E. Fuller, 216n39
transcendence, internal, 158, 171, 178
translation: anxiety of influence in, 27; as criticism, 16; Dryden on, 17; Arnold on, 18; Pound on, 16–17; theory of etymographic interpretation, 30–2; translatability, 40–1, 208n64; translator-angel, 34
Troubadours, 56–7, 58
Tu Wei-ming, 9, 43, 120, 123; on *cheng*, 71; on religiousness of Confucianism, 147; on self, 89–90; on 'third-epoch development' of Confucianism, 197–8
tuan, four. See *si duan*

Upward, Allen, 4, 92, 210n18
usury, 65, 77, 112, 151, 155; as invisible hand, 185; as 'perverters of language,' 81; as sin against nature, 159–60; usurocracy, 184–5; versus sharing, 139

verbal precision. *See* linguistic precision
Villion, 100–1
virtù: as innermost energy, 100; as self-knowledge, 117–18
virtue. See *virtù*
volitionism. *See* will
Voltaire, 26, 190, 193
Vorticism, 92

Waley, Arthur, 21, 22, 38, 207n57; on *zheng ming*, 209n9; translation of *Dao*, 175; translation of *ke ji fu li*, 86
Wang Yangming, 87, 214n14
Weber, Max, 10, 191–2, 194
Whitman, Walt, 100–1
Wilhelm, James, 8, 216n39
will: towards order, 12, 119, 122, 124–5; to power, 120; volitional determinism, 125
Williams, William Carlos, 105
Wolfe, Cary, 92
Wordsworth, William, 59

xin (faith), 65
xin (heart/mind), 7, 151; learning of, 149; exertion of and service to Heaven, 179–80, 181
Xiong Shili, 202n23
Xu Fuguan, 218n48
Xunzi: on human nature, 149

Yang Bojun, 207nn57, 58; on *zheng ming*, 209n7
Yang Zhu (Yang Chu), 4
Yeats, William Butler, 110, 223n3
yi (righteousness), as 'equity,' 153–4; versus *li* (profit) in Mencius, 154–5. See also *si duan*
Yi jing (Book of Changes), 54
Yong Zheng (Iong Ching), 167–8

Zhang Dainian, 55
Zhang Junmai (Carson Chang), vii, 218n48
zheng ming (to rectify names), doctrine of, 11, 195; and social reform, 66–7; as counterforce to usury, 77; as 'new Paideuma,' 45; as recorded in *Lun yu*, 46–7; as 'revolution of word,' 66; first appearance in *Cantos*, 65; three historical interpretations of, 47–50; Pound's translation of, 50–1. *See also* linguistic precision
Zheng Xuan, 48
zhi (wisdom), 155. See also *si duan*
Zhong yong (Doctrine of Mean), 5, 18, 41, 149; Pound's abridgment of, 42–4; *Chiung Iung. L'asse che non vacilla*, 19; *Unwobbling Pivot*, 6, 19
Zhou Dunyi (Tcheou Tun-y), 173, 179
Zhu Xi (Chu Hsi), 17, 18, 20, 38, 88, 89; as editor of *Zhong yong*, 41–2; 44; interpretation of *cheng*, 71; on *Dao*, 150; on human nature, 149; on *ke ji fu li*, 87; on *zheng ming*, 47
Zielinski, Thaddeus, 220n18
Zisi, 41, 149

www.ingramcontent.com/pod-product-compliance
Lightning Source LLC
Chambersburg PA
CBHW052019070526
44584CB00016B/1813